TRAUMA MODEL THERAPY

A Treatment Approach for Trauma, Dissociation and Complex Comorbidity

Colin A. Ross, M.D.
Naomi Halpern, C.Q.S.W.

Manitou Communications, Inc.

Library of Congress Card Number: 2009936442

Ross, Colin A.
Halpern, Naomi

    Trauma Model Therapy
    A Treatment Approach for Trauma, Dissociation and Complex Comorbidity

ISBN-10: 0-9821851-2-X
ISBN-13: 978-0-9821851-2-4

1. Psychological Trauma   2. Dissociation   3. Treatment Techniques

TABLE OF CONTENTS

APPENDICES

INTRODUCTION

This book is a treatment manual for Trauma Model Therapy. It builds on a previous book, *The Trauma Model: A Solution to the Problem of Comorbidity In Psychiatry* (Ross, 2007) by greatly expanding on the ideas and providing concrete, practical skills on the 'how to' of therapy. CDs and DVDs of role plays of therapy sessions are also available from Manitou Communications and The Ross Institute.

Trauma Model Therapy is written primarily for therapists, but it can also be read by clients, friends, and relatives. To this end, we have attempted to write with a minimum of jargon and in a conversational style. The hope is that it will have the feel of a case consultation or workshop discussion. It is not designed or presented as an academic text and therefore is not referenced as such.

The book provides hands-on techniques, strategies, and interventions in two ways: through description and discussion, and through transcripts of therapy conversations. The conversations are composite case histories drawn from thousands of hours of clinical experience. No individual person is the basis of any given therapy vignette, although many people may recognize parts of their therapy in these pages.

The research, clinical interventions and ideas presented are a combination of the authors' experience, original ideas and a composite of the work of many prominent researchers and clinicians in the field. We would like to acknowledge and thank these professionals for their work and for informing and influencing our understanding of trauma and dissociation.

In particular, we would like to make special mention of the following people, whose ideas and research are incorporated in this manual and who have played a significant role in informing and developing our understanding of trauma and dissociation:

John Briere, David Calof, Eve Carlson, James Chu, Christine Courtois, Charles Figley, Jennifer Freyd, Eliana Gil, Judith Herman, Richard Kluft, Warwick Middleton, Ellert Nijenhuis, Laurie Anne Pearlman, Ken Pope, Frank Putnam, Kathy Steele, Roland Summit, Onno van der Hart and Bessel van der Kolk.

Many of the above have over the years made the long trip to Australia to present their research and clinical expertise, through The Delphi Centre. They have played a substantial role in the education and development of professionals 'Down Under.'

There are numerous others, too many to mention, who have made significant contributions to the field. There is an extensive recommended reading list at the end of the book. We encourage people to read these texts for more in-depth information about particular research, theory and practice that is of interest to them.

Finally, Trauma Model Therapy is suitable for a wide range of mental health problems and addictions. In this book we emphasize dissociation because it is a core component of the trauma response, and because dissociation is not as widely understood and recognized as depression, anxiety, psychosis, substance abuse, eating, and personality disorders.

The techniques in this book can be used in the treatment of dissociative identity disorder (DID) and dissociative disorder not otherwise specified (DDNOS), and also in the therapy of individuals who do not have dissociative disorders. Approaches to talking to the voices and direct work with dissociated parts, can be adapted to work with internal aspects of self, thoughts and perspectives in the non-dissociative client.

The Trauma Model predicts the existence of a dissociative subtype of schizophrenia treatable with psychotherapy (Ross, 2004). The techniques in this book are those advocated for the treatment of dissociative schizophrenia.

ABOUT THE AUTHORS

Naomi Halpern is Co-Director of The Delphi Centre, Melbourne, Australia. She qualified as a Social Worker in the U.K. in 1983. Prior to entering private practice at The Delphi Centre in 1987, she worked with homeless youth, children in State care and convicted offenders, in government and charity organizations in the U.K. and Australia.

Naomi has specialized in therapy, case consultations and professional development training in the areas of severe trauma, abuse and dissociative disorders for over two decades. She has presented her work nationally and internationally. Naomi has also provided emergency consultation related to the development of trauma and psychosocial training programs for the United Nations.

www.delphicentre.com.au

Acknowledgments

I thank Dr. Colin Ross for the invitation to write with him, for his patience, humour, and openness to discuss and explore different perspectives.

Deepest thanks to my colleague and business partner of over two decades, Susan Henry, for her great insight, understanding of trauma and dissociation, friendship and a journey into the unknown that couldn't have been predicted or anticipated!

Thanks and gratitude to Dr. John Spensley, Gillian Nikakis, Dr. Susan Brann and Patricia Danko for walking the talk. They have been great professional supports and wonderful friends.

Thank you to Dr. Warwick Middleton, for putting and keeping dissociation on the agenda in psychiatry in Australia, his enormous contribution to the field, ongoing collaboration with The Delphi Centre professional development training, and unwavering friendship.

Finally, a heartfelt acknowledgment to my clients for their courage, persistence, and humour. They have challenged and inspired me to keep learning and developing my understanding of trauma and the long road to healing.

This book is dedicated to the memory of Dr. John Spensley, 31/7/1938 - 10/8/2008, much loved and greatly missed.

Colin A. Ross, MD received his degree from the University of Alberta in 1981 and completed his psychiatry training at the University of Manitoba in 1985. He moved from Canada to Texas in 1991 and has been running a Trauma Program in the Dallas area since then. Besides his work at Timberlawn Hospital in Dallas, Dr. Ross consults to Trauma Programs at Forest View Hospital in Grand Rapids, Michigan, and Del Amo Hospital in Torrance, California.

Dr. Ross is the author of a series of books on trauma and dissociation, including *The Trauma Model: A Solution to the Problem of Comorbidity in Psychiatry*. He has spoken in Australia for The Delphi Centre on three occasions.

Acknowledgments

And I thank Naomi Halpern, for her professional and personal support and friendship. Like Naomi, my greatest teachers have been the trauma survivors I have worked with, and I thank them for providing me the opportunity to learn, sharpen my skills, and find meaning in my work.

I would also like to thank Melissa Caldwell-Engle for her contributions over the last fifteen years. These include countless conversations about the Trauma Model and Trauma Model Therapy, in which she contributed ideas and insights of her own. The chapter on expressive therapies is based entirely on her work and the expressive groups she has developed for the Trauma Programs.

Both authors would like to thank Lynn Wasnak for her excellent work editing the manuscript, which improved the text greatly.

Naomi and Colin would both like to thank John Briere, Christine Courtois, Warwick Middleton, Ellert Nijenhuis, Laurie Anne Pearlman and Eli Somer for giving their valuable time and expertise in reading and offering their thoughts and opinions about this book.

ASSESSMENT OF DISSOCIATION

1
What Is Dissociation?

This chapter will provide an overview of dissociation. In this chapter we will cover

- The Four Meanings of Dissociation

- Continuum and Taxon Models of Dissociation

- Examples of Dissociative Symptoms

- The Difference Between Dissociation and Repression

The word *dissociation* is used in different ways by different authors. This can be confusing. Dissociation has four basic meanings.

THE FOUR MEANINGS OF DISSOCIATION

A general systems meaning—the opposite of association

An operationalized meaning—the items in measures of dissociation

A technical term in cognitive psychology

An intrapsychic defense mechanism

The General Systems Meaning of Dissociation

In this meaning, dissociation is the opposite of association. When two things are associated, they are in a relationship with each other. They are linked, connected, or interacting. This can apply to two companies that are doing business with each other, two molecules that are bonded to each other, or anything else in the universe.

When two things are dissociated, they are disconnected from each other, out of relationship with each other, and not interacting.

This general meaning of dissociation is accepted throughout the physical sciences. For instance, in chemistry there are *dissociation constants* that are used in chemical formulae and calculations.

We all dissociate in this general sense. For instance, a therapist might say of a client, "He's really disconnected from his feelings. He's all in his head."

Alternatively, another therapist might say, "This client exhibits a dissociation of affect from cognition."

Both therapists are saying the same thing. Throughout this manual, we will give examples of how to say things without too much jargon.

A client is "out of touch with how her behaviour affects other people." This is a disconnection or dissociation within the client's psyche. It can happen in anyone and does not necessarily mean there is a dissociative disorder.

Other examples of the general systems meaning of dissociation include

"I spaced it—I completely forgot our appointment."

"I can't feel it in my heart."

"He says he feels fine but he looks really sad."

"His arm is twitching but he isn't aware of it."

"She's put it on the back burner for now."

"She's bleeding badly but she doesn't feel any pain."

The last two examples are adaptive survival strategies.

Sometimes dissociation is normal, sometimes not. Sometimes it is a good thing, other times it interferes with function. Sometimes it is done consciously, other times it happens automatically.

You couldn't get through the day without healthy, normal dissociation. On the other hand, if you put everything on the back burner for life, or were always and only in your head, it wouldn't be possible to live a balanced, healthy life. It's all a matter of balance and degree.

The ability to dissociate is a skill. Throughout this manual we will provide examples of normalization strategies, which we use frequently. The following is one way that we explain the adaptive, survival-oriented benefits of dissociation:

DISSOCIATION AS AN ADAPTIVE SURVIVAL SKILL

Years ago, an Inuit hunter in the Arctic had to be successful, or he and his family would starve. During the winter, he had to hunt and kill seals. This was done by standing at a seal hole for up to eight hours at a time, silent and motionless. The seal could come up for air at any one of a series of different holes in the ice. The hunter would stand at a seal hole in the middle of the Arctic winter, at forty below zero, and he could not move because any sound would frighten the seal away. The packed snow he was standing on would creak or squeak if he moved around. During these eight hours, the hunter had to be ready to react quickly and accurately within a couple of seconds—that was all the time he had to spear the seal before it saw him and dove under water.

During these eight hours, do you think the hunter ever got a cramp, or an ache, or a full bladder? In order to survive he had to stay alert and focused, and he had to dissociate his fatigue, his muscle pain, and even his own thoughts, which might distract him from his task. Dissociation is normal, healthy, and built-in through evolution. It is not a defect or a disability, if you use it in a flexible, healthy fashion.

How handy would it be to be able to dissociate the pain of childbirth and not feel it at all?

Any similar story can be used to explain normal dissociation. The ability to dissociate is built into all mammals. When a gazelle is run to ground by a lion, it may curl up and freeze—this is a dissociative response. People who have survived lion attacks describe being calm, feeling no pain, and remaining still while in the lion's jaws.

One of the ways to survive a grizzly attack is to freeze and play dead. When you are faced with a grizzly, fight and flight aren't going to work. There is a third option built into mammalian survival systems, however—freeze, offer no resistance, and play dead. The opossum is a master of the freeze response, which means it is a master of dissociation.

At times, however, dissociation can be overused, or used in the wrong context. When it becomes maladaptive, we start talking about "dissociative symptoms." The story about the Inuit hunter does not explain what makes dissociation unhealthy.

The goal of treatment is not to eliminate the person's skill at dissociation. Rather, it is to help the individual learn more fluid, flexible, adaptive, coping and survival strategies.

An Operationalized Meaning of Dissociation—Dissociative Symptoms

When dissociation becomes maladaptive, therapy may be required. As always, it's a matter of degree. Someone who gets drunk once every two years doesn't need to seek assistance for a drinking problem. Someone who gets drunk every day definitely does.

In order to understand dissociative symptoms and dissociative disorders, one must understand the continuum and taxon aspects of dissociation. The same logic applies to anxiety, depression, substance abuse, anorexia nervosa, and every other mental health problem or addiction. Take alcohol as an example:

One person is a complete teetotaler who never consumes any alcohol. The next person drinks a litre of vodka every day. These two people belong to two separate, distinct categories—in statistical jargon, each is in a separate *taxon*. The two categories are easy to tell apart. Trying to decide which person needs to seek assistance for a drinking problem is simple and obvious.

Looking at alcohol this way, alcoholism is a taxon. You either are an alcoholic, or you aren't.

The problem is, alcohol intake also occurs on a continuum. One person never drinks, the next has one beer a month, the next one beer a week. Going further out the continuum, we find a person who drinks two beers a day during the week, and five beers each Saturday. Next comes a person who drinks five beers Monday to Friday and twelve beers each Saturday and Sunday. Finally, we find the person who drinks twelve beers every day; this person is clearly an alcoholic.

There is a gray zone in the middle of the continuum. There, different people, including different "experts," will disagree about who is an alcoholic, and who is not. In statistical terms, the *inter-rater agreement* for the diagnosis of alcohol abuse will be low for people in the gray zone. It will be high when we compare two people at opposite ends of the continuum.

A person classified as an alcoholic when he really isn't has received a *false-positive diagnosis*. When authorities conclude someone is not an alcoholic when he really is, this is a *false-negative diagnosis*.

There are different research and statistical strategies for reducing the number of false-positives and false-negatives, but it is impossible to get rid of either completely, for any addiction or mental disorder. This is true for dissociation. Dissociation occurs on a continuum but it is also a taxon. There are false-positives and false-negatives in research and in clinical practice. The goal is to make as few errors as possible, but perfection is unattainable.

The continuum of dissociation was well described in the literature in the 1980's. At the far left was normal dissociation, at the far right was multiple personality disorder (MPD). MPD was officially renamed dissociative identity disorder (DID) by the American Psychiatric Association, when the DSM-IV was published in 1994.

Normal dissociation includes common experiences such as zoning out and missing part of a conversation or movie. We all dissociate a little bit. As you move right on the continuum, the dissociative experiences become more frequent, more severe, and increasingly interfere with function. If you zone out for 45 minutes during an exam and then fail, this is obviously not a good thing. If this zoning out happens during most tests, then it can be a serious problem and may require treatment.

In the late 1990's two research papers established that dissociation is also a taxon. Using a statistical procedure called *taxometric analysis*, it was shown that there are two types of dissociative experiences. There is normal dissociation. These are experiences we all have once in a while. Then there is *pathological dissociation*. These are experiences most people never have. Examples of pathological dissociation include

- Looking in a mirror and not recognizing yourself

- Not remembering putting on the clothes you are wearing

- Not recognizing friends or family members

- Suddenly becoming aware in a strange location and not knowing how you got there

Like anxiety, depression, substance abuse, and psychosis, dissociation occurs on a continuum but is also a taxon. The logic of the taxon–continuum aspect of dissociation is the same as the wave–particle duality in physics. Under certain experimental conditions, light behaves as a wave, but under other conditions, it behaves as a particle. Light is both a particle and a wave, but also it is neither. This logic is accepted in physics based on rigorous experiments. In our view, the same logic should be accepted for dissociation, so debates about whether dissociation "really" occurs on a continuum or "really" is a discrete taxon are misconceived: Both ways of looking at dissociation are correct, but neither captures the whole story.

In this manual, in the DSM-IV-TR, and in the dissociative disorders literature, dissociation is psychological. If dissociative experiences are caused by drugs, alcohol, brain disease, or specific medical problems, then they don't count as psychological dissociation. These symptoms are dissociative, but they are medical symptoms not psychological symptoms.

Telling the difference between medically caused dissociation and psychological dissociation can be tricky or impossible, but most of the time it is fairly straight-forward because the person has no specific brain disease or abnormality. The same difficulty applies to anxiety, depression, and all other types of symptoms. The difference between physical and psychological symptoms is usually clear, but sometimes can be quite murky.

We will describe dissociative symptoms in more detail throughout the manual. Here we are providing an overview.

Dissociation as a Technical Term in Cognitive Psychology

In experimental cognitive psychology, dissociation refers to a disconnection within memory. Memory is not one thing. Rather, it is an overall system composed of two major subsystems. These are called *procedural memory* and *declarative memory*. Procedural memory corresponds to unconscious or implicit memory, while declarative memory corresponds to conscious or explicit memory.

Dissociation between procedural and declarative memory is one of the most rigorously proven phenomena in cognitive psychology. What does this mean?

It means that the normal human mind can store an accurate memory of a real event in procedural memory, while there is complete amnesia for this information in declarative memory. Not only is the memory there in the unconscious mind; it affects behaviour and speech in a measurable fashion.

This fact has been demonstrated over and over in thousands of experiments over decades. There are many different types and designs of experiment in this literature, and they have been described in many different journal articles and textbooks.

As well, countless experiments demonstrate that by giving cues, the memory stored in procedural memory can be transferred to declarative memory, so that the person is consciously aware of it. Also, repeated effort to recall the information can bring it to conscious awareness.

This property of the human mind is demonstrated by the common experience of having a name on the tip of your tongue. By concentrating, or by thinking of related things, the name pops back into conscious awareness. Similarly, it is common to be unable to remember something until a reminder spontaneously triggers the memory.

Like everything in the mind, memory is not perfect and errors can occur. However, a great deal of evidence demonstrates that recovered memories are often accurate. Basic findings are described in the accompanying table.

DISSOCIATION IN COGNITIVE PSYCHOLOGY

- Real events are accurately stored in the unconscious mind

- There is no conscious memory for this information

- The information nevertheless affects speech and behaviour in a measurable fashion

- The memory can be recovered through cued recall or repeated recall effort

- Such recovered memories are often, but not always, accurate

---

Recovered memories will occur during trauma therapy, no matter what techniques and procedures are used. The therapist cannot prevent this from occurring. Simply taking a history of the person's childhood, or returning to an event to process it a second time, involves repeated recall effort and cueing of memories.

Dissociation as an Intrapsychic Defense Mechanism

In its fourth meaning, dissociation is an intrapsychic defense mechanism. Other classical defense mechanisms include projection, acting out, denial, identification with the aggressor, and rationalization. We all use defenses. Some are relatively mature and healthy, others are less so. In some situations, a defense can be healthy; in others not. For instance, laughing uproariously at a funeral in order to avoid one's grief is obviously not healthy.

The problem with defense mechanisms is that they are hard to prove scientifically. Equally, they are hard to disprove. Defense mechanisms are not unscientific. Rather, they are *ascientific*. They can't be directly tested scientifically. For instance, if the phenomenon of dissociation is demonstrated in a cognitive psychology experiment, how do you know if it is caused by the defense mechanism of repression, or the defense mechanism of dissociation?

This is where a lot of the confusion about dissociation and repression comes in: the *phenomenon* of dissociation between procedural and declarative memory is a proven scientific fact, but the *mechanism* causing the dissociation does not have to be the defense mechanism of dissociation.

In this manual, we will focus on the first three meanings of dissociation.

The Difference Between Dissociation and Repression

At one level, repression, splitting, blocking, and dissociation are the same thing. They are all synonyms for the first and third meanings of dissociation. There is a disconnect between material in the conscious mind and material in the unconscious mind, and the disconnection is causing a problem of some kind. At a common sense level, it doesn't matter which term a therapist uses to describe the phenomenon of dissociation.

We prefer to use the word *dissociation*, because we treat dissociative disorders, not blocking disorders or repression disorders; because dissociation can be measured with questionnaires; and because dissociation is a proven scientific fact. Using the word dissociation keeps our treatment grounded in clinical and experimental research.

However, *repression* and *dissociation* are also technical terms in psychoanalysis. It is important to understand the difference between repression and dissociation at the level of intrapsychic defense.

Freud divided repression into two subtypes: primal repression and repression proper.

- *Primal repression*—an unconscious ego defense against unacceptable id impulses and wishes.

- *Repression proper*—an unconscious defense mechanism used by the ego to push unacceptable thoughts, feelings, and memories down into the id, or unconscious.

The easiest way to keep repression and dissociation straight is to remember the difference between *vertical splitting* and *horizontal splitting*.

In horizontal splitting, there is a horizontal barrier in the mind (this is a metaphor, not a literal fact). Above the barrier is the conscious mind (Freud's ego), and below it is the unconscious mind (Freud's id).

In repression proper, impulses and wishes that are threatening to well up from the id are kept out of the ego by the horizontal splitting barrier. They never get into the ego.

In primal repression, unacceptable material in the ego is pushed down into the id to hide it. In vertical splitting, however, there is a vertical barrier within the ego. Nothing gets pushed down into the id, therefore no primal repression is taking place. Instead, mental contents are dissociated from each other and stored within separate compartments of the ego.

Repression and dissociation are not the same thing. Repression is different from all four meanings of dissociation. It is important to keep the different meanings of dissociation straight, otherwise unnecessary confusion, debate, and disagreement can occur.

2
The Different Dissociative Disorders

This chapter provides a review of the Dissociative Disorders section of the DSM-IV-TR plus the provisional diagnosis of dissociative trance disorder. The rules for making DSM diagnoses will be reviewed briefly and some of the common conceptual errors about dissociative identity disorder (DID) will be discussed: for instance, the mistaken ideas that people with DID literally have more than one person living inside them, or are not accountable for their actions.

Also, we will discuss the relationship between the dissociative disorders, PTSD, and acute stress disorder, as well as the inclusion of dissociative symptoms in other DSM-IV-TR categories, including somatization disorder and borderline personality disorder.

We will provide a brief historical and anthropological review of the universality of trance, possession, amnesia, and switches of executive control. The symptoms and experiences in the dissociative disorders section of the DSM-IV-TR have been around for millennia, are universal, and have been understood in many different ways—as mental disorders, as possession, as transcendental spiritual experiences, and as brain disease.

This chapter will include

- Historical and anthropological aspects of dissociation

- Review of the DSM-IV-TR dissociative disorders

- Relationship of dissociative disorders to other disorders, especially PTSD and ASD

- Common conceptual errors about DID

Historical and Anthropological Aspects of Dissociation

"Verily, verily, I say unto you, there is nothing new under the sun."

That quotation from Ecclesiastes could be applied to the dissociative disorders. The core features of DID have been around since time immemorial. Most cultures throughout history have recognized trance and possession. The core features of DID and possession states are the same, no matter what culture, belief system, or particular entity is involved.

In a given culture, the possessing entity may be a demon, ancestor, animal spirit, alien, or god. Or, the possession state may be regarded as a seizure disorder or a mental health problem. In our practices, we view the entities we talk to as psychological aspects of the person, or parts of the self. That is how we will approach them in this manual.

In another society, time, or place, a possession model might be culturally acceptable and therapeutic. In fact, more people on the planet believe in possession than in DID.

Unfortunately, we have seen examples of exorcism used in a destructive, harmful way by people who mistook DID for demon possession. In our experience, dramatic, coercive exorcisms increase the internal fragmentation and conflict of people with complex, chronic dissociative disorders.

The following case example illustrates the potential harm of exorcisms or deliverance rituals.

A woman was sexually abused by her father, who was a clergyman. As an adult she belonged to the same charismatic Christian church as her father. This church, and her controlling, abusive husband, defined her alter personalities as demons and tried to exorcise them. The demons tried to talk about the childhood incest, but their disclosures were dismissed as tricks of Satan.

In order to be a "good Christian," within that church, the woman had to deny the truth of her childhood, deny the validity of her anger, and make a pseudo-reconciliation with her father. She had to view parts of herself as alien and evil.

Treatment of DID is about accepting parts of the self into a blended, unified whole—not getting rid of them.

When angry, disavowed parts of the self are defined as demons, the "treatment," in the form of exorcism, reinforces denial and internal conflict. During the Inquisition, when women made socially unacceptable statements, or practiced unacceptable forms of folk medicine, they were burned at the stake. This form of genocide was defined as the righteous work of God.

The same error is made, at a more subtle, psychological level, when anger and resentment about child abuse are defined as the speech of a demon.

There is nothing new under the sun. The form that DID takes varies from culture to culture, but the basic structure (switches of executive control, amnesia, and dramatic changes in behaviour) are constant. Being "possessed" has been a common aspect of human psychology throughout history. In the mental health field, the possessing entities are called "alter personalities," "dissociative identities," "dissociative states," "parts," "parts of self," or some similar term. The entities are viewed as dissociated aspects of the person's psyche.

Dissociated parts of the self are not demons, nor are they separate people. They are all aspects of one person and there is only one person.

CORE FEATURES OF DID AND POSSESSION

- Switches of executive control from one identity to another

- Changes in behavior depending on "who" is in control of the body

- The "person" has full or partial amnesia for the period of possession

- Treated by a healer or priest within the conceptual system of the culture

The DSM-IV-TR Dissociative Disorders

DSM stands for the *Diagnostic and Statistical Manual of Mental Disorders*. The Manual is the official diagnostic manual of the American Psychiatric Association. It contains all the rules for how to make various psychiatric diagnoses. The DSM has gone through a series of editions. DSM-III came out in 1980, a revised version, DSM-III-R, came out in 1987, DSM-IV came out in 1994, DSM-IV-TR came out in 2000, and DSM-V is expected to be out in 2012.

A separate section of DSM for dissociative disorders first appeared in DSM-III in 1980. In 1994, with DSM-IV, the names of the disorders were changed, except for depersonalization disorder, which remained the same. There has also been a gradual evolution in the diagnostic criteria for dissociative disorders from 1980 on, but it basically consists of fine-tuning. There have been no major conceptual changes.

There are five DSM-IV-TR dissociative disorders:

- Dissociative amnesia

- Dissociative fugue

- Depersonalization disorder

- Dissociative identity disorder

- Dissociative disorder not otherwise specified

In this treatment manual, we are talking about dissociative identity disorder (DID) and dissociative disorder not otherwise specified (DDNOS). These are chronic, complex dissociative disorders linked to chronic, severe trauma in almost every case.

DDNOS has a number of subtypes described in the DSM. We are concerned here with one subtype: forms of DDNOS that are partial forms of DID. Here, DDNOS means a clinical picture that is the same as DID, but just not quite as much. The parts are not quite so separate and distinct, the amnesia between them is not as severe, the switches of executive control are less clear-cut, and the parts are less likely to have specific different names and ages.

People with DDNOS are clearly in the dissociative taxon. They have numerous other disorders and addictions, intensive trauma histories, and are in need of treatment. DDNOS could be described as DID, but not as obtrusive. The treatment for both is the same. In research studies, DDNOS is more common than DID, so factually DID could be seen as a subset or extreme example of DDNOS.

The DSM-IV-TR criteria for DID can be summarized as follows:

DEFINITION OF DISSOCIATIVE IDENTITY DISORDER

- The person exhibits distinct, separate identity states.

- The identities take turns being in control of the body.

- Some kind of amnesia occurs between the different identities.

- It cannot be explained by imaginary companions, alcohol blackouts or medical conditions.

The diagnostic criteria for DID and the core features of possession states are the same thing. What varies from culture to culture is how they are understood and treated. We believe that many indigenous healers have probably done an excellent job of treating dissociative disorders throughout history. Also, no doubt, many have *not* done a good job. But, overall, many indigenous healers have probably provided humane and effective treatment, especially for the simpler, more time-limited dissociative disorders.

The DSM-IV-TR also contains a provisional diagnostic category included for further study and discussion: trance possession disorder. This is American psychiatry's attempt to recognize the existence of dissociative states in other cultures. The criteria and text for trance possession disorder are not perfect but they are a start.

Rules for Making DSM-IV-TR Diagnoses

The purpose of the DSM is to provide standardized rules for making psychiatric diagnoses. Without a system like the DSM, different psychiatrists would make diagnoses in an inconsistent, hit-and-miss fashion. There would be no way to study different disorders scientifically, because you could never be sure who had what disorder, or if they would get the same diagnosis elsewhere.

The DSM is set up so that diagnoses do not depend on theories, personal opinions, or different schools of thought. The diagnostic criteria are behavioural, and are based on symptoms the patient reports, not on interpretations made by the psychiatrist. Of course, this is true only in theory, because psychiatry is not a hard science. Nevertheless, the DSM tries to be as objective as possible.

If we make a diagnosis of DID, what are we saying?

All we are saying is that the person meets the criteria for DID. They exhibit different, distinct identity states; there is switching of executive control between states; some kind of amnesia is involved; and the behaviour cannot be explained by conscious faking, imaginary companions, alcohol blackouts, or a specific medical disease.

If we make a diagnosis of DID, what are we *not* saying?

We are not saying what caused the DID. Stated more technically, theories of etiology are not relevant to making DSM diagnoses. It doesn't matter what you believe caused a given disorder: if the person meets the criteria for the disorder, they have it.

This is true for all DSM diagnoses. If a person meets the criteria for depression, they have depression.

Whether the depression was caused by a virus, a defective gene, a bad childhood, errors of thinking, a bad marriage, or any possible cause, doesn't matter.

Controversies or disagreements about the causes of DID and DDNOS are not relevant to making the diagnoses, according to the rules of the DSM system. As long as the diagnostic criteria are applied consistently, based on what the patient or client says and does, different mental health professionals should agree on who does, or does not, have DID (or DDNOS).

Relationship of DID and DDNOS to Other Disorders in DSM-IV-TR

A person with DID, cannot have another dissociative disorder as well. A person with DID will always meet criteria for dissociative amnesia, for instance, but since the amnesia is part of the DID, there is no need for a separate diagnosis.

For DDNOS, the rule works the other way around: a diagnosis of DDNOS cannot be made if the person meets criteria for one of the other dissociative disorders. The NOS (not otherwise specified) category exists specifically to describe people who do not meet criteria for one of the other dissociative disorders, but nevertheless have serious dissociative symptoms. The NOS category is a grab-bag category that is included at the end of most sections of the DSM—there is an anxiety disorder NOS, a mood disorder NOS, and so on.

If you have DID or DDNOS, you can also have any other non-dissociative disorder in the DSM. In fact, almost everyone with DID or DDNOS meets criteria for numerous other diagnoses, including depression, posttraumatic stress disorder, acute stress disorder, obsessive-compulsive disorder, panic disorder, substance abuse, and eating disorders.

Posttraumatic stress disorder, acute stress disorder, DID, and DDNOS, in our opinion, all belong to the same family of diagnoses. It would be appropriate for them all to be in the same section of the DSM-V. Indeed, when acute stress disorder was first presented to the DSM-IV dissociative disorders committee for consideration, it was called *brief reactive dissociative disorder*. The name was changed to acute stress disorder and it was moved to the anxiety disorders section of DSM-IV later in the process of revising DSM-III-R.

By definition, acute stress disorder can only last one month. If it lasts longer, the diagnosis is changed to posttraumatic stress disorder (PTSD). About 80% of people with DID meet criteria for PTSD. The relationship does not hold the other way around, however. A much smaller, but unknown percentage of people with PTSD also have DID. More studies are needed on the relationship between DID and PTSD.

At the moment, the rules of DSM-IV-TR require that we think of these as distinct, separate disorders, but that does not seem realistic to us.

Common Misconceptions About DID

There are a number of common misconceptions about DID. Some people do not "believe" in DID because they do not believe in one or more of these misconceptions. But DID isn't a matter of belief. If a person acts like someone else, claims to have a different name and age, and then later doesn't remember that behaviour, then he or she has DID. The only exceptions are if the person is consciously faking, if the behaviour happens only with drugs or alcohol, or if it is caused by a specific medical condition.

A questionable diagnosis generally boils down to two options: the person has DID, or the person is consciously faking. In practice, such behaviour is rarely or never caused by a specific medical condition, or drugs and alcohol. The common misconceptions about DID are as follows:

COMMON MISCONCEPTIONS ABOUT DID

- There are literally different people inside the person with DID.

- The person literally has more than one personality.

- The person can't be held responsible for her behaviour.

- It will go away if you ignore it.

- It can't be treated.

- Treatment involves getting rid of the alter personalities.

- If you buy into the DID, you will make it worse.

- DID isn't real.

- The person is just making it up.

- The person is just doing it to get attention.

If a person is behaving as if she has DID, but is just making it up or doing it for attention, then the diagnosis is *factitious disorder*, not DID.

Once these misconceptions are set aside, then DID can be seen for what it is: a set of behaviours, and a psychological structure, designed to help the person cope with life. Almost always, that life has been full of abuse, trauma, neglect, misfortune, and misery. It is always important to remember that DID isn't literally real. One way to explain this is to say:

"If we took an X-ray of your head, we wouldn't see a whole bunch of little skeletons in there. There aren't literally any two-inch tall little people living inside your head. They are parts of you. You have only one brain."

"On the other hand, DID is very real psychologically. People truly do come out of blank spells in strange locations, not knowing how they got there. So while DID describes your internal, personal experience, it isn't literally real. Does that make sense to you?"

3
How Common Are the Dissociative Disorders?

In this chapter we provide a brief review of the epidemiology of the dissociative disorders. The dissociative disorders are not rare. In fact, they are part of the daily caseload of most mental health professionals, but usually go unrecognized.

This chapter covers

- Epidemiology of dissociation in the general population

- Epidemiology of dissociation in clinical populations

- Unrecognized dissociation is common in most mental health caseloads

Dissociation in the General Population

Studies of the dissociative disorders in the general population have been conducted in Canada, Turkey, and China. Studies in college students have been conducted in Canada and the United States. In each of these studies, the Dissociative Experiences Scale and Dissociative Disorders Interview Schedule were administered to 300-500 participants.

Complex, pathological dissociation was found in all three of these distinct cultures and languages. Overall, in North America, somewhere between 3% and 11% of people in the general population have had, or currently have, a dissociative disorder. We need more studies in larger samples to narrow this figure down, but based on the available evidence, the lifetime prevalence of pathological dissociation is not less than 3% in North America.

DID appears to affect 1% of the general population. This does not mean that complex, severe DID such as we see in inpatient programs affects one person in a hundred. The 1% figure for the general population includes many cases that are mild and do not require inpatient care. The prevalence of full, complicated DID with severe trauma and extensive comorbidity is uncertain. An educated guess based on the general population studies and studies among psychiatric inpatients would place it at between 1 in 500 and 1 in 1000.

Dissociation in Clinical Populations

There are now 11 published studies in 7 countries in which either the Dissociative Disorders Interview Schedule (DDIS) or the Structured Clinical Interview for DSM-IV Dissociative Disorders (SCID-D) have been administered to general adult psychiatric inpatients. In each of these studies, patients with previously diagnosed dissociative disorders were excluded. The results of these studies are as follows:

PREVALENCE OF DISSOCIATIVE DISORDERS IN INPATIENT SETTINGS IN SEVEN COUNTRIES

Study	DID (%)	Dissociative Disorder (%)
USA		
Ross, 1999 (N=201)	7.5	40.8
Rifkin, 1998 (N=100)	1.0	n/a
Latz, 1995 (N=175)	12.0	46.0
Saxe, 1993 (N=110)	3.6	15.0
Canada		
Horen, 1995 (N=48)	6.0	17.0
Ross, 1991 (N=299)	3.3	20.7
Turkey		
Tutkun, 1998 (N=166)	5.4	10.2
Switzerland		
Modestin, 1996 (N=207)	0.4	5.0
Norway		
Knudsen, 1995 (N=101)	4.7	7.9
Netherlands		
Friedl and Draijer, 2000 (N=122)	1.7	8.2
Germany		
Gast et al., 2000 (N=115)	0.9	4.3
Total (N=1,644)	3.7	15.3

Source: Adapted from Ross, 2004.

In addition to these studies among general adult inpatients, four similar studies have been conducted among people in treatment for drug and alcohol problems. In these studies, the percentage of people with previously undiagnosed DID averaged about 7%. Dissociative disorders appear to be more common in chemical dependency populations than among general adult inpatients.

Other studies using the Dissociative Experiences Scale, Multidimensional Inventory of Dissociation, and the Dissociation Questionnaire have found pathological dissociation among college students, the general population, people with eating disorders, and other samples.

Unrecognized Dissociative Disorders are Common in Mental Health Caseloads

There is now a considerable body of research showing that dissociative disorders are common in mental health caseloads. About one in five psychiatric inpatients has a dissociative disorder. Most of these cases are DID and DDNOS. Therefore the treatment techniques we describe in this manual are relevant for a large number of individuals in western societies.

The Trauma Model is designed to be useful for a wide range of mental health problems and addictions, not only the dissociative disorders. Treating DID and DDNOS always means treating numerous other symptoms, diagnoses, addictions, and self-defeating behaviours.

Also, severe dissociative symptoms commonly occur in people who do not meet criteria for a dissociative disorder. For instance, depersonalization is common in schizophrenia; amnesia is one of the symptoms of somatization disorder; and transient dissociative symptoms are one of the criteria for borderline personality disorder.

Anyone treating severe personality disorders or trauma survivors of any kind is bound to be treating pathological dissociation. In our opinion, dissociation is one of the common, everyday, major symptom categories in the mental health field. These categories include

- Depression

- Anxiety

- Psychosis

- Dissociation

- Addiction

Rather than being subspecialty techniques, the strategies and interventions in this manual aim, in our opinion, at the core of general mental health practice.

4
The Dissociative Experiences Scale

The Dissociative Experiences Scale (DES) is by far the most widely used measure of dissociation. The DES is included in an Appendix. All the measures in the Appendix can be photocopied and used without permission.

This chapter covers

- The DES: How to use it as a screening tool

- The DES-Taxon

How to Use the Dissociative Experiences Scale (DES) as a Screening Tool

You can't use the DES to make a diagnosis. The DES was designed as a screening tool. Its purpose is to help spot dissociative disorders, not to make actual diagnoses. It also works well to track treatment outcome.

To administer the DES, you simply give it to the person, and ask him to read the instructions and fill it out. If the person is vision impaired or has literacy problems, the questions can be read out loud. The DES takes about 10 minutes to fill out and 5 minutes (or less) to score. It can be administered by anyone, including clerical or volunteer staff.

To score the DES, you add up each of the 28 item scores, then divide the total by 28 (eg., 528/28 = 18.9). DES scores are reported to one decimal place. The average score in the general population in North America is 10.8. For adults, any score below 15 is normal. A rough guide to interpreting DES scores is:

INTERPRETING DES SCORES	
• 0 – 15	Normal
• 15-20	Slightly above normal
• 20-30	Elevated: possible PTSD or DDNOS
• 30-40	Definitely elevated: possible DID
• 40 or higher	High: increased likelihood of DID

The higher the DES score, the more likely it is that the person has a dissociative disorder. However, a person with DID can have a score under 20, and a person with a score over 40 does not necessarily have DID or DDNOS. Tests of DES reliability and validity show that the odds of having a dissociative disorder go up with the score.

Sometimes a person will have an extremely high score on the DES, like 85. This is unlikely to be an accurate, valid score. Probably, the person is exaggerating or doesn't understand the questions or instructions. Alternatively, very high scores are a red flag for a factitious disorder.

Sometimes the overall DES score may be realistic but one or more individual item scores are out of line. For instance, a person may respond that she stares off into space and misses part of a conversation 90% of the time—if this was really true, she would be catatonic.

Another person responded that she was able to do things with amazing ease and spontaneity that she would ordinarily not be able to do, 100% of the time. This is self-contradictory. If you can do something 100% of the time, then it can't be something you ordinarily cannot do.

We always make a point of looking at the question on auditory hallucinations, because elevated scores on that item strongly increase our suspicion that the person has DID.

It is useful to look at the pattern of responses to individual items, to get a feel for the types of symptoms the person experiences. Also, administration of the DES tool may be followed by a clinical interview, to inquire about specific items and responses on the DES in more detail.

The DES-Taxon (DES-T)

Eight items on the DES form the DES-T. Taxometric analysis is a statistical technique that was used to analyze DES scores in two large studies (Waller, Putnam, and Carlson, 1996; Waller and Ross, 1997). In the two studies, the DES-T divided participants into two separate categories: normal, and pathological dissociation. There were very few intermediate cases. DES-T analyses can be done using a program that is available on the web page of the International Society for the Study of Trauma and Dissociation (ISSTD) at www.isst-d.org.

For clinicians, a more practical way to use the DES-T is simply to add the item score for the 8 DES-T items, then divide by 8 (e.g., 164/8 = 20.5). This simpler, numerical DES-T score can vary from zero to 100, just like the overall DES score using the entire 28 items.

However, the 8 DES-T items are clearly much more abnormal than many of the non-DES-T items. Therefore, a score above 20 on the DES-T means the person is quite likely to have a dissociative disorder. It is not definitive, but the odds of a person having a dissociative disorder are greater with a DES-T score of 20.5 than if the overall DES score is 20.5.

The 8 DES-T items are as follows:

THE EIGHT DES-T ITEMS

DES-T item	DES-T item number
• Finding oneself in a place but unaware how one got there	3
• Finding new belongings but does not remember buying them	5
• Sees oneself as if looking at another person	7
• Does not recognize friends or family members	8
• Feeling that other people, objects, and the world are not real	12
• Feeling that one's body is not one's own	13
• Feeling as though one were two different people	22
• Hearing voices inside one's head	27

Using the DES as a Treatment Outcome Measure

Several studies show that the DES can be used to track treatment outcome. Most studies find average DES scores above 40 for people with DID and above 25 for people with DDNOS.

At the beginning of treatment for DID or DDNOS, the DES score will probably not drop right away. Symptoms of anxiety, depression, suicidal ideation, and hopelessness will usually begin to ease off before there is any change in the DES score. However, over a period of years, the DES score will drop gradually. It will become normal if the person reaches integration and completes a successful course of therapy. Post-integration, DES scores usually will be in the normal range—15 or less.

5
The Somatoform Dissociation Questionnaire

The Somatoform Dissociation Questionnaire (SDQ) is an easy-to-use, 20-item questionnaire that addresses the somatic dimension of dissociation. The DES focuses more on the cognitive aspects of dissociation.

This chapter will cover

- The Difference Between Somatoform and Psychoform Dissociation

- The SDQ: How to Use It as a Screening Tool

The Difference Between Somatoform and Psychoform Dissociation

As explained in Chapter 1, any two elements of the psyche can be dissociated from each other: thought from feeling; physical sensation from conscious memory; movement from sensation; smell from behaviour, and so on. As defined in DSM-IV-TR, the dissociative disorders focus on memory, identity, and consciousness. The diagnostic criteria and text for dissociative disorders mention little about somatoform dissociation. Instead, the description of somatoform dissociation can be found in the somatoform disorders' section of the DSM, under *somatization disorder* and *conversion disorder*.

However, in ICD-10, the diagnostic manual used outside the United States, dissociative disorders and somatoform disorders are grouped together in the same section. This makes sense to us. According to the DSM-IV-TR, if you dissociate a memory you have dissociative amnesia. If you dissociate the ability to move your left arm, or feel touch below the navel, you have a conversion disorder. Conversion disorder is diagnosed when there is a single symptom reminiscent of a neurological problem.

By DSM-IV-TR rules, if you have many different psychosomatic symptoms, you have somatization disorder. However, the symptoms listed under somatization disorder include amnesia, a hallmark of dissociative disorders. This confusion in the DSM system need not interfere with therapy, because all forms of dissociation can be treated the same way, as we will explain in later chapters.

Many people with DID experience various conversion symptoms, as cited on the list of symptoms in DSM-IV-TR somatization disorder. Treatment of DID and DDNOS routinely involves paying attention to both somatoform and psychoform dissociation.

Psychoform dissociation involves disconnections in consciousness, identity, feelings, perception, and identity. Somatoform dissociation involves disconnections between mind and body. Since mind and body are elements of a unified field, the distinction between somatoform and psychoform dissociation is somewhat artificial. There is overlap between the two categories. Separating them out is important, though, because somatoform dissociation often gets overlooked. Separating the two helps the clinician keep both in mind.

There are high levels of correlation between scores on the SDQ and scores on measures of psychoform dissociation like the DES. This confirms that the two types of dissociation often overlap, but are nevertheless somewhat separate. The full form of the SDQ—the SDQ-20—has 20 items. A short form of the SDQ, called the SDQ-5, has five items, as shown.

THE SDQ-5 ITEMS

- Pain during urination

- Insensitiviy to pain

- Seeing things differently than usual (e.g., as if looking through a tunnel)

- Feels the body, or part of it, has disappeared

- Cannot speak or can only whisper

The overlap between somatoform and psychoform dissociation is evident in the SDQ-5. Pain during urination, insensitivity to pain, and being unable to speak are classical conversion symptoms. Seeing things differently than usual and parts of the body disappearing are perceptual symptoms typical of depersonalization disorder.

As a rule of thumb, somatoform dissociation involves the body, usually physical movement or one of the five senses. Both the SDQ-20 and the SDQ-5 are reproduced in the Appendix.

How to Use the SDQ as a Screening Tool

Like the DES, the SDQ is a screening tool. It cannot be used by itself to make diagnoses. The SDQ helps identify and track symptoms that might otherwise be overlooked.

Like the DES, the SDQ is short; it can be completed and scored easily. Each item can be scored from 1 to 5; therefore the total score for the SDQ-20 ranges from 20 to 100.

DES AND SDQ-20 SCORES IN DIFFERENT DIAGNOSTIC CATEGORIES

	SDQ-20	DES
• Bipolar mood disorder	27.2	21.3
• Somatoform disorders	33.9	18.9
• DDNOS	40.3	34.1
• DID	51.2	47.2

Source: Adapted from Nijenhuis, 2004.

As in the DES, the higher the SDQ score, the more likely it is that the person has a dissociative disorder. Average DES and SDQ-20 scores for four different diagnostic categories are:

From these scores, one can see that somatoform dissociation occurs more frequently in somatoform disorders than does psychoform dissociation. That makes sense. However, it is also clear that both forms of dissociation are common in DDNOS and DID. That is why neither should be overlooked.

Also, although SDQ-20 and DES scores are much lower in bipolar mood disorder than in DDNOS and DID, such symptoms do occur in bipolar disorder as well. Indeed, as in anxiety and depression, both forms of dissociation occur in many different DSM categories. It is not surprising that they are most frequent in somatoform and dissociative disorders. A detailed discussion of the SDQ and somatoform dissociation can be found in Nijenhuis (2004).

6
The Dissociative Disorders Interview Schedule

The Dissociative Disorders Interview Schedule (DDIS) is a structured interview that diagnoses all of the five DSM-IV-TR dissociative disorders, somatization disorder, major depressive episode, and borderline personality disorder. It also inquires in detail about psychotic symptoms, childhood physical and sexual abuse, paranormal/ESP experiences, and secondary features of dissociative identity disorder. The DDIS and its scoring rules are included in the Appendix. The DDIS can be used by any mental health professional without formal training.

This chapter also includes a section on the Structured Clinical Interview for DSM-IV Dissociative Disorders (SCID-D). The SCID-D is a structured interview with good reliability and validity, but its use requires considerable training and it cannot be photocopied or used without permission. Information on how to purchase the SCID-D is included. Data on the DES, DDIS and SCID-D can be found in the American Psychiatric Association's *Handbook of Psychiatric Measures* (Pincus, Rush, First, and McQueen, 2000).

In this chapter we cover

- Reliability and Validity of the DDIS

- How to Use and Score the DDIS

- Clinical Findings With the DDIS

- Brief Review of the SCID-D

Reliability and Validity of the DDIS

The DDIS has good reliability and validity. In a sample of 296 people with DID, the DDIS correctly identified 96% as having DID. This is well above the standard for structured interviews for other Axis I diagnoses. The false positive rate of DID is under 1% on the DDIS. This means that the DDIS very rarely identifies someone as having DID when the clinical diagnosis is something else. Using statistical analysis, the DDIS can differentiate DID from DDNOS.

Using the scoring rules in the Appendix, the DDIS can differentiate DID from non-dissociative disorders very well. In a study by Ross, Ellason, and Duffy (2002), there was an excellent level of agreement between the clinical diagnosis, the DES-T, the DDIS, and the SCID-D. In this study, each method of diagnosis was asked to categorize the study participants as having DID or DDNOS versus no dissociative disorder.

It is always true, however, that the clinical interview provides the gold standard. If careful interviewing over time indicates that a person does not have DID or DDNOS, then the DDIS, Multidimensional Inventory of Dissociation (MID), or SCID-D are wrong if they say otherwise. A structured interview cannot override clinical evaluation. These rules apply to all diagnoses in DSM-IV-TR and all structured interviews.

How to Score the DDIS

The DDIS has 16 different sections. The ones that make DSM-IV-TR diagnoses are scored using the rules of the DSM. The questions in these sections are taken straight out of the DSM. For borderline personality disorder and somatization disorder, we always count the number of positive symptoms in addition to making the DSM-IV-TR diagnosis.

Other sections, such as Positive Symptoms of Psychosis, Secondary Features of Dissociative Identity Disorder, and Extrasensory/Paranormal Experiences yield scores based on the number of items in the section, i.e., there are 16 secondary features, therefore scores can range from zero to 16 for this section. The Psychiatric History section is descriptive and is not scored.

The childhood physical and sexual abuse sections are descriptive but can also be analyzed to yield numbers. We commonly add up the number of different types of sexual abuse reported, for instance. For research purposes, a total Trauma Dose Score can be calculated using the formula in the Appendix. Details on scoring are in the Appendix. Average scores for selected sections of the DDIS in different diagnostic categories are as follows:

AVERAGE DDIS SYMPTOM SCORES FOR DIFFERENT DIAGNOSTIC CATEGORIES

	DID	DDNOS	Schizophrenia	CD	General Population
Somatic	15.4	9.7	2.8	4.4	1.1
Psychotic	6.6	3.8	4.6	1.8	0.5
Secondary Features of DID	10.6	5.2	3.6	1.7	0.6
Borderline	5.5	3.9	2.6	3.4	0.6
ESP/Paranormal	5.8	4.1	4.5	2.4	1.4
Substance abuse	1.1	0.8	0.9	2.2	0.1

CD = chemical dependency. Source: Adapted from Ross and Ellason, 2005.

It may seem odd that people with DID report more psychotic symptoms than people with schizophrenia, but this is a consistent finding in the literature. Ross (2004) discusses the relationship between dissociation and schizophrenia in detail.

Besides the psychosis section, the symptom scores on the DDIS are as expected. Except for chemical dependency items, people with DID report more symptoms in the different sections of the

DDIS. As expected, people with a primary diagnosis of chemical dependency report the most drug and alcohol use.

Although there is no exact cutoff, the more symptoms a person reports on the DDIS, the more likely it is they have DID or DDNOS. The actual diagnoses are made using the sections of the DDIS that follow the DSM-IV-TR rules for dissociative disorders. The other sections provide supporting information. The scores on the different sections of the DDIS can be added up to yield an overall score. Scoring methods are described in Ross and Ellason (2005).

Clinical Findings with The DDIS

During an initial assessment, we generally give the DES first, then the DDIS, then do a clinical interview. The DDIS usually takes 30–40 minutes, depending on the complexity of the case. However, many questions on the DDIS are ones you would want to ask in the clinical interview, so the net additional time for administering the DDIS is roughly 20 minutes.

The DDIS was designed to be practical and user-friendly in terms of its training requirements, time to administer, and ease of scoring. Once the DDIS has been completed, it can be scanned visually in a few minutes. The sequence of observations is as follows:

INFORMAL SCANNING OF THE DDIS

- Count the number of positive somatic symptoms

- Check whether at least one substance abuse item is positive

- Skim the psychiatric history section

- Count the number of positive psychotic symptoms

- Check for major depressive episode—check if currently active

- Check for physical abuse and sexual abuse

- Count the number of secondary features of DID

- Count the number of ESP/paranormal experiences

- Count the number of borderline symptoms—note if there are five or more

- Check each dissociative disorder—especially DID

This informal scanning of the DDIS can be done in a few minutes after a little practice. A person with DID should meet the DSM-IV-TR criteria for DID and have a typical symptom profile on the DDIS. Some mild cases will have fewer than the usual symptoms. If the person does not meet the actual DSM-IV-TR criteria for DID, he may still have DID or DDNOS. DDNOS is diagnosed based on the interviewer's judgment. To diagnose DDNOS you should look at the overall DDIS profile; it should be like DID but not as severe.

After looking at the overall profile, you should carefully read the section that describes the secondary features of DID. A person with DID or DDNOS may say "No" to the DSM-IV-TR criteria for DID, but answer "Yes" to key questions in the secondary features section. If the person has someone else inside with a different name who takes control of the body, combined with voices and blank spells, you can confidently diagnose DDNOS.

DDNOS is often a preliminary diagnosis; later in therapy it may become clear that the person has full DID. Since the treatments for DID and DDNOS are basically the same, there is no reason to be too concerned about whether you are missing full DID.

You should also look at the childhood physical and sexual abuse histories. If both are negative but the symptom profile looks like DDNOS, check the answers to the amnesia questions: one in somatization disorder; three in the secondary features of DID section; one in the dissociative amnesia criteria; and one in the DID criteria. The more of these amnesia criteria are positive, the more you should consider the possibility that a history of childhood abuse will emerge in therapy.

Over 90% of people with DID describe childhood physical and/or sexual abuse on the DDIS during the initial interview. Those who do not fall into three categories: 1) were never physically or sexually abused, 2) were abused, remember, but do not want to talk about it, and 3) were abused but have complete amnesia for the abuse.

This latter complete amnesia group is small—probably 1% -2% of DID cases at most. Even within this group, it is hard to tell the difference between actual amnesia, extreme denial, conscious suppression, and simple misunderstanding of the questions.

It is important to recognize that if the person says "No" to childhood physical and sexual abuse, but meets criteria for DID or DDNOS, it is quite possible that no such abuse ever occurred. The trauma may have involved verbal or emotional abuse, family violence, death of caretakers, other threats to secure attachment, serious disease or injury, or some other form of misfortune.

In theory, a person could develop DID or complex DDNOS without trauma, but in our experience this never happens. The DDIS asks about only two of the many different forms of trauma, so it is not surprising that a few respondents do not report physical or sexual abuse.

The SCID-D

The Structured Clinical Interview for DSM-IV Dissociative Disorders (SCID-D) was developed by Marlene Steinberg (1995). Information about the SCID-D can be found at www.strangerinthemirror. com. The SCID-D was designed to supplement the Structured Clinical Interview for DSM-III-R (SCID), a widely used structured interview that makes many different Axis I and II diagnoses, but does not diagnose dissociative disorders. The SCID-D is a semi-structured interview that inquires about a wide range of dissociative symptoms in great detail.

The SCID-D has five subscales and an overall score. Each subscale score and the overall score can range from zero to 20. The five subscales of the SCID-D are

- Amnesia

- Depersonalization

- Derealization

- Identify confusion

- Identity alteration

The SCID-D has excellent reliability and validity. Among its advantages, it makes a very detailed inquiry about many dissociative symptoms; it has five easy-to-understand subscales; it yields an easy-to-understand overall score; it is semi-structured, so allows for probing and clarification by the interviewer; it is well accepted in the dissociative disorders field; and norms for DDNOS and DID are available.

There are some disadvantages to the SCID-D: It requires training to administer; it can take several hours to administer; and it cannot be photocopied and used without permission.

The DDIS and SCID-D are complementary to one another. It is good for the field to have two structured interviews with different formats and scoring. The validity of each structured interview provides concurrent validity for the other. Neither of the two structured interviews is superior to the other. Each has different advantages and disadvantages. Both can be used to make reliable, valid dissociative disorder diagnoses.

7
The Multidimensional Inventory of Dissociation

The Multidimensional Inventory of Dissociation (MID) is a computer-scored self-report measure that is somewhat like the MMPI or MCMI. It provides a comprehensive inquiry about the full range of dissociative symptoms and yields a set of subscales that have well-established norms and cutoff scores. The MID is practical to use because it is filled out by the client and scored by computer, so little professional time is required to administer it.

Information on how to have the MID scored by its developer, Paul Dell, PhD, can be obtained from him at pfdell@aol.com. Additional information is available at www.isst-d.org. The MID can be scored on the International Society for the Study of Trauma and Dissociation web page, but only members of the organization can access the scoring program.

This chapter will cover

- How to Use the MID

How to Use the MID

The MID was developed more recently than the DES, DDIS, and SCID-D (Dell, 2000). It has several features that make it an important addition to the field:

FEATURES OF THE MID

- Covers the full range of dissociative symptoms

- Is a computer-scored self-report measure like the MMPI or MCMI

- Yields a graphical profile

- Includes numerous subscales

- Includes validity scales

- Includes a large database

Because the MID is filled out by the respondent and scored by computer, it is especially welcomed by busy researchers and clinicians.

The brevity of this chapter has nothing to do with the importance or usefulness of the MID. It is so easy to use and score that no longer explanation is required. Besides a graphical summary of the data, Paul Dell can provide a narrative summary that can be useful for diagnosis and treatment planning, research, or forensic evaluation.

Typical MID profiles for DID, DDNOS, and a normal control are displayed in chart form:

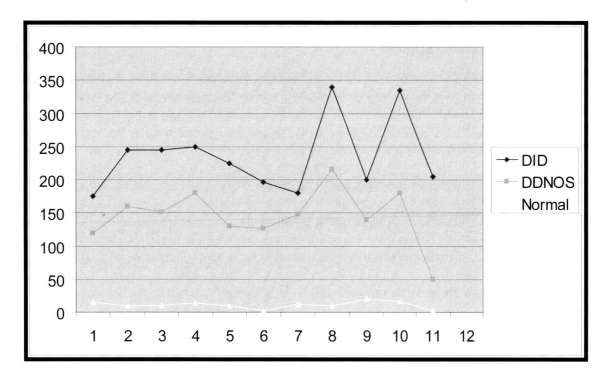

8
Dissociation and Borderline Personality Disorder

The relationship between dissociation and borderline personality disorder (BPD) is complicated. Much more research is required to develop a fuller and clearer picture of the inter-relationship between these clinical pictures. In this chapter we provide an overview geared to the actual work of therapy. We cover

- Definition of Borderline Personality Disorder

- Frequency of Borderline Personality Disorder

- What Percentage of People with BPD Have a Dissociative Disorder

- What Percentage of People with DID Have Borderline Personality Disorder

- How to Understand the Relationship Between Dissociation and BPD

- Genes Versus Environment

Definition of Borderline Personality Disorder

The word *borderline* is like the word *dissociation*, in that it has different meanings or usages. The three meanings of borderline range from factual to highly negative, as follows:

THE THREE MEANINGS OF BORDERLINE

- The DSM-IV-TR criteria

- A theoretical psychological structure

- A condescending, demeaning insult

DSM-IV-TR Criteria for Borderline Personality Disorder

There are nine criteria for borderline personality in DSM-IV-TR. In order to be diagnosed with borderline personality disorder, a person must meet five of these criteria on a stable, long-term basis. A person cannot be categorized as BPD for behaviour that occurs every once in a while.

We believe there are several problems with the DSM-IV-TR definition of borderline personality disorder. First, since there are nine criteria, but only five are required to satisfy the diagnosis, two people can both be diagnosed with BPD, while sharing only one symptom out of nine. It is hard to see how those two people can fit the same category when they have so little in common. Second, the requirement for five criteria is conceptually arbitrary. Why is a person identified as BPD who meets five criteria, but not BPD if meeting four? It is not realistic to jump from normal to a severe personality disorder by adding one criterion.

According to the DSM definition, borderline personality disorder is an entity that one exhibits or does not. In reality, everyone displays some borderline characteristics, and we all behave more "borderline" when we are stressed out. This is another example of the taxon-continuum problem we discussed in the first chapter regarding dissociation. In our view, the DSM-IV-TR criteria for BPD encompass a behavioural trauma-symptom checklist. This checklist describes how we would expect an adult to look after a childhood of chaos, abuse, neglect, violence, and highly disturbed family dynamics. In our view, borderline personality traits are usually a matter of degree, not something one either has or does not have. That is, it is more useful to think of a BPD diagnosis as a continuum rather than as a taxon.

A third problem with the DSM criteria is that taken together, they do not define a separate category of behaviour. People diagnosed with BPD tend to fit criteria for several other DSM personality disorders, especially histrionic, narcissistic, and antisocial. They also have numerous comorbid diagnoses on Axis I, including PTSD, dissociative disorders, substance abuse, anxiety, and depression.

The main advantages of the DSM-IV-TR criteria for BPD diagnosis are that they are individually clear, operationalized, and behavioural. The criteria can be applied with reasonable consistency. A mnemonic for the nine diagnostic criteria is: ABCD, four I's, and dissociation.

NINE DIAGNOSTIC CRITERIA FOR BORDERLINE PERSONALITY

- A – Angry outbursts

- B – Boredom and emptiness

- C – Cutting, self-damaging acts

- D – Devaluation/idealization (all-or-nothing, black-and-white thinking)

- I – Identity disturbance

- I – Impulsivity

- I – Instability of affect

- I – Intolerance of being alone

- D – dissociation or paranoid ideation

The DSM-IV-TR rules don't tell you how much dissociation there has to be before a separate dissociative disorder diagnosis is made on Axis I. We recommend making a separate Axis I diagnosis whenever a person meets criteria for one of the five dissociative disorders. The dissociation in the borderline criteria should be relatively mild, transient, or occasional, for no separate dissociative disorder to be diagnosed.

The Psychological Structure Meaning of Borderline

The second meaning of borderline is a theoretical psychological structure. Everyone who treats or writes about borderline personality agrees with this meaning of borderline. Basically, the person is split into two separate modes of being. There is a positive, "I'm OK-You're OK" mode, in which the person feels good emotionally, and has a positive image of herself and the outside person. Then there is a second, negative, "I'm Not OK-You're Not OK" mode, in which the person feels abandoned, empty, depressed, rejected, anxious, angry, or all of the above. In this mode, the self is bad and unlovable, and the other person is bad, rejecting, and cruel.

The person diagnosed with BPD bounces back and forth from mode A to mode B in a chaotic fashion, and uses numerous unhealthy defenses, addictions, and behaviours to try to get back into the positive mode. She cannot integrate the two modes into a blended, stable, balanced, fluid self. Each of the two modes has different thoughts, beliefs, behaviour, feelings, and views of the self and the world.

Different authors use different theories and vocabulary to describe the psychological structure of borderline personality, but the basic description is the same. We will talk about this structural meaning of borderline in later chapters, especially Chapter 11 on the problem of attachment to the perpetrator.

The Third Meaning of Borderline

The third meaning of borderline, unfortunately, is used widely in the mental health field. It is a term of insult and slander. "Borderlines," in this use of the term, are not legitimate patients in psychiatric hospitals. They are seen as hysterical, manipulative, demanding, dependent nuisances. Some professionals speak in a cruel, belittling fashion about "borderlines," who are always female.

This hostile counter-transference toward people diagnosed as BPD is communicated through facial expression, tone of voice, and similar mechanisms, not through theory, data, or science. Too often, in the mental health system, people with borderline personality disorder are laughed at, put down, "managed" in a rejecting, uncaring fashion "for their own good," or denied the respect and compassion provided for people with psychiatric disorders like depression and schizophrenia.

This institutionalized negative attitude toward "borderlines" needs to be addressed both in training and within the mental health system. It is true that people who meet six, seven, or eight DSM-IV-TR criteria for borderline personality disorder can be demanding, manipulative, chaotic, and stressful to deal with. They certainly require limit-setting and behavioural management, but they do not deserve the dismissive treatment they too often get from mental health professionals. Too often, the mental health field inflicts more abuse, neglect, devaluation, and rejection on top of the life experience that gave rise to the borderline criteria to start with.

In clinical practice, two good reasons to make an official diagnosis of borderline personality disorder are to refer the person for dialectical behaviour therapy (DBT) (Linehan, 1995) or Trauma Model Therapy (Ross, 2007). Otherwise, the diagnosis is too often a black cloud that follows the person around the mental health system.

Epidemiology of Borderline Personality Disorder

The relationship between dissociation and borderline personality disorder can be summarized at an epidemiological level. More research is needed, but the findings to date follow:

- About 3% of adults in the general population in North America meet criteria for BPD.

- Rates of childhood abuse, neglect, violence, family chaos, and loss of primary caretakers are very high in BPD.

- About two thirds of people with BPD have a dissociative disorder.

- About two thirds of people with DID have borderline personality disorder.

- DID and BPD have similar patterns of extensive comorbidity on Axis I and II.

- The childhoods of people with DID and BPD are similar.

The basic epidemiological facts tell us that DID/DDNOS and borderline personality disorder are not neat, distinct categories. They are related to each other in some kind of complicated, overlapping fashion.

How to Understand the Relationship Between Dissociation and Borderline Personality Disorder

It is impossible to find someone who fits DSM-IV-TR borderline personality criteria who never dissociates. All people diagnosed with BPD trance out, experience depersonalization, disconnect from themselves at numerous levels, get lost in their own distress, and experience a failure of integration. Logically, borderline personality disorder and complex dissociation (DID or DDNOS) may be related or described as follows:

- Separate disorders that co-occur, i.e., frequently comorbid with each other

- Variations of the same disorder

- One or the other, or both, are not legitimate

There are many schools of thought concerning people called "borderline," and academic debates about them. From our point of view, in terms of actually doing the work of therapy, borderline personality can be worked with in the same way as a dissociative disorder. We treat it the same way that we treat DDNOS or DID, except for a few details. This will become clear in later chapters. We see borderline personality disorder as an adaptation to trauma.

From a treatment perspective, BPD is a simple form of dual personality in which the parts are not as distinct and personified as they are in DID. Actually, if you look carefully, there are often more than just two parts—there are other child and adolescent ego states besides the basic modes A and B.

Reciprocally, DID is a complex form of borderline personality disorder in which there are more ego states, and the states are more distinct, personified, and separate. It's all a matter of degree. What makes DID a dissociative disorder is not really the fact that the ego states have different names, ages, hair color, heights, genders, favorite TV shows, foods, and so on. All of this is a secondary elaboration on the basic dissociation. The internal disconnection is the core of a dissociative disorder. The number and elaboration of the ego states does not determine whether there is a dissociative disorder.

In BPD, a core defense is splitting. In our view, splitting is a synonym for the fourth meaning of dissociation—an internal defense mechanism. Or, one might say, splitting is a type of dissociation. While in mode A, the person with BPD exhibits "denial" about the negative, hostile behaviour she has exhibited in mode B. Is this denial or lying? How complete does the denial have to be before the BPD client actually can't remember her previous behaviour—before she has amnesia?

In our view, the denial of the client with BPD could be described as the beginning of amnesia. It is all dissociation, occurring in various forms and degrees.

One might object that people with borderline diagnoses don't have distinct parts, which makes them different from people with DID. At one level, this is true. Someone who fits the borderline personality criteria doesn't suddenly become a "different person" with a different name and age. But people with DID do not literally switch back and forth from one person to another. DID is a compelling subjective illusion, a way of coping with life, not a literal fact.

A person with DID, DDNOS, or borderline personality disorder, switches back and forth from one unintegrated ego state to another. This is the core feature of both BPD and complex dissociative disorders.

The diagnostic criteria and secondary features of both DID and borderline personality disorder follow logically from a common psychological structure. There are dissociated, disconnected, unintegrated ego states. The states intrude on each other causing impulsivity, identity disturbance, instability of affect, auditory hallucinations, depersonalization, and other symptoms. The states attack each other in an endless inner civil war, due to self-hatred and self-rejection. Ego states that are disconnected or driven away leave other ego states feeling empty, abandoned, hypersensitive to being alone, and desperate to form attachments they simultaneously long for, fear, and hate. All of this is the logical, predictable fallout of a chaotic, abusive, neglectful, violent childhood filled with loss and betrayal.

Genes Versus Environment

There are disagreements about the roles of genes versus environment in mental illness. Everyone agrees in theory that life is a mixture of genes and environment. In practice, however, some mental health professionals adopt and operate out of extreme genetic reductionism or extreme environmental reductionism.

Everything in life depends on genes. You couldn't exist without genes. You couldn't get out of bed and brush your teeth in the morning without genes. However, this does not mean that there is a specific gene or set of genes for brushing teeth. In our view, few if any people have a genetically specific abnormality that dooms them to have a specific DSM-IV-TR disorder.

However, it is obvious that people are born with different temperaments. These are certainly genetically determined, but a temperament is not a DSM-IV-TR diagnosis. We believe that people are born with certain temperaments, or perhaps a general tendency towards addictions and mental health problems, but not that they are doomed or genetically programmed to have a specific DSM-IV-TR disorder. Exceptions are rare.

In response to similar childhood experiences (which are never exactly the same), a person with one temperament may be more likely to develop borderline personality traits while another is more likely to become anxious and phobic. But most people assigned to the borderline personality category are anxious, depressed, dissociative, and addictive, resulting in numerous diagnoses. They have a tendency to react to trauma in one way more than another. This is not a sign of biological programming for specific DSM-IV-TR disorders, which are really not separate medical diseases.

Not every child exposed to certain stressors develops borderline personality disorder. Therefore BPD has a genetic component. At the same time, the disorder is environmental. The Trauma Model predicts that almost all cases of BPD could be prevented by adoption at birth into a stable, healthy family. This is a scientifically testable prediction of the Trauma Model, but not a known fact. The truth is that DID, DDNOS, and borderline personality disorder are treatable with psychotherapy. This is not true for real genetic diseases like cystic fibrosis or Huntington's chorea.

Why do we have AA for the "disease" of alcoholism? Because AA often works. Why don't we have AA for treating cancer of the pancreas, Alzheimer's, or coronary artery disease? Because AA doesn't work for physically-based diseases. Talking about alcoholism, or any other addiction or mental health problem, as a disease, is a *metaphor*. The metaphor has financial, sociological, political, and funding implications, but it is a metaphor, not a scientific fact. This is true throughout the DSM, not just for borderline personality disorder and alcoholism.

On the other hand, it is possible that certain cases of some DSM disorders are genetically programmed at conception. We know there are real genetic disorders. Some of them affect the brain in a way that causes psychiatric symptoms. Huntington's chorea is the best example. We also know that there are brain diseases that are non-genetic, like Parkinson's disease and multiple sclerosis. Both can cause psychiatric symptoms.

We are not "against" biology or genetics. But at this time we don't think the evidence supports the opinion that specific genes cause most specific mental disorders. We think psychiatry has overemphasized the impact of genes, brain chemicals, and medications on mental and emotional stability. It would be an equally serious error to completely ignore inherited influences, or to forgo the scientific study of brain chemistry and medications. However, the psychiatric pendulum definitely needs adjustment in the direction of environmental causes of mental disorders and addictions.

9
How to Ask About Dissociation

Many mental health professionals have had little training in how to ask about dissociation. This chapter provides a practical guide for how to do so. The reader will learn specific, detailed questions to ask, but will also see that most of the questioning involves standard principles of history-taking, with specialized content.

This chapter covers

- General Overview: How to Ask About Dissociation

- A Set of Initial Open-ended Questions for the Core Dissociative Symptoms

- Closed-ended Questions for Dissociation

General Overview of How to Ask About Dissociation

Throughout the mental health field, the general approach is to start with open-ended questions, then narrow down to more and more specific and closed-ended questions. The first requirement is to think about and consider dissociation. The second is to know what questions to ask.

The specific dissociative symptoms can be found in the measures in the Appendix: the DES, SDQ, DDIS, and MID. These items provide a full inventory of the domain of dissociation. From a practical perspective, in planning therapy, the main question is whether the person has either DDNOS or DID. DDNOS and DID, lumped together, can be thought of as the dissociative taxon, discussed in Chapter 4.

At first, it may be unclear whether the person has DDNOS or DID. There is no exact dividing line between the two. Basically, DDNOS is DID, but not quite as much. The symptoms are the same but less frequent, severe, and crystallized. The initial goal is to determine whether the person has a severe, chronic dissociative disorder, not to decide whether the diagnosis is DDNOS or DID.

The main reason that dissociative disorders are under-diagnosed is that mental health professionals, by and large, were not trained to ask about dissociation (or a history of trauma or abuse) in a thorough, systematic manner. There are three core symptoms of pathological dissociation.

THE CORE SYMPTOMS OF PATHOLOGICAL DISSOCIATION

- Amnesia

- Depersonalization and derealization

- Voices

Amnesia

The pattern of questioning is always the same. For instance, to find out about amnesia, one starts with a general open-ended question. A typical line of inquiry follows:

Therapist: Do you have any problems with your memory?
Client: Yes.
Therapist: Can you describe some of the problems you have?
Client: Sometimes I forget things.
Therapist: Can you give me some examples?
Client: I forget where I put my keys.

At this point, all the client has described is normal forgetting. In order to be a dissociative symptom, such forgetting would have to happen frequently, it would have to involve a variety of different objects and situations, and it would have to cause distress or interfere with function. The interview continues:

Therapist: How often does this happen?
Client: A couple of times a year.
Therapist: Do you ever forget other things?
Client: Yeah, pens.
Therapist: How often does that happen?
Client: Maybe once a month.
Therapist: Any other things you forget?
Client: Appointments. That happens every few months.
Therapist: Anything else?
Client: No, that's about it.
Therapist: Any other problems with your memory?
Client: No, I don't think so.
Therapist: OK, thanks. I want to ask about some other things now.

This client does not report amnesia. With a DID client, however, the interview might go like this:

Therapist: Do you have any problems with your memory?
Client: Yes.
Therapist: Can you describe some of the problems you have?
Client: Sometimes I forget things.
Therapist: Can you give me some examples?
Client: I forget where I put my keys.
Therapist: How often does this happen?
Client: Every time I'm getting ready to drive to my mother's.
Therapist: How often is that?
Client: A couple of times a week.
Therapist: Do you end up finding your keys, or what happens?
Client: I have to look all over. I'll find them hidden in a drawer, or in the pantry, or anywhere. Sometimes I have to look for half an hour.
Therapist: How do your keys get in those places?
Client: I have no idea. I always leave them on my dresser, then they just aren't there.

Therapist: What do you think is going on with that?
Client: I'm afraid I'm losing my mind.
Therapist: Do you ever forget other things?
Client: All the time.
Therapist: Like what?
Client: My journal. It disappears and I'll find it stuffed down in the sofa, or under my mattress, all kinds of places.
Therapist: Any other examples of forgetting things?
Client: Sometimes I forget getting dressed in the morning.
Therapist: How do you mean?
Client: It's like I come to and I look down at my clothes and I can't remember putting them on.
Therapist: How often does that happen?
Client: Sometimes not for weeks, sometimes every day for a while.
Therapist: How long is a while?
Client: It can happen every day for weeks.

At this point, we are well beyond normal forgetting. This is a good time to ask about head injuries, seizures, drugs and alcohol:

Therapist: Have you ever had a serious head injury?
Client: No.
Therapist: Ever been knocked out or had a concussion?
Client: No.
Therapist: Have you ever had a seizure?
Client: No.
Therapist: Have you ever had any neurological disorder like MS or Parkinson's disease?
Client: No, I'm in pretty good health.
Therapist: Any other serious medical problems, like diabetes for instance?
Client: No, my physical health is OK.
Therapist: Do you drink or use drugs?
Client: No, just a little marijuana when I was in college.

Setting aside the possibility of denial about drugs and alcohol, it appears at this point that the client experiences a lot of dissociative amnesia. There is probably conflict about visiting her mother, and there is probably some sort of conflict about journaling. Both these themes will be returned to later in the interview, and during the ongoing therapy.

Now the task is to find out more about the amnesia—its frequency, structure, and degree of interference with function. The client seems to have described coming out of a blank spell and finding herself dressed in clothes she can't remember putting on. However, this is a little vague at the moment. The interview continues:

Therapist: Do you ever have blank spells or periods of missing time?
Client: Yes.
Therapist: How long do they last?
Client: Usually a few hours. Sometimes a couple of days.
Therapist: How often does this happen?
Client: It varies. Sometimes every day, sometimes not for weeks.
Therapist: On average, over the last five years, how many blank spells would you have per month?

Blank spells lasting at least a couple of hours?

Client: Per month? Maybe six or seven, I guess.

Therapist: Have they been getting more frequent recently, staying about the same, or getting less frequent?

Client: I started having more after I withdrew from my evening class three months ago.

Therapist: Oh, I'll ask more about that later. Right now I have a few more questions about the blank spells. What's the longest stretch you've gone without a blank spell—one lasting at least a few hours—since you turned 18?

Client: I didn't have any for a few years during my first marriage.

Therapist: How were things going overall during that period?

Client: Good. My husband hadn't started cheating on me yet.

Therapist: That must have been rough when you found out about that.

Client: Yeah, I got really depressed and suicidal. That's when I had my first admission.

Therapist: Back to the blank spells—how old were you when they first started?

Client: I don't know. I've had them for as long as I can remember.

Therapist: Going back how far?

Client: Before ten, I think. I don't remember much before age 12.

Therapist: Did anything happen when you were 12?

Client: My dad left us.

Therapist: Oh, I'll make sure to ask you more about that too.

Now the clinician needs to ask about related items from the secondary features of DID section of the DDIS:

Therapist: Do you ever come out of a blank spell in a different location, unable to remember how you got there?

Client: Yeah, that happens a lot.

Therapist: Can you give me some examples?

Client: When I was in college I used to wake up in some guy's dorm room, but I had no idea how I got there. Last thing I remembered, I was in class or in my dorm.

Therapist: Did you see any evidence that you had had sex with the guy?

Client: Yes. There was no doubt.

Therapist: Can you give me some more recent examples?

Client: Last week I came to sitting on my couch. On the floor were a bunch of shopping bags with stuff I'd bought at the mall, but I couldn't remember going there.

Therapist: What kind of stuff had you bought?

Client: Dumb stuff. Coloring books, lots of candies, kids books.

Therapist: Was that stuff you would normally buy?

Client: No way.

Therapist: Do people ever tell you about what you've done during periods of time you can't remember?

Client: Yes. It's embarrassing.

Therapist: What do they describe?

Client: Sometimes I'm really angry, sometimes I'm just out of it. Sometimes I act like a little kid. It makes me feel crazy. I wonder if people are just making it up.

Therapist: These kinds of experiences don't mean you're crazy. I've met other people with similar memory problems, and they weren't crazy. Do people ever come up to you and claim to know you, but you don't know them?

Client: Yeah, that happens. I think there's somebody who looks like me named Margie. Quite a few

people have called me Margie. I just tell them they've got the wrong person.
Therapist: How long have these things been going on—people telling you about stuff you don't remember, mistaking you for someone else?
Client: On and off since I was a teenager.

At this point, the odds are very slim that the client does not have DID. The next area of inquiry is "objects missing and present." Objects missing was covered earlier in the discussion about keys, and the shopping bags from the mall were an example of objects present that the person cannot account for. The clinician will ask for other examples, and their frequency.

Then it is time to ask about auditory hallucinations.

Voices

One way to think of the mental status examination of auditory hallucinations, in DID and DDNOS, is to imagine you are sitting in front of a house with a person who lives there. An unknown number of other people live in the house, but the person may not know anything about some of them. The goal of the interview is to gather a preliminary picture of who lives in the house, how old they are, how they behave, and how they interact with other residents of the house. This inquiry must be done in a sequence that starts with indirect questions and narrows down to increasingly more closed-ended, direct questions.

Therapist: Now I want to ask you about voices. Do you ever hear voices talking out loud that no one else can hear?
Client: Yes.
Therapist: Do the voices seem to come from inside your head or outside?
Client: Mostly inside.
Therapist: Does the voice feel like you talking to yourself, or like someone else talking?
Client: It's definitely not me. I wouldn't say that shit.
Therapist: What kinds of things does the voice say?
Client: It tells me I'm a piece of crap. It tells me to kill myself. It's always putting me down.
Therapist: Do you hear any other voices or is that the only one?
Client: Nobody ever asked me about this before? Does it mean I'm crazy?
Therapist: No, it doesn't. It's not unusual for people with memory problems like yours to also hear voices.
I was asking if you hear any other voices.
Client: Yeah.
Therapist: Could you tell me about them?
Client: There's a nice voice. I call her my Angel. She talks to me and tells me it's OK, it'll be all right.
Therapist: How long have you been hearing these two voices?
Client: Since I was a kid.
Therapist: What's the longest period of time you've ever gone without hearing the voices?
Client: They were gone for a few years early in my first marriage.
Therapist: Same time period as when the blank spells stopped?
Client: Yeah, come to think of it.

The odds that this client has DID are increasing. The clinician needs to gather a little more detail about the voices before asking about other "people" inside. The sequence of questions follows:

SEQUENCE OF QUESTIONS ABOUT DISSOCIATION

- Memory problems—general, open-ended questions

- Blank spells

- Coming out of blank spells in a different location

- Objects missing and objects present

- Strangers telling you about things you can't remember

- Strangers claiming to know you

- Voices—number, characteristics, interactions

- Depersonalization and derealization

- Other people inside—genders, ages, characteristics

- Switching

The exact sequence of questions can be varied to some degree. For instance, depersonalization and derealization can be asked about first, or left to the end. The main points are:

- Start with open-ended questions and narrow down

- Always ask about other people inside and switching after asking detailed questions about memory problems and voices.

Leaving explicit questions about other people inside and switching until later allows you to gather the maximum amount of information about amnesia and voices without directly suggesting DID to the person. This is especially important if any third party will be questioning the validity of the DDNOS or DID diagnosis. The interview continues:

Therapist: Do the two voices ever talk to each other?
Client: Yes.
Therapist: What do they say to each other?
Client: They argue about me. My Angel tells the bad voice to leave me alone.
Therapist: Do you hear any other voices besides those two?
Client: I hear a little girl crying and sometimes I hear someone else laughing and making fun of me.
Therapist: So there are four distinct voices that you can tell apart from each other?

Client: Yeah. I think there might have been some other ones when I was a teenager.
Therapist: OK. Just so I'm clear—these voices are just like another person talking out loud, except they come from inside your head. Is that right?
Client: Yes.
Therapist: Do you feel that you have any control over what the voices say or when they talk?
Client: No, they pretty well do what they want.
Therapist: Do any of the voices have a particular gender? You said it's a little girl crying—what about the other three? I think you referred to the Angel voice as "she."
Client: Yeah, she's a woman. The angry voice is male and the laughing one sounds like a teenage girl.
Therapist: Do the Angel and the angry voices have particular ages?
Client: No.
Therapist: Could you say whether they seem to be children, adolescents or adults?
Client: Adults. The little girl is five.
Therapist: How do you know that?
Client: She told me one time.

The diagnosis of DID is almost certain at this point. Now the clinician wants to know the client's theory or model of what's going on with the voices:

Therapist: What do you think these voices are? How do you understand them?
Client: What do you mean?
Therapist: I mean how do you explain these voices to yourself? What do you think is going on that you hear voices like this?
Client: I think I'm nuts.
Therapist: It's common for people who hear voices to think that. But you're not crazy. Your conversation makes perfect sense, it's logical, and you answer my questions clearly. Your thought processes seem rational and well organized. You have a lot of disturbing symptoms, but you aren't psychotic, insane or crazy.

This conclusion by the clinician is based on past history and records, other aspects of the interview not transcribed here, and a standard general mental health assessment. It isn't simply a casual reassurance. The interview continues:

Client: OK, if you say so.
Therapist: You don't sound convinced.
Client: I'm not.
Therapist: That's fine. This is something we will go over again in the future.
Now I would like to ask some additional questions.

Other People Inside and Switching

Therapist: Do you ever feel like there are other people inside you?
Client: You mean the voices?
Therapist: Well, yeah, do you feel like the voices are other people?
Client: I don't know. I know there is somebody inside who gets real angry.
Therapist: How do you know that?
Client: I can feel her.
Therapist: Feel her where?

Client: Inside me.

Therapist: Do you feel like this angry person has a specific location inside?

Client: What do you mean?

Therapist: If you had to point to where she is, is there somewhere you would point?

Client: Yeah, here in my stomach.

Therapist: Does this angry person ever take control of your body and do things?

Client: Yeah, I can feel her coming out, then I blank out. People sometimes tell me about what she's done. They say I'm like another person.

Therapist: Would it be possible for me to interview any of these people who've been with you during periods you don't remember?

Client: Yeah, my best friend would come in if you wanted, and you could talk to my sister on the phone.

Therapist: Good, it's always helpful to get an outside perspective on things. Before we finish today, I'll ask you to sign a consent form allowing me to talk to your friend and your sister.

Client: OK.

Therapist: Now I want to ask about a few more symptoms.

Depersonalization and Derealization

Therapist: Do you ever feel like you're outside your body looking at it?

Client: Yes.

Therapist: Can you describe that a little?

Client: Sometimes when I feel the angry girl taking over, I don't go away completely. I feel like I'm floating just outside of my body. I can watch what's going on and I can hear what's she's saying, but I can't control it.

Therapist: When this angry part takes over, what percentage of the time are you completely gone, and what percentage of the time are you aware of what's going on?

Client: I'm gone most of the time—I can watch maybe 10% of the time, I guess.

Therapist: Did you ever have this experience of being outside your body when you were young?

Client: Yeah, when my brother was having sex with me.

Therapist: Yeah, I read about that in your records. That's called an out-of-body experience. The technical term for it is depersonalization. It's a very common experience during trauma, whether the trauma is sexual abuse, a car accident, a tornado, military combat, or whatever.

Client: So I'm not crazy?

Therapist: No, these are common experiences for people who have had a lot of trauma.

Client: Oh.

Therapist: People who have out-of-body experiences sometimes feel that their body has changed, or part of it is missing. Have you ever had that experience?

Client: When I have sex, sometimes the bottom half of my body goes numb and it feels like it isn't there anymore.

Therapist: Any other experiences like that?

Client: If I get really scared and I'm starting to go away, sometimes my body seems to get small like a child's body. It's really weird.

Therapist: These are all feelings that are common in trauma survivors. Do you ever have the opposite experience? Instead of feeling you aren't real, it seems like the world isn't real, or you're looking at it through a fog?

Client: Yeah, that happens a lot. It got really bad when I smoked pot in college. That's one reason I stopped.

The clinician can continue to ask for more examples, then can inquire about the age at onset and frequency of these symptoms. It is always important to ask whether they have gotten better, worse or stayed the same recently, and how they are linked to trauma, general stress, or other events. As with voices and amnesia, it is a good bet that the depersonalization improved during the early years of the first marriage.

The same features must be documented for any symptom, whether it be anxiety, depression, substance abuse, binge eating, or dissociation. Note these features:

GENERAL FEATURES OF ALL SYMPTOMS

- Present or absent

- Several different examples

- Frequency

- Duration

- Age at onset

- Interference with function

- Degree of subjective distress

- Association with other symptoms

- Triggering —to stressful events

- Soothing events—what makes the symptoms ease off

- How the person understands what is going on

A person with a dissociative disorder and a person with a florid psychosis may both hear voices talking to them, but the overall picture will be different. The relationship between dissociation and psychosis is complex, and is covered in detail in Ross (2004). However, extreme, florid psychotic states will include:

- Bizarre, delusional explanations of the voices—e.g., Martians talking through a computer chip implanted in a tooth by the mother's gynecologist

- Disorganized, incoherent speech

- Thought processes that are disconnected, illogical, or very difficult to follow

- Voices tend to be more rigid and fixed—say the same few things over and over

- Voices are not described as if they are other "people" inside who have interactions, histories, functions and attitudes

In order to confirm a diagnosis of DID, it is desirable to directly observe switching to another identity, and to engage the alternative identity in conversation. This is not required by the DSM-IV-TR rules for diagnosing DID. Similarly, one can diagnose bipolar mood disorder by history, without directly observing a manic episode. Direct observation of a switch provides clear confirmation of the diagnosis. If no switch has been observed, a provisional diagnosis of DDNOS can be made, with a notation like "Rule out DID," or "Probable DID."

Asking about dissociation is no more mysterious or arcane than asking about any other set of symptoms. Nor are dissociative symptoms inherently more exotic than checking all the light switches and door locks three times before going to sleep, taking 30 minutes to make the bed perfectly, or common symptoms of a severe manic episode.

Like any form of history taking, asking about dissociation requires practice. There are many variations and subtleties but this chapter provides the basic principles. A good way to practice asking about dissociation is to administer the DDIS, or at least the sections on secondary features of DID and the five dissociative disorders. Alternatively, one could read questions aloud from the DES, SDQ, or MID.

10
How to Ask About Trauma

This chapter does for trauma histories what the preceding chapter did for dissociation. Many mental health professionals have never been taught how to inquire about trauma. The chapter begins with a review of the types of childhood trauma including physical, sexual, verbal and emotional abuse, neglect, family violence, and loss of primary caretakers. In many parts of the world, the major burden of childhood trauma comes from extreme poverty, disease, high infant mortality, starvation, genocide, war, and natural disasters. These will be mentioned but the main focus will be on abuse, neglect, and family trauma. Adult trauma will also be discussed.

The same approach of open-ended questions followed up with increasingly closed-ended questions applies in asking about trauma. We include examples of specific questions.

This chapter covers

- Overview of Types of Trauma

- Overview of the General Strategy of Interviewing

- Detailed Open and Closed-ended Questions About Trauma

Types of Psychological Trauma

In terms of chronic childhood trauma, in North America and Australia we tend to focus on child abuse and neglect. For adult trauma, much of the early focus in the posttraumatic stress disorder (PTSD) field was on military combat in Vietnam. But these are only thin slices of the overall pie of psychological trauma. In chronic, complex dissociative disorders, there is never just one type of trauma. There is usually a mixture of many different forms of trauma which occur in varying degrees.

There is no simple equation such as "DID is caused by sexual abuse."

Rather than being caused by a single type of trauma, DID and DDNOS involve a complex web of numerous different factors that interact in countless different feedback loops. The three basic factors that go into formation of DID and DDNOS are:

- Innate dissociative capacity

- Traumatic events

- Soothing, healing, restorative events

Individuals vary in their responses to trauma. Some people are born with a greater tendency to dissociate. Also, two people with the same amount of trauma may turn out differently because one had more frequent counter-balancing, healing, soothing, restorative experiences—a good grandmother, school teacher, spouse, or employer. Plain luck is involved. Also, one person may have the same amount of childhood trauma as another, but much more trauma in adulthood, such as military combat, a rape, or a serious car accident.

DIFFERENT FORMS OF CHRONIC CHILDHOOD TRAUMA

- Sexual abuse

- Physical abuse

- Emotional and verbal abuse

- Neglect

- Loss of primary caretakers

- Family violence

- Family chaos and highly disturbed family dynamics

- Violence outside the family

- War

- Famine

- High infant mortality

- Disease, surgical procedures

- Natural disasters

- Extreme poverty

- Slavery—child labor, sex trade, human trafficking

At age 35, one person who experienced similar childhood traumas as another may be less dissociative than that person, because of choices and decisions made in adulthood—to get into therapy, to stop abusing substances, to leave a bad marriage, and so on. There is no simple, direct, linear relationship between traumatic events and the long-term outcome. Some people seem to be born more resilient than others. Even so, we have never met a person with DDNOS or DID who has not experienced a great deal of trauma and loss.

The Overall Strategy for Asking About Trauma

The overall strategy for asking about trauma follows the usual pattern of history-taking. Start with open-ended questions, then narrow down to more detailed and specific questions. However, childhood sexual abuse is a much more sensitive, delicate subject to explore than where you went to school, or where you have worked, so more caution is required. It is possible to err in two directions: asking too much about childhood trauma, and asking too little.

Overall, practitioners in the mental health field have erred in the direction of asking too little about trauma. Reasonable caution and sensitivity are required in asking about trauma, but one must also be sensitive and tactful when asking about unpleasant symptoms of any kind. It is not easy for people to disclose hallucinations, bulimia, severe OCD, addictions, or suicidal thinking.

There is controversy about how accurate or unreliable reports of childhood trauma are, especially sexual abuse. It is necessary to maintain neutrality about trauma reports, as we will discuss in detail in later chapters. However, in our opinion, trauma histories are no less reliable than reports of symptoms. How accurate do we expect a symptom history to be when the person is manic, severely depressed with extreme negative thinking, psychotic, or delusional? How accurate do we think the histories are when the diagnosis is bulimia or substance abuse?

Reasonable caution about the accuracy of trauma histories is necessary, but not an extreme level of incredulity or disbelief. There is no evidence that childhood trauma histories are less accurate than histories of depression, anxiety, psychosis, or substance abuse. Diagnoses of bipolar mood disorder, for instance, are routinely made by history alone when mania has not been observed directly. Outside evidence and collateral history are desirable, but not essential. Trauma histories should not be held to a higher standard than histories in general.

In this chapter we are referring to trauma histories that are contained within the treatment setting, not to legal or forensic situations. If outside parties are going to be accused of abuse in public, then different standards apply and different responsibilities and consequences come into play.

How to Ask About Psychological Trauma

An inquiry about childhood trauma could look like this:

Therapist: What was it like when you were growing up?
Client: Fine.

That response could be given by someone with a healthy, supportive, nurturing childhood, or by someone with an extreme trauma history. More exploration is required.

Therapist: What was it like when you were growing up?
Client: Fine.
Therapist: Can you describe the general atmosphere in your family when you were growing up?
Client: What do you mean?
Therapist: I mean, what was it like on a day-to-day basis for you, growing up?
Client: Lonely.
Therapist: You said you were an only child, right?
Client: Right.
Therapist: That's bound to be somewhat lonely just because of the structure of the situation.
Client: It was, but my parents were good people. My dad coached a lot of my teams and my mom was really involved at my school.
Therapist: That's good. How did your parents get along with each other?
Client: Good. They never fought or yelled or anything like that.

Therapist: How were feelings expressed in the home?

Client: They weren't.

Therapist: Oh, well, were your parents affectionate with you?

Client: They took good care of me.

Therapist: I understand that. I'm just trying to get a better sense of the emotional atmosphere in your home growing up. Did your mom ever hug you, cuddle you, or tell you she loved you?

Client: Kind of . . . not really. She made my lunches, and looked at my report cards, and shopped for me, and everything. Neither of my parents showed many feelings. They're just not touchy-feely people.

Therapist: OK, that gives me a clearer picture. Did any specific bad events happen to you as a kid?

Client: My dog died when I was eight. Other than that, nothing.

Therapist: Did anybody ever abuse you or assault you in any way?

Client: No, nothing like that.

Therapist: OK, thanks. I'll come back to your childhood more later. Has anything bad happened to you since you turned 18?

Client: I was raped in college.

Therapist: Oh, I'm sorry to hear that. Was it a stranger or someone you knew?

Client: It was a guy I dated a few times.

Therapist: A rape is going to affect anyone, everyone, deeply. Do you feel that the effects of the rape are still with you?

Client: It was ten years ago.

Therapist: I know, but sometimes it takes a long time for things like that to go away. Probably they never do, completely.

Client: I got therapy at a Rape Crisis Center for a year. It helped a lot.

Therapist: That's good. Did you report the guy?

Client: No, it would have been my word against his and he was a football player. The counselor and I talked about it a lot.

Therapist: Often not reporting is the best decision. Why get trashed in public if he's likely to get off? On the other hand, some people feel they have to try. There's no one way that's always right—you have to do what's best for you. Do you feel you did that?

Client: Yeah, I do.

Therapist: Well, good.

Client: I had trouble with sex for a few years but I got over that. My boyfriend helped a lot—he was very supportive.

Therapist: Sounds like you've done a lot of hard work. Let me ask a few questions about your eating now.

Client: Oh, that.

This client has an eating disorder that she uses to avoid feelings of loneliness, sadness, and emptiness. She was never abused or neglected at the Child Protective Services level, but her parents failed to nurture her emotionally, to bond with her at a feelings level, and to model and teach healthy communication of emotions. She never experienced "trauma" in the PTSD sense, but her experience affected her deeply, nevertheless.

This client's trauma was the opposite of the PTSD model. It wasn't what happened that affected her, it was what didn't happen. She never bonded with her parents in a full, reciprocal, expressive fashion; her dog died; and she had no siblings. Her parents were not perpetrators of abuse, they were perpetrators of inadequate nurturing, even though everything was provided for at the material level.

Whether or not this childhood experience should be called *trauma*, it affected the client deeply and underlies her eating disorder. She is suitable for Trauma Model Therapy because her eating disorder is her addiction. It is her unhealthy strategy for suppressing and managing intolerable feelings. She needs to work on desensitization to the underlying feelings and developing healthy, more fluid, more flexible, coping skills.

In a sense, Trauma Model Therapy could be called *Intolerable Feelings Therapy*, but since a large percentage of intolerable feelings come from trauma, it boils down to the same thing no matter what it's called. The "trauma" need not be the dramatic, big-event, PTSD style of trauma. The absence of love can hurt as much as the presence of abuse.

Returning to the open-ended phase of the trauma interview, but now with a different client—one referred for assessment of borderline personality disorder— the questioning might go like this:

Therapist: What was it like when you were growing up?
Client: Fine.
Therapist: You seem pretty angry when you say that.
Client: I am.
Therapist: Why?
Client: Because no one ever wants to hear my sob story.
Therapist: No one? No one like who? Who do you mean?
Client: Not my parents, that's for damn sure.
Therapist: Have you had trouble with mental health professionals not wanting to hear about it?
Client: Hello . . . what do you think?
Therapist: I'd say the odds are pretty high you have.
Client: So why are you any different?
Therapist: I specialize in psychological trauma. I believe that most mental health problems and addictions come from trauma and neglect. That's why I work here. That's why you were referred to me.
Client: OK, I get it.
Therapist: So, I was asking what it was like when you were growing up.
Client: It sucked.
Therapist: Can you fill me in a little, give me some details?
Client: It sucked real bad.
Therapist: I'm sorry to hear that. Can you describe it in a little detail so I can get a clearer picture? By the way, you called it your "sob story"—I imagine there are a lot of genuine tears inside you, not just a sob story.
Client: Why do you imagine that?
Therapist: Because it's sad to have a childhood that sucks real bad; would be for anyone.
Client: You got that right.
Therapist: At this point, I get it that you had a really rough childhood. I don't necessarily need the details right now. Would you prefer I move on to some other questions?
Client: Yeah, I really don't want to talk about it.
Therapist: That's fine, we can come back to it another time.

This client obviously has a childhood trauma history, but the top priority is trying to form a treatment alliance with her, not extracting information. The main techniques used were hardly even "techniques"— they were genuine positive regard, accurate empathy, and congruence—basic Rogerian principles, common elements of every psychotherapy.

In another case, the interview might go as follows:

Therapist: What was it like when you were growing up?
Client: Pretty bad.
Therapist: Can you fill me in a little?
Client: I was abused a lot.
Therapist: Actually, I saw that in the intake notes. What kind of abuse was it?
Client: Physical, sexual, emotional, you name it.
Therapist: Was it family members?
Client: Sexual abuse by my dad and two brothers, physical abuse by my mom and dad. Sexual abuse by a baby sitter.
Therapist: Sounds bad. How old were you when the sexual abuse started?
Client: Four.
Therapist: How old were you when it stopped?
Client: When I moved out—I was 18.
Therapist: Did it involve intercourse?
Client: Intercourse, oral sex, you name it. My brothers brought their friends in, too.
Therapist: Did your mother know what was going on?
Client: My dad beat her, and me, and my brothers. I think she knew but she was too afraid and too out of it to do anything.
Therapist: Did any of them ever admit it or talk about it?
Client: One brother did a few years ago. He said he was sorry. Everybody else is in denial.
Therapist: Do you have contact with your parents currently?
Client: A few times a year. I talk to my mom on the phone every couple of weeks.
Therapist: What about your brothers?
Client: One brother is in jail. I talk to my other brother every few weeks, visit him and his wife once a month.
Therapist: Do they have any kids?
Client: Yeah, my niece is six. She's wonderful. I really love her.
Therapist: How do the two of you get along?
Client: Great. I'm her favorite aunt. I'm also her only aunt.
Therapist: Well, she's lucky to have you in her life then.
Client: Thanks.
Therapist: You're welcome. Getting back to the physical abuse—did your dad hit you hard enough to cause bleeding or bruising, or leave welts?
Client: Yeah, lots of times.
Therapist: Any broken bones?
Client: My mom and my brother had that, but not me.
Therapist: Which brother?
Client: The one who's in jail.
Therapist: What's he in jail for?
Client: Drugs. He's been in for three years; could get out on parole in two.
Therapist: How old were you when the physical abuse started?
Client: I'm not sure—five or six.
Therapist: And when it stopped?
Client: It stopped when I was 14. My brother threatened Dad with a knife and told him he'd kill him if he ever touched one of us again.

Therapist: Good for your brother—not that threatening someone with a knife is OK—but standing up to him was great.

Client: Yeah, that was cool.

Therapist: Roughly, how often did your dad hit one of you hard enough to cause bleeding, bruising, or welts?

Client: Hardly a month would go by that one of us didn't get it.

Therapist: Was it that way the whole time up to age 14?

Client: Pretty well.

Therapist: How about yelling, screaming, fighting?

Client: Lots, all the time. I used to hide in the closet.

This is enough to establish a history of severe, chronic childhood trauma. It isn't necessary to get more details at this point. They will come out over time in the therapy. In this interview, the questions are pretty straightforward. As for any aspect of the history, you want to know the who, what, where, when, and why of it, although the "why" can never really be answered. Standard elements of a trauma history include

- What type of trauma?

- Who were the perpetrators?

- When did it start?

- When did it stop?

- Why did it stop?

- What was the frequency?

- Who knew about it?

- Was anything done about it?

- Did you ever disclose and to whom?

- What reaction did you get to disclosure?

This is the history of the events. The thoughts, feelings, self-blame, and other aspects of the psychology are the focus in later chapters of this manual. It isn't necessary to tiptoe around the subject of trauma, but one shouldn't be a bull in a china shop either. The trauma history is taken in the course of asking about family dynamics, current relationships, and other matters. It is woven into the interview. Asking about trauma is a bit like asking about suicide. The standard recommendation is to ask directly about suicide in a sensitive fashion. The same applies to trauma histories, beginning with open-ended questions and narrowing down.

THE TRAUMA MODEL OF DISSOCIATION

11
Survival Strategy No. 1: Attachment to the Perpetrator

The ordering of the clinical chapters does not imply that The Trauma Model is a linear process. At each stage of therapy many issues will be revisited time and again. The following chapters describe the presentations, stages, processes, issues, and therapeutic strategies for assisting clients with a trauma history.

Inherent in working with abused individuals is the powerful and pervasive dynamic of attachment to the perpetrator. Resolving the conflict of attachment to the perpetrator is a core aspect of trauma therapy.

This chapter will cover

- Healthy Attachment

- Attachment to the Perpetrator, Defined

- The Problem of Attachment to the Perpetrator

- Attachment Styles: Preoccupied; Ambivalent; Avoidant; Disorganized

- Identification With the Aggressor and Passive Victim: Two Sides of the Same Coin

- The Love-Hate Conflict

- Grief and Loss

Healthy Attachment

Attachment is a fundamental biological drive necessary for survival. Successful attachment is the foundation for the development of psychological, emotional, social, and spiritual well-being and functioning. Normal child development sees the infant move from having no sense of differentiation between self and other, to recognition that mother is not an extension of self, to an evolving sense of agency, autonomy, and independence at each stage of development.

In a stable and secure environment, mother, father, and other caregivers provide a sense of safety and protection in an ever expanding world of new experiences. The growing child can test, experiment, explore, learn, and gain greater independence in the knowledge that there is a soothing voice and a hand to comfort when experiments go wrong. Praise and encouragement fuel the child to get back up on the horse. This girl feels safe enough to explore her world and develops an increasing sense of independence and confidence in her abilities. She has safe attachment figures who engender within her a sense of efficacy from which she grows to develop healthy and positive relationships as an adult.

Attachment to the Perpetrator, Defined

A child growing up in an abusive, neglectful, or chaotic family is faced with a double bind. She has two opposing survival needs. First, she needs to develop and maintain attachment to her caregivers. Second, she needs to defend herself emotionally and mentally from the very people to whom she is attached. She may also need physical protection. A child clearly has no capacity to defend herself physically and has limited capacity to defend herself emotionally and mentally.

To compound her confusion and conflicts—invariably, an abusive parent is not abusive all the time. Episodes of abuse may be followed by periods of nurturing and affection. This girl lives in a continual state of tension, trying to anticipate whether it will be "good" mummy or "bad" mummy when she gets home from school.

To maintain her attachment to mum and dad the child needs to find a way to deny and avoid the deep pain associated with the reality that her parents repeatedly hurt and betrayed her. This is the impossible double-bind of the child.

To maintain the attachment necessary for survival, she needs to develop a range of defenses. Dissociation of unacceptable feelings and experiences allows her to maintain attachment. This ensures her emotional, psychological, and sometimes physical survival. However, it sets the stage for destructive patterns of relating to self and others later in life. These destructive relationship patterns serve to maintain, and paradoxically are attempts to master, a deep inner conflict.

The Problem of Attachment to the Perpetrator

So why is attachment to the perpetrator a core issue in therapy? A client may present with an idealized love or vengeful hate toward an abusive parent. These seemingly polar presentations equally reflect a problem with attachment to the perpetrator. Extremes of idealized love and vengeful hate defend against memories and powerful feelings of betrayal, terror, helplessness, loss, grief, and rage. These emotions are experienced as overwhelming, and perceived as "life threatening." The client stuck in idealized love or vengeful hate cannot face her painful feelings or resolve the conflict of feeling both love and hate for her abusive parent(s).

Attachment Styles

The attachment style of an individual is likely to be a combination of biology, personality, and environment. The four attachment styles below are not ranked from better to worse. They are simply different approaches that come naturally to different people. Each style describes an adaptive strategy to negotiate a hostile and unpredictable environment.

Preoccupied/Fearful

The person with a preoccupied attachment style presents as very needy. She will seek approval, and be clingy and emotionally demanding. In her relationships, she might be experienced as "high maintenance" and emotionally draining to others. The person with a fearful attachment style also seeks validation and approval but she gives out seemingly contradictory messages, seeking validation while simultaneously keeping others at arm's length. She avoids any real intimacy and emotional connection with others.

Ambivalent

The person with an ambivalent attachment style oscillates between drawing people close and pushing them away. She will approach a relationship to seek the attention she craves and then pull away at the prospect of any real intimacy with another. She will give out contradictory messages—come close, stay away—in a never ending dance that will confuse herself and others.

Avoidant

The person with an avoidant attachment style will give out a strong message that she doesn't need you. She doesn't let anyone get close, remaining aloof and uninvolved emotionally, even with people she would describe as close friends or her partner. She presents as if she doesn't care about anything or anyone. She has a strong need to be able to do everything herself and dismisses others with a casual shrug of her shoulders and moves on.

Disorganized

The person with a disorganized attachment style Is extremely dissociated and fragmented. In a client with DID or DDNOS, all the above attachment styles will likely manifest in different parts of the personality system. She is so disconnected from self that her lack of cohesion internally is reflected in her relationships. The disorganized attachment style probably reflects greater emotional damage and inability to defend against a severely abusive environment.

People's attachment styles are not always so clear-cut. It is common to find people with variations of the above broader definitions.

Identification with the Aggressor and Passive Victim: Two Sides of the Same Coin

A client may present as either identifying with the aggressor, i.e., hostile and blaming toward herself for the abuse, or as the passive, helpless victim who has difficulty taking responsibility for her life. While these presentations appear to be opposite and contradictory, they are two sides of the same coin. Both presentations reflect attachment to the perpetrator. Further, one does not have to explore too far into the DID or DDNOS structure to find the part of the personality who holds the counter viewpoint.

Each presentation reflects a defense against unacceptable thoughts, feelings, and memories. Identifying with the aggressor defends against feelings of powerlessness and helplessness. Feelings of anger can "safely" be turned inward rather than directed toward the perpetrator(s). As a child these feelings were too dangerous to acknowledge, let alone express.

Identifying herself as the passive victim allows for rationalizing, minimizing, and excusing abusive behaviour so that some positive feelings of love and connection can remain intact. It also defends against unacceptable feelings of rage and hate toward the perpetrator(s).

To resolve these conflicts the client needs to be able to hold all her intense and contradictory feelings consciously, in the present.

The Love-Hate Conflict

Understanding the dynamic of attachment to the perpetrator is fundamental to successfully working with a trauma survivor. The keys to the problem of attachment to the perpetrator are resolving the love-hate conflict and accepting disavowed feelings. However, this conflict is unlikely to be resolved until later stages of therapy. It cannot be pushed or forced. The therapist needs to keep resolution of the love-hate conflict in mind as the ultimate goal, but allow the process to unfold in the client's own way and at her own pace. In reality, she will bounce backwards and forwards around this issue.

As a child, the dilemma of both loving and hating her perpetrator(s) was too great for her internal resources. These feelings needed to be held separately to allow the attachment required for her survival. To move beyond surviving to thriving in all aspects of her adult life and relationships, the adult survivor needs to resolve the love-hate conflict. This requires her to bring forth her previously dissociated thoughts, feelings, and memories of those who abused her, and to feel both her love and her hate for her perpetrator(s) simultaneously.

Invariably, she will think she has resolved it and then inexplicably find herself back at square one, her ambivalence and preferred defense as strong as it ever was. This does not mean she has not progressed. As with most issues in therapy, the same conflicts will require revisiting time and again. It can be helpful to view therapy as a progression through the levels of a spiral, with each new level bringing the client back to the same issue but at a different place.

The board game, Snakes and Ladders, is another useful analogy. The client will climb ladders only to find herself land on a snake and appear to be further back than where she started. If both the therapist and client are cognizant of this process it can be seen as an intrinsic and valuable part of the journey that can help minimize feelings of despondency and the feeling of making no progress.

Grief and Loss

Grieving and mourning the loss of the parent(s) she never had is also bound up in untangling attachment to the perpetrator. When the client not only understands intellectually but can also feel for the defenseless child that she was, she begins to tap into an ocean of grief about the parent(s) she never had and will never have: grief for her lost childhood; for losses she may have as an adult, such as loss of time, career, financial stability, relationships, and perhaps the possibility of children; and for damage to her body through self harm, substance abuse, and destructive relationships.

This emotional work is also part of the later stages of therapy. However, it is important to understand how all these issues are connected with the intricate web of attachment to the perpetrator. Later chapters will provide practical guidance on how to assist a client to explore and work safely with complex and painful feelings and emotions.

Briere, J., & Scott, C. (2006). *Principles of trauma therapy: A guide to symptoms, evaluation and treatment*. Newbury Park, CA: Sage Publications

Ross, C.A. (2007). *The trauma model: A solution to the problem of comorbidity in psychiatry*. Richardson, TX: Manitou Communications.

Solomon, J., & George, C. (1999). *Attachment disorganization*. New York: Guilford Press.

12
Survival Strategy No. 2: "It Happened Because I Am Bad"—The Locus of Control Shift

In this chapter we will explore how a "normal" child in an abusive and dysfunctional environment learns to adapt and to make sense of his "abnormal" experiences. The core belief of the traumatized child is: "Bad things happened to me because I am bad." The logical conclusion that follows from this belief is: "I deserved what happened to me because I am bad." This is one of the most pervasive cognitive distortions among survivors of childhood abuse. Such erroneous beliefs arise from developmentally normal childhood cognitions.

This chapter will cover:

- Locus of Control

- Development of Normal Childhood Cognitions

- "I Am Bad"—Compensating for Feelings of Powerlessness and Loss of Control

- "I Am Bad"—Avoidance of Overwhelming Pain, Grief, and Anger

Locus of Control

Locus of control is a concept in the social learning theory of personal;ity developed by Rotter (1954). It refers to a person's beliefs about what causes good and bad things to happen.

Locus of control is categorized as internal or external. If a person has a 'high internal locus of control' he or she determines that his or her own behaviour and actions are the primary factors influencing events.

The person with a 'high external locus of control' has the belief that events are determined by influences or people outside of himself - this might be understood to be 'God's will,' karma, fate, chance or people who are perceived to have, or who actually do have, power over his life.

The circumstances of a child's environment will inform the child's sense of locus of control. The child growing up in a dysfunctional or abusive home or an environment characterized by poverty, civil unrest or war may be more prone to develop a high external locus of control. His experience is that nothing much he does influences the outcome of his situation. This may lead to beliefs and feelings of powerlessness and helplessness.

In abusive, disruptve and chaotic environments there is ample opportunity for a child's perception of events and experiences to become distorted in an attempt to make sense of his experiences. One way a high internal locus of control may become distorted is in how a child comes to attribute meaning and responsibility. For example, the child who believes, "I control events that happen, if bad things happen it must be because I am bad." This understanding is developed and built upon to compensate for a high external locus of control. "Others control my world and this makes me feel helpless," is an intolerable concept for the child who has no control over stopping bad things happening.

Other factors to consider that may influence a child's perception and experience of locus of control are gender, and cultural, political and social forces.

Development of Normal Childhood Cognitions

Between the ages of 2–7 years, the developmentally normal child has the perception that he is the centre of the universe. He has a magical belief that he is all powerful. He is the cause of everything that happens to him and around him. These developmentally normal beliefs can be seen as a byproduct of healthy attachment. As an infant, the child cries and mummy feeds him, changes his nappy, and soothes him. He smiles, and daddy smiles back and lifts him up over his head. The more he laughs, the more daddy repeats this fun game. He's in charge and all is well in his world.

Life will show this little boy, in small and big ways that he does not have the control he believes he possesses. His every want and need will not always be immediately attended to by others. One day he will cry and mummy will stay talking on the phone and he'll have to wait for her to come. A baby brother or sister will arrive on the scene and suddenly he will not be the centre of attention.

In a loving and stable family, normal magical thinking will naturally transition into a more complex and realistic perception of relationships and the world. The child will come to understand that other people have their own feelings, wants, and needs. He will learn to tolerate disappointments and develop skills and competence in attending to his own needs. He will learn to consider the needs of others through the modeling he observes and experiences.

"I Am Bad"—Compensating for Feelings of Powerlessness and Loss of Control

The abused child will learn different lessons. Physical, sexual, and emotional abuse and neglect overwhelm this child. He feels powerless, terrified, alone, and helpless. To make sense of his experience he draws on his limited understanding of the world. As described above, he comes to the conclusion that "This bad thing happened to me because I am bad."

This makes perfect sense to him. What other reason could there be other than "I am bad" or "I am stupid" or "I am ugly" or "I am sexy" or "I made daddy do it because I am a dirty boy?"

Every time something bad happens, these beliefs are reinforced. The beliefs are often reinforced by the perpetrator projecting responsibility onto the child, explicitly or implicitly. The child may be told "You made me do it," "It's your fault," "You wanted it," or "You like it."

Paradoxically, the belief of being bad and responsible for bad things happening is a protective device. The child's magical thinking leads to the conclusion, "If I have the power to make these things happen because I am bad, I also have the power to stop them happening by being good."

In the short-term this creates the illusion of having some power and control, where in fact he has none. He can try and try to be better behaved, smarter, and more likeable. When his attempts fail and the abuse continues, he can conclude that he just hasn't tried hard enough. He will do better next time. This is called the "locus of control shift."

Based on developmentally normal thinking, and childhood narcissism, the child shifts the control and power from inside the adults in his world to inside himself.

The downside to creating a sense of power and control through the belief "I am bad," is that this belief in essential badness will carry forward into adulthood and manifest itself through destructive behaviours toward self and others. The belief that "I am bad and deserved the abuse, so I don't deserve good things in life," can present as sabotaging his prospects at work and in relationships, substance abuse, and any number of other apparently self-defeating behaviours. The entrenched self-blame can appear to both client and therapist to be an insurmountable obstacle to healing.

"I Am Bad"— Avoidance of Overwhelming Pain, Grief, and Anger

Clients hold onto a belief in their inherent badness with an almost fanatical zeal. To unlock the stranglehold of "I am bad" is to understand its dual nature. "I am bad" not only serves as a defense against feelings of powerlessness and loss of control; "I am bad" also protects against facing very painful truths.

The cognition, "I am bad and deserved the abuse" protects both the child and adult survivor from facing the pain of betrayal, abandonment, and hurt by the people who should have been there to love, care, nurture, and protect him. Turning feelings of rage toward his parents for their abuse and neglect inward, and transforming them in to self-loathing and self-hate, protects his survival need to maintain his attachment.

Resolution of how the child attributes responsibility, and of the locus of control shift, necessitates addressing the dual nature of its function and interaction with attachment to the perpetrator. By shifting all the badness to inside himself, the child creates the illusion that his parents are safe attachment figures. It is better to be a bad boy with good parents, than a good boy with bad parents.

How to work with the interaction between responsibility, the locus of control shift and attachment to the perpetrator will be outlined in the chapters related to specific treatment strategies.

Ross, C.A. (2007). *The trauma model: A solution to the problem of comorbidity in psychiatry.*
        Richardson, TX: Manitou Communications.
Rotter, J.B. (1954). *Social learning and clinical psychology.* New York: Prentice-Hall.

13
Treatment Outcome Data for Dissociative Identity Disorder

We have published treatment outcome data for dissociative identity disorder in eight different sources (Ellason and Ross, 1996; 1997; 2005; Ross, 1997; 2004; Ross and Dua, 1993; Ross and Ellason, 2003; Ross and Haley, 2004). The data are reviewed in Ross (2005). In this chapter we will briefly review these data—the interested reader can consult the original papers for more details. The study by Ellason and Ross (1997) is posted at www.rossinst.com and can be downloaded from there. We will also review the basics of treatment outcome study design, and compare the state of the art for DID to the data available in the mental health field as a whole.

This chapter covers

- The Design of Treatment Outcome Studies

- Treatment Outcome Data in the Mental Health Field as a Whole

- A Review of Treatment Outcome Data for DID

The Design of Treatment Outcome Studies

For both medication and psychotherapy, the best design for treatment outcome studies is a *randomized prospective double-blind placebo-controlled trial*. This means

- Randomized—participants are randomly assigned to active treatment or placebo

- Prospective—the study begins at a starting point and follows participants forwards in time

- Double-blind—neither the researchers nor the participants know whether an individual is getting active treatment or placebo

- Placebo-controlled—some subjects receive a placebo

Additional treatment outcome study criteria not included in the phrase *randomized prospective double-blind placebo-controlled trial* are as follows:

- The study participants are well-defined diagnostically.

- Well-defined inclusion and exclusion criteria are used.

- Valid and reliable measures of treatment response are used.

- The treatment is well-defined and can be copied or replicated by other investigators.

- Adequate statistical analyses are conducted.

Inclusion criteria are the things that have to be true of the participant in order for her to get into the study, e.g., meets DSM-IV-TR criteria for the diagnosis being treated; scores above a certain cutoff on a symptom measure; and has given written informed consent. In an antidepressant study, for instance, the person would have to meet DSM-IV-TR criteria for a currently active major depressive episode and score above 20 on the Hamilton Depression Rating Scale.

The *exclusion criteria* are things that prevent a person from participating in a study. In a typical antidepressant study, these would include: under 18 or over 65 years of age; not taking birth control; currently abusing substances; serious medical problems; currently actively suicidal; and meets criteria for any other Axis I disorder.

In practice, it is hard to meet all the desired criteria in psychotherapy studies because it is fairly easy for participants to figure out whether they are getting active treatment or placebo. Also, a typical drug study lasts only 6–8 weeks, whereas a course of psychotherapy for DID takes years. The ethics and logistics of a treatment outcome study for DID are complicated. Retaining participants in a study for five years is far more difficult than retaining them for eight weeks, and it is not feasible or ethical to offer someone who is in need of meaningful assistance, a placebo treatment for five years. Additionally, obtaining funding for a large-scale DID treatment outcome study is a major hurdle.

Treatment Outcome Data in the Mental Health Field as a Whole

To evaluate the treatment outcomes for DID, they must be compared to two standards:

- The randomized prospective double-blind placebo-controlled trial

- The state of the art in the mental health field as a whole

Compared to well-funded drug studies that cost millions of dollars, the treatment outcome data for DID are preliminary. The fact that antidepressants are more effective than placebos has been proven scientifically. It is a fact, not an opinion or theory. However, it is equally true, and scientifically proven, that antidepressants are not very effective. Overall, 50% of depressed people respond to an antidepressant while 30% respond to placebo. The greater effectiveness of antidepressants compared to placebo is proven, and is statistically significant, but it isn't very impressive. The same is true for all psychiatric medications.

Also, the ecological validity of the world's data on psychiatric medications is very weak. This means that the results of the studies funded by drug companies don't tell us much about whether the medications help most patients. This is true because of the exclusion criteria.

If you have a drug or alcohol problem, serious medical problems, are actively suicidal, or have other Axis I disorders, you are not allowed into an antidepressant study. This excludes almost all the people admitted to psychiatric hospitals for depression, and almost all the people treated by psychiatrists. That is why psychiatrists have to advertise in newspapers and on the radio to recruit people for drug studies—they can't find them in their practices.

Basically, we have very little scientific data on whether antidepressants help the depressed people seen by psychiatrists in clinical practice. If the gap between antidepressants and placebo is small in simple, clean, neat-and-tidy outpatients who are allowed into drug studies, it is likely smaller in real-world patients. This is even more likely if we add in all the people who don't get diagnosed:

people who refuse to see a psychiatrist, the homeless, prison inmates, and people without health care insurance.

In one of the few real-world-style antidepressant studies, which involved a large number of patients treated at many different facilities throughout the United States, only about 10% of patients were still in treatment and still in remission after a year of treatment. Comparable results were found in a similar study of antipsychotic medication for schizophrenia. So treatment outcome in real-world clinical settings, as one would expect, is poorer than in the standard drug studies submitted to the Food and Drug Administration, with their rigorous exclusion criteria.

One can compare study data funded by drug companies to the DID treatment outcome data, but how relevant is that comparison? Why would a drug treatment lasting 6–8 weeks for a cooperative outpatient who is not suicidal, and has no other disorders or addictions, be expected to work for someone with DID, DDNOS, complex PTSD, or borderline personality disorder?

One can read the entire psychiatric literature and find almost no treatment outcome or follow-up data on complicated, highly comorbid psychiatric inpatients. Most people with DID have been inpatients at some time, or been suicidal at some time, and all have other Axis I disorders and addictions. The treatment outcome data for DID are as strong as any other body of data for any treatment method involving highly comorbid inpatients.

This is the context in which the treatment outcome data for DID should be evaluated: not the ideal standard of drug studies funded by multi-billion dollar drug companies, but the actual data available for real-world treatment of difficult, highly comorbid clients. The purpose of reviewing the treatment outcome data in the mental health field as a whole is to provide legitimate responses to critics of Trauma Model Therapy and the dissociative disorders.

Treatment Outcome Data for DID

The treatment outcome data for DID are prospective but they are not randomized, double-blind, or placebo-controlled. They meet all the additional criteria listed above. All the studies we have published except Ross and Dua (1992) involve giving measures to inpatients at admission, then again either at discharge, at three months post-discharge, or at two-years post-discharge.

Data at admission into the Trauma Program in Dallas, Texas, at discharge an average of 18 days later, and at 3-month follow-up (Ross and Haley, 2004) are presented in the following table:

TRAUMA MODEL THERAPY TREATMENT OUTCOME DATA

	Admission	Discharge	3-Months	F	p
		Average Score (S.D.)			
SCL-90-R	2.20 (.78)	1.57 (.80)	1.47 (0.85)	55.0	.00001
BDI-II	41.6 (11.0)	23.3 (13.6)	23.2 (13.3)	13.3	.00001
BSS	21.6 (11.9)	12.1 (9.2)	11.9 (8.6)	45.6	.00001
BHS	13.4 (5.2)	7.3 (5.2)	7.4 (4.9)	52.4	.00001
DES	42.1 (24.4)	34.9 (24.6)	33.8 (24.3)	16.5	.00001

SCL-90-R = Symptom Checklist-90-Revised; BDI = Beck Depression Inventory-II;

BSS = Beck Scale for Suicidal Ideation; BHS = Beck Hopelessness Scale;

DES = Dissociative Experiences Scale.

Reprinted with permission of the Haworth Press, Ross and Haley, 2004.

In this study, all of the 46 participants had major depressive disorder, all had a dissociative disorder, 85% had borderline personality disorder, 59% had somatization disorder, and 48% had substance abuse. Therefore, all would have been excluded from drug-company sponsored drug trials. The data demonstrate that the improvement seen during admission is maintained at three-month follow-up. The data at two years show even further improvement (Ross and Ellason, 1996; 1997).

What does a successfully treated case of DID look like on standard measures of psychopathology? During our two-year follow-up study, twelve people out of 54 reached integration. Only twelve reached integration because people were at all stages of recovery at baseline—some had only been diagnosed a few months earlier, and the treatment usually takes five years or more.

The percentage of people with DID who reach stable integration is unknown at this point, but if it is 12/54 = 22% at two years, it should be over 50% at five years. Therefore one can reasonably say that at least 50% of people with DID can reach stable integration if offered treatment for it. This is as good or better than the percentage of outpatients with simple straightforward depression who respond to antidepressants. Data for people with DID treated to integration look like this:

OUTCOME DATA FOR DID TREATED TO INTEGRATION

Measure	Admission	Two-Year Follow-Up
	Average Score	
DES	50.5	15.4
DDIS		
Somatic symptoms	14.3	4.3
Borderline criteria	5.9	1.7
Schneiderian symptoms	6.2	1.4
Secondary features of DID	11.2	4.1
ESP/paranomal experiences	5.8	1.9
Beck Depression Inventory	27.9	9.7
Hamilton Depression Scale	36.5	16.0
Structured Clinical Interview for DSM-III-R		
Active Axis I disorders	7.8	1.3
Active Axis II disorders	3.6	0.7
SCL-90-R	1.95	0.71
MCMI-II		
Borderline	88.8	50.0
Anxiety	71.9	39.0
Major depression	78.5	40.6
Thought disorder	72.3	43.6
Drug dependence	63.0	42.4
Alcohol dependence	62.6	30.5

At two-year follow-up, not one person out of the twelve who reached integration had abused drugs or alcohol in the preceding year. The treatment techniques described in this manual are supported by a body of prospective data in a well-defined population using valid and reliable measures of psychopathology.

14
The Stages of Recovery

The process of trauma recovery is divided into three stages. Although the terminology may vary, the basic stages of recovery are described consistently throughout the trauma field. It is important to be aware of the stages of recovery in order to maintain stability and function. The motto of therapy is *Slow and steady wins the race.*

Going too fast in treatment can result in flooding, which in turn can cause destabilization and regression; this in turn can activate maladaptive addictions, defenses, and coping strategies. The net result is that the person stays further behind than if the pace had been slower to begin with. Sound treatment involves a balance between opening up and containment, movement forward and consolidation of gains to date.

The three stages of recovery overlap; one does not progress through them in a purely linear fashion. However, the overall arc of recovery can be divided into these three sections despite the overlap and re-working inherent in the process.

This chapter covers

- The Three Stages of Recovery

- Goals of Each Stage

The Three Stages of Recovery

The three stages are commonly known as

- Initial Stage

- Middle Stage

- Late Stage

Initial Stage

Treatment begins with the first session, even if it is defined as an initial consultation or diagnostic assessment. The first goal of treatment is to establish a therapeutic alliance. Therapist and client need to form a working relationship. This is done through body language, tone of voice, attitude, and mannerism as well as through content and technique. The therapist practices the three basic Rogerian principles: congruence, genuine empathy, and unconditional positive regard. The therapist needs to be sincere, genuinely interested in the client, and see her as suffering and in need of assistance. At the same time, clear rules, boundaries, and limit setting are required. Empathy does not mean an "anything goes" attitude, being soft on the rules of therapy, or being indulgent.

Empathy, in trauma therapy, means seeing the person as exhibiting a normal, understandable reaction to trauma and misfortune. Normal outcomes of bad childhoods can include manipulative and self-destructive behaviour, testing of limits, negative transference reactions, acting out, resistance to the work of therapy, ambivalence about commitment to recovery, pressure on the therapist to become the rescuer, and acting out in many forms.

Therapist and client need to agree on common treatment goals. If the therapist is committed to the client's becoming sober, for instance, but the client is not, the therapy will not be productive. The goals need to be discussed in detail and reviewed periodically, especially if there is an impasse or the client seems stuck.

Goals need to be broken down into manageable steps. The ultimate goals are to be functional and productive, without active DSM disorders or addictions, to have a meaningful life and relationships, and to contribute to the lives of friends, family, and loved ones. However, one cannot work directly on these global goals; instead one works on a series of finite tasks and goals, moving through the three stages of recovery. The ultimate goals are met as a byproduct of successfully completing the series of finite, therapy tasks.

In the first few sessions therapist and client will need to agree on the logistics of therapy including fees, frequency of sessions, availability of the therapist outside hours, homework expectations, basic rules and boundaries, billing procedures, and the like. The therapist will need to explain the expected duration of therapy—it will be years, not weeks and not months. The client will need to understand that healing is painful, complicated, and difficult, and requires a lot of hard work. The client is undertaking to make a fearless inventory of her addictions, unhealthy defenses, and maladaptive behaviours. A lot of very intense feelings and conflicts will be worked through.

The therapist will need to review the client's hierarchy of needs: basic safety and stability need to be ensured before anything resembling "trauma work" can be the focus. For some clients, housing, income, food, and freedom from spousal battery may need to be first in the work of therapy. Once these are secured, which may take months, then basic psychological stabilization becomes the next priority. The client will need to learn and practice skills for grounding, containment, and self-soothing.

Teaching the client basic principles of trauma therapy such as the problem of attachment to the perpetrator, "the problem is not the problem," and the Victim-Rescuer-Perpetrator triangle is fundamental to assisting the client to identify and work with these core issues. These can be taught didactically in sessions and by assigned reading, which can include chapters of this book. Overall, the goal of the initial stage of therapy is to establish safety and stability, and to form a solid working alliance. These tasks are reviewed and reworked throughout the rest of treatment.

A conversation early in the initial phase might go like this:

Therapist: I want to go over the basic outline of therapy with you, just so you know what to expect.
Client: OK.
Therapist: First, it's going to take a long time. This is a really big project you are launching into here. It's do-able, but it's really hard work. It can't be done in weeks or months—it takes years. I can't say exactly how many years.
Client: Great.
Therapist: Well, I want you to have realistic expectations. If you work hard, and stick with it, you have

a realistic chance to make an amazing recovery. You have the basic ingredients for it: you're smart, you have a good work ethic, you basically understand how things work inside you, and you certainly have enough pain to motivate you. If you stick with it, and work hard, you will make a lot of progress. I'm not giving you a guarantee; I'm just saying that recovery is realistically possible for you.

Client: I wanted the guarantee.

Therapist: I'll see if I can get one for you by next week.

Client: I'd appreciate it.

Therapist: So, the first thing is, we need to agree on some initial treatment goals. We need to agree on what we are working toward, and what we need to do to get there. For instance, I see getting the self-mutilation under control as a high priority.

Client: Me too, but I don't know how to cope without cutting.

Therapist: We can work on that. Right now I'm just trying to set up some goals for early on. In fact, defining clear attainable goals is the first step in meeting those goals. We have to be working off the same map in order for you to move forward. So, the cutting—what else?

Client: I'd like to feel better.

Therapist: That's the whole point of therapy. The problem is, one can't work on "feeling better"—one can only work on defined, specific tasks. It's by working on the little things that one feels better in the end. What specifically is making you unhappy right now?

Client: My boyfriend is treating me bad.

Therapist: Bad like how?

Client: He yells a lot; he puts me down a lot.

Therapist: Does he ever hit you? Is he physically abusive in any way?

Client: Yeah, sometimes.

Therapist: Describe that in a little more detail for me.

Client: Well, half the time I deserve it, because I'm a real bitch sometimes.

Therapist: OK, hold it. There is never any justification for physical abuse. No matter how unpleasant you are, he needs to walk away, or cope some other way. How hard does he hit you, and how often?

Client: It only happens once a month or so.

Therapist: Does he hit you hard enough to cause bruises?

Client: Yeah.

Therapist: How about bleeding or broken bones?

Client: No.

Therapist: OK, so, as far as I am concerned, you are currently being abused by two people: your boyfriend and yourself. Both forms of abuse need to stop. You don't deserve either. You've already had way too much trauma and abuse in your life.

Client: Tell me about it.

Therapist: You say that, but your actions don't fit with your words. The one form of abuse you could stop right away is the self-mutilation.

Client: I don't know how to stop.

Therapist: I realize that, and we can work on how. But there's a stage before how, and that's deciding that you want to stop, for real. So I'd say the first goal of therapy is you getting serious about stopping the self-mutilation. Your boyfriend isn't treating you much worse than you are treating yourself.

Client: My boyfriend won't listen to me or you.

Therapist: But I'd like to at least consider inviting him to a session or two in the next few weeks. Before that, though, what about saying "no" to self-mutilation?

Client: I'm willing to work on it. I'm sick of living this way, with all this shit inside my head and shit from my boyfriend.

Therapist: I'm glad to hear that. I firmly believe that being fed up enough is the main motivator for

recovery. Sounds like you've got that down.
Client: Yeah, I do.
Therapist: Well, good then. How about this Thursday at two?
Client: It's a date.
Therapist: Good. See you then.

The purpose of that vignette was to illustrate the specifics and also the general principles of the early initial stage. The therapist's interventions included a mixture of education, confrontation, validation, reframing, humour, goal-setting, and working on the treatment alliance. Specific techniques and tasks of the initial stage are dealt with in later chapters.

There are no exact time frames for the stages of recovery. A danger of providing even rough time frames is that some people will feel behind schedule if the pace is specified. It is highly variable, and depends on severity of past trauma, current life situation, physical health, presence or absence of supportive relationships, financial situation, work ethic, commitment to recovery, and other variables, many of which are not under the client's control. Random trauma, illness, or misfortune can occur during therapy, and will slow down the process.

That said, the initial phase lasts either months or a year or two. If it lasts longer, therapy may not be productive, a consultation should be obtained, referral to another therapist may be required, or more limited treatment goals may be required.

The Middle Stage

The middle stage of therapy is where the hard work of recovery is done. The work of the middle stage begins in the second half of the initial stage and gradually becomes the primary focus as the tasks of the initial stage are completed. In clients with DID or DDNOS, initial work on internal communication and cooperation was already underway in the initial phase, but now it becomes a regular feature of most sessions. Treatment alliances are formed with an increasing number of alternate identities, and the system learns to solve small current life problems in a team fashion.

As well, the painful work of confronting, owning, and mastering the past begins. This involves integrating trauma memories in the full sense including information, visual pictures, emotions, physiological arousal, and sensation. Heart and head, body and mind become more connected, and as a result a lot of painful feelings are felt. This needs to be done without regression or decompensation, so the skills learned in the initial phase are put to the test, practiced, and re-learned in an ever-deeper fashion.

During the middle stage, which takes years (not months), there is a lot of symptom reduction. Most of the acting out stops, the active PTSD settles down a great deal, most of the major addictions are under control, and the need for inpatient treatment starts to disappear, or may be gone by the end of the middle stage. If the need for hospitalization occurs frequently or flashbacks, self harm, substance abuse or other harmful behaviours increase, the pacing of trauma processing may be beyond the clients' capacity to manage and tolerate the work. Pacing and exploration of any other contributing factors is warranted. Many clients don't ever require hospitalization.

By the later parts of the middle phase, major gains are readily evident to the client and her loved ones. This is a big relief, and it reinforces the commitment to therapy. During the initial phase, sometimes a lot of work is done without as much visible payoff, which can be discouraging. Realistic optimism and some signs of peace and contentment begin to emerge in the middle phase. There is now light at the end of the tunnel. The techniques and goals of this stage of recovery are described in later chapters.

Late Stage

The late stage is less arduous in terms of dealing with trauma and difficult defenses, but no less essential to recovery. It involves consolidation, finalizing the tasks of the middle stage, and working on the present and the future. An imagined positive future is a major motivator throughout therapy, but now one is actually working on making it happen. However, many trauma clients have difficulty imagining a future, let alone a positive one. The therapist may need to hold this hope and possibility for the client until such time he or she can begin to imagine it for him or herself. Much of the work involves therapy tasks for the average neurotic person (i.e., life challenges we all face).

Building and practicing more mature and healthy defenses and relationships, improving new life skills, and learning the identity of "regular person" as opposed to "trauma victim" are the fundamental tasks late in therapy. Near the end, processing the loss of the therapist becomes part of the work.

In the person with DID or DDNOS, the fragmented identities gradually blend together into an ever more unified whole. This occurs as a gradual, overall process, but specific personality states may integrate at specific points in time. The amount of amnesia in present-day life becomes minimal, then zero. Now the task of dealing with life as a single person is undertaken.

There is a lot of grief work throughout all three stages. In the late stage, the client may mourn relationships that ended as a consequence of healing, internal friends who are no longer there, the realization that some dreams will not come true, and the lost years between the end of childhood and the beginning of healing. All of these things are sad and deeply felt.

Thankfully, the grief is counter-balanced by the new joys of being normal, having a life, getting out of the mental health system, and having a stable sense of self. One can debate the meaning of "normal." There is no cookie-cutter definition available, no "one size fits all," but we have never met an integrated person who thinks it is better to be in the early initial stage of recovery.

For the person with DID or DDNOS, full integration may not be attained or desired. This is up to the client, not the therapist. However, we suggest that a desire not to integrate is a defense against aspects of trauma and/or feelings that have not yet been faced or processed. An outcome of a cooperative, co-conscious system with no ongoing amnesia and full orientation of all parts to the body and the present may be what some clients choose. While we personally advocate full integration, this cannot be legislated. We believe that full integration reduces the risk of relapse back into dysfunctional, pathological dissociation in response to future stress or trauma. We believe that integration is the goal for all therapies.

The final stage brings the end of therapy, the tapering down of sessions, and a review of the hard work done, the gains made, and the comedy and tragedy encountered along the way.

15
Consent, Contracts, and Treatment Goals

In the late eighties and early nineties there was more discussion of written contracts than one hears in the field today. This may be because formal contracts have been de-emphasized a bit, but, nevertheless, consent, contracts, and treatment goals remain vital components of therapy. Treatment goals were discussed in the previous chapter, but their incorporation in the consent and contracting process will be discussed here. We used the word *process* in the previous sentence on purpose: consent and contracting are not one-time events. They will be reworked and updated periodically throughout therapy.

In this chapter we cover

- Consent

- Contracts

- Treatment Goals

Consent

Written informed consent is required for participation in research, obtaining records, disclosure to third parties, admission to hospital, medical procedures, and often for medications prescribed. There are ethical guidelines and procedures for use of hypnosis and other specific therapeutic procedures. Here we are talking only about consent to therapy in general. Although written consent forms are not an absolute requirement, they certainly provide clarity and protection for both therapist and client.

Informed consent to therapy requires an explanation to the client of what is involved. Some of this was covered in the previous chapter. As for medical procedures, key components are the expected risks and benefits of treatment, and of declining treatment. Not all of this need be spelled out in writing, but at minimum it needs to be covered verbally. The record should contain a detailed note on the consent discussion.

The basic ideas are straightforward. Declining treatment could result in some degree of spontaneous remission but also involves the risk of prolonged symptoms and deterioration; the prediction made will vary from case to case. Someone who has been drinking heavily for fifteen years, and who does not see a need for treatment, is highly likely to continue drinking and experience more complications, for instance. On the other hand, a high-functioning person who is coping reasonably well may continue to experience an acceptable status quo without treatment.

Therapy involves a risk of flooding and decompensation (which can also occur in response to future trauma without therapy). The client needs to be informed that the work is painful and difficult, that it may drain time and energy from other duties, and that significant financial sacrifice is involved. Relationships may improve but others may end as the person moves through the stages of recovery. The possibility of flashbacks, new memories, and new feelings about old memories should be touched on.

The client needs to be advised that at some points, some reduction in hours at work, domestic duties, school attendance, or participation in relationships or hobbies may be required because of the demands of the therapy process. This needs to be balanced against the gains in function that can be expected. The realistic but not guaranteed benefits of recovery should be outlined. However, if a client's degree of functioning and capacities declines dramatically during therapy, this is a clear signal that some aspect of the therapy process has gone awry and requires reviewing.

Finally, there needs to be some discussion of duty to warn, emergency situations in which confidentiality may be broken, and behaviours that may result in termination of therapy, such as assault on the therapist, other professionals, or office furniture or property, or criminal or dangerous behaviour outside therapy. Duty to report to Child Protective Services overrides all other considerations—the client needs to know this if she has children herself, or has contact or involvement with nieces, nephews, or other children.

A conversation about consent might go as follows:

Therapist: There are some rights and responsibilities about therapy that I want you to understand. I am not saying these things because I think you will do any of them, it is my duty to explain this to all my clients. The first thing is, if you were ever to attack, threaten or abuse me in any way, harm yourself or anything else in the office during therapy sessions I would terminate the session immediately and would not continue therapy with you. This also includes the receptionist, other professionals and people in the building.

Client: What else?

Therapist: I will keep your confidentiality absolutely, except under certain circumstances. If I think you are a serious danger to yourself or another person, I may call the police whether you want me to or not. That's called *a duty to warn*, and I take it very seriously. If any child is in danger because of you, or if you tell me that a child you know is in danger from someone else, I will make sure that is reported to Child Protective Services immediately.

Client: I agree with that one.

Therapist: Good. Most of the rest can be worked out and negotiated as we go along. For instance, I may think it's important to bring someone into a session and you may disagree. If you do, I may explain why I disagree with you, but we'll continue to work together.

Client: So I have some control here.

Therapist: You have lots of control, but I have some too. This is your therapy; It has to make sense and be helpful to you for it to work. I also wanted to give you some idea of what to expect.

Client: Pain and suffering, I bet.

Therapist: Unfortunately, too much pain and suffering is why you're here—trauma and abuse you didn't choose or deserve. And healing does involve a lot of painful work, that's for sure. But it's worth it if you can get out the other side and have a life.

Client: Yeah, well we'll see about that.

Therapist: I think it's smart to be skeptical. You've had far too many betrayals and disappointments in life. It would suck if therapy was one more. All I'm asking is that you give it a try, one step at a time. In order to consent to treatment, you need some idea of what you're getting into.

Client: So when am I going to be better?

Therapist: I can't give you any guarantee you'll improve at all. I'm confident you will, if you work hard and stick with it. But that's the catch—you have to stick with it and do the work.

Client: I'm not a quitter.

Therapist: I can see that from the fact that you are here talking to me, and from your survival so

far—against tough odds.
Client: Well, thanks.
Therapist: You're welcome.

Contracts

Written contracts signed by client and therapist can be useful, but they are not cure-alls. Contracts can be broken in therapy, as they can in life generally, whether written or verbal, explicit or implicit. Most often, contracts are used for no-suicide, no-cutting or other target behaviours. They can be for set time periods. For instance, a common contract in an Emergency Department is for no self-harm until the outpatient appointment the next day. The payoff of the contract is not being admitted to the hospital, being in control of oneself, and getting an experience of self-mastery, even if only for 24 hours.

The simpler and more straightforward a contract is, the better. Lengthy clauses and sub-clauses foster a hunt for loopholes. A contract formalizes the consent and collaboration that runs throughout therapy. At the more global level, the contract of therapy needs to be reviewed periodically, as mentioned previously, especially when there is an impasse or progress seems to be too slow.

If the therapist seems to be working a lot harder than the client, there may be something wrong at the implicit contract level. The client may have made a commitment to abstinence from an addiction, but may have internally disavowed or denied it, in which case the therapist is working on abstinence but the client is not. In this situation, the contract to work on abstinence will need to be reviewed. It is better to have an agreement to work together on other things than to work at cross purposes on a commitment that has lapsed.

Often, when discouragement, doubt, and despair gain the upper hand, a review of progress to date, and a renewing of the contract to keep working can be helpful. Being stubborn, and refusing to quit, can be redefined as tenacity and commitment. The duty to interrupt the cycle of abuse, not to pass it on to future generations, and not to let the perpetrators win, can all be reviewed under the heading of the therapy contract. Like all other techniques and interventions, contracting is interwoven with many other components of the process. Contracts need to be viewed as both specific, finite, time-limited agreements, and at the more global, implicit level as well. As in all relationships, the most important elements of the contract may seldom be spoken about; this is fine, if everything is working well enough. When there is trouble, all levels of the contract will need reviewing, at least in the therapist's mind.

A conversation about the therapy contract might go as follows:

Therapist: It seems like we are off base somehow. You don't seem to be making the progress you were before, especially on the drinking.
Client: I can't help it.
Therapist: Why do you say that?
Client: Because my parts come out at night and drink while I'm asleep.
Therapist: So you have thirsty parts?
Client: Very funny.
Therapist: Well, why do your parts come out and drink? It's safe to assume that it's not because they're thirsty.
Client: They probably don't want to remember the abuse.

Therapist: Do you?

Client: No, would you?

Therapist: I don't think anyone would. So their drinking helps them push the memories away?

Client: I think so.

Therapist: When your parts push the memories away with alcohol, do the memories get further away from you too?

Client: Yes.

Therapist: So you share in the benefit from the drinking, then?

Client: Well, I guess if you put it like that, yeah.

Therapist: So I wonder if you are sending your parts a double message: you take the stance of being committed to sobriety, and you don't drink yourself, but then you benefit from the parts drinking. I imagine they see this.

Client: That could be.

Therapist: And that pattern of communication seems pretty similar to how your mother communicated with you when you were a child. It's called a double bind. There is the surface message—*I don't drink*—then the underneath message, which is denied or disavowed—*Thanks for drinking; I don't want to remember*. The parts can't escape from the situation, and no one comments on the fact that the surface message is contradicted by the underneath message. It's really the underneath message that is controlling things.

Client: So you're saying I treat my parts the way my mother treated me?

Therapist: Exactly. This isn't surprising: we all learn to treat ourselves by copying how our parents treated us. How did it feel when your mother put you in those double binds?

Client: Lousy.

Therapist: How do you think it makes your parts feel when you blame them for drinking, but tacitly assign them the job of drinking at the same time?

Client: OK, I get it.

Therapist: So I see two solutions here: 1) get real about not drinking at both the surface and the deeper levels, or 2) stop pretending to be committed to sobriety, and stop coming down on your parts for drinking. It's not like you're fooling your parts.

Client: No, they aren't stupid.

Therapist: That's because they are part of you.

Client: Thanks, I guess. OK, so you're saying I have to decide whether I'm going to get serious about quitting drinking?

Therapist: You don't "have" to do anything. It's up to you. But if you want to go down the path of sobriety, then you do have to get real with yourself and with your parts.

Client: I didn't realize I was treating my parts like that. What a loser!

Therapist: You're only a loser if you keep repeating the patterns of the past forever. In fact, you're a winner because you're working hard to change. It takes time.

Client: Well I do want to quit. So I guess I'll have to lighten up on the parts and learn some better ways of coping.

Therapist: Good. We're back on track, then.

Notice that reviewing the contract is not a separate activity from the work of therapy. The vignette includes the techniques of interpretation, confrontation, reframing, education, humour, empowerment, and contracting.

Treatment Goals

Treatment goals were discussed in the previous chapter, and the details are dealt with in later chapters. At the global overall process level, consent, contracts, and treatment goals are intertwined. The client needs to consent to a contract that specifies the treatment goals. In addition, an initial treatment goal is to form a contract and obtain informed consent. All of these elements are ongoing and can remain implicit much of the time.

THE SEQUENCE OF TREATMENT GOALS IN COMPLEX DISSOCIATIVE DISORDERS

- Form a treatment alliance

- Obtain consent

- Establish a contract

- Obtain a commitment to abstinence from addictions and acting out

- Secure basic safety and needs

- Educate the client about the model of therapy

- Educate the client about dissociation and comorbidity

- Establish inter-personality communication and cooperation

- Orient parts to the body and the present

- Practice problem solving as a team or system

- Engage an increasing number of parts in the therapy process

- Teach and practice new coping strategies

- Desensitize the client to previously intolerable feelings

- Learn to tolerate ambivalence

- Reconstruct a trauma narrative

- Complete the process of integration

- Consolidate gains

- Practice coping as a unified person

At the microscopic level, treatment goals proceed in a sequence, bearing in mind that the process is not purely linear, but involves reworking and revisiting themes already gone over in previous sessions. The following outline of treatment tasks is broad and general, and not exhaustive. The specifics are described in later chapters:

Note that "memory work" is not a treatment goal. Remembering the trauma is not an end in and of itself. Rather, the task is to construct a coherent life narrative that has meaning, order, and purpose. The trauma is an important part of the narrative, but it is only one element. At the end of therapy, the role of trauma in the life story should be more limited and less important than it was at the beginning, when flooding, flashbacks, intrusions, and re-enactments dominated.

The ultimate treatment goal is to be a person, not a "trauma survivor" or a victim. The trauma needs to be remembered, acknowledged, and felt, and this is an intense, painful undertaking. However, the goal is no longer to be dominated, determined, or controlled by the trauma or its perpetrators. This cannot be accomplished through amnesia, nor can it be accomplished by abreaction and flooding. There is a middle path of intense recollection that leads to healing.

16
Navigating Boundaries with the Dissociative Client

Boundaries in therapy can be a contentious issue for both client and therapist. Dissociation and other trauma responses such as borderline behaviours can intensify transference and counter-transference and affect boundaries in the therapeutic relationship.

Clients with a history of trauma and abuse have experienced boundary violations, most often by the people who should have been safeguarding and protecting them. At best, boundaries were inconsistent and at worst, non-existent. To create a space for the client to feel "safe enough" to undertake the hard and scary work of healing, the therapist needs to be sensitive and consistent with the rules, rights, and responsibilities of therapy, for both therapist and client. Boundaries for trauma clients follow the same ethical rules and guidelines as for general psychotherapeutic practice. However, navigating boundaries with dissociative clients can be more challenging.

Some boundaries are obvious, clear cut, and non-negotiable. These include: no sexual relationship; no socializing; and no giving legal or financial advice (other than perhaps to suggest that a client may benefit from seeking such professional advice). Other boundaries may legitimately differ according to the working environment of the therapist.

For instance, the role of a youth outreach worker may include activities such as taking a client for a cup of coffee. A nurse therapist may leave the hospital grounds with a patient as part of a therapy plan. Counselors in sexual assault centres may also act in an advocacy role as part of their mandate. Therapists working in rural areas, small communities, in pastoral care, and gay and lesbian therapists working specifically with gay and lesbian clients, may find themselves in community or social situations with clients. Boundaries for working with children may differ from boundaries for working with adults. Finally, the personality and particular style of the individual therapist, and the use of discretion on a case by case basis, may result in some boundary variations.

This chapter is aimed primarily at therapists consulting in private practice, and in government and non-government agencies during regular business hours. Therapists working in other settings where there may be acceptable or necessary variations on the boundaries outlined in this chapter will benefit from seeking case consultation with an experienced trauma therapist to clarify boundaries for their particular setting.

This chapter will cover the following

- Boundary Violations by Therapists

- Boundary Testing by Clients

- Setting and Maintaining Boundaries

Boundary Violations by Therapists

Boundary violations and the damage they cause can range from minor to extremely serious. Boundary violations are committed by both novice and experienced therapists. Mostly, minor boundary violations appear to be committed unintentionally and are not designed to deliberately hurt or exploit the client. Some other violations appear to arise from the therapist's own unresolved trauma history and/or counter-transference. Vicarious trauma and/or compassion fatigue may be a contributing factor in some boundary violations. In all boundary violations, the therapist has become a player in the Victim-Rescuer-Perpetrator dynamic (see Chapter 18—The Victim-Rescuer-Perpetrator Triangle).

The following are the most common boundary violations by therapists:

BOUNDARY VIOLATIONS BY THERAPISTS

- Running late for sessions

- Regularly going over time in sessions

- Not giving adequate notice when going on holiday

- Not offering an emergency contact therapist while on holiday

- Taking telephone calls while in session

- Frequent lengthy phone calls between sessions

- Phone calls after hours (may be acceptable in some settings)

- Sessions regularly last over 60–90 minutes (other than planned therapy work)

- More than two sessions per week (other than short-term in emergencies)

- Sharing detailed personal information

- Giving and receiving gifts (other than accepting small tokens such as at Christmas)

- Going for a walk, coffee, meal, or social outing

- Attending client's personal or professional events

- Sessions outside of the consulting room (some situations may be acceptable, i.e., if the client is in hospital or a session outside the office for a planned therapeutic purpose)

- Confidentiality violations

- Minimizing a client's experience and/or undermining her abilities

- Bartering therapy for client's personal services

- Employing client

- Involving client in therapist's personal life

- Providing supervision to a client when the client is a therapist

- Involving a client in the personal life of other clients and/or as a consultant on other clients and/or as co-therapist for other clients

- Living with a client

- Going on holiday with a client

- Sexual involvement with a client

Length and Frequency of Sessions

The length and frequency of sessions is an important boundary in therapy.

Allowing for a longer lead-in to a therapy task and for grounding and reviewing at the end of the session is a useful practice in general and very important at different points in therapy. Examples of planned therapy work that may benefit from scheduling a longer session are: exploring a specific memory, working with feelings and emotions, or to video a role-play—either a rehearsal for handling a current situation, or to process a past experience and then to review the video in the same session.

Factors impacting the number of sessions an individual client may require are finances/insurance coverage, the clients' functioning and stage of therapy, and work/study/family and other commitments. Clients may need more or fewer sessions at different stages of therapy.

The ISSTD guidelines for treatment recommend 1–2, 45 to 55 minute sessions per week with up to 3 sessions for limited periods to maintain adaptive behaviour, prevention of hospitalization, or post discharge from hospital. Sessions of 75–90 minutes are considered helpful for some clients depending on functioning and the stage and focus of therapy. Alternatively, for some clients two sessions, one 45–55 minutes and one 75–90 minutes, may be a useful combination. It is recommended that sessions do not exceed 90 minutes. A combination of excessive number of sessions and/or duration of sessions can lead to regression in the client and is indicative of problems with boundaries and the pacing of therapy.

Acknowledging Boundary Violations

When a therapist recognizes that he or she has committed a boundary violation, it can give rise to intense feelings. In case consultations, therapists have expressed feeling foolish, embarrassed, and ashamed. These feelings are often accompanied by sincere regret and an eagerness to explore how to address the consequences of the violation with their client, and to understand what was driving their own behaviour. Many clients are very generous when a therapist acknowledges and apologizes for making a mistake. Sometimes the client may not have recognized that a boundary had been crossed. In less serious boundary violations the breach in the therapeutic relationship may be easily repaired.

The authors have consulted on cases in which the therapist has been defensive when a boundary violation has come to light. Complaints to Licensing Boards and legal action tend to occur when the boundary violation has been more serious. In such cases, the therapist may be more likely to respond with denial that the violation occurred and/or blame the client's "borderline" behaviour for the violation, and to see themselves as the "victim" of the "seductive client."

Boundary violations make the work in therapy harder for both the client and therapist. Particularly with more serious boundary violations, the impact for the client can be devastating. The nature of therapy is that it is intimate, gives rise to intense feelings, and is conducted in private. The therapy relationship is unequal. The nature of being a client is that it is a vulnerable position, more so when the client has a history of trauma and abuse. While acknowledging the vulnerability of, and risk taken by clients, it is also important to be cognizant of the vulnerability of, and risk taken by therapists. Vicarious trauma, personal safety and professional reputation are all potentially risked and challenged by the most ethical and competent of therapists.

When a client enters a therapist's room, it is an act of great courage. Clients have experienced various combinations of emotional, psychological, spiritual, physical, and sexual violation, commonly perpetrated by the people who were meant to care for and protect them. Trust has been broken and boundaries violated. When a client takes the risk in reaching out for help, it is unacceptable for her to be hurt again by the professional who was meant to assist.

The therapist's duty of care is to be qualified (through knowledge and experience); to pursue regular professional development reading, study, and/or case consultation; to be transparent with clients and colleagues regarding practice; to attend to his/her own personal issues; and to act with integrity. It can be hard to acknowledge making a mistake. However, as a profession, therapists need to be open, talk about our experiences and learn from our mistakes. If you are aware that you or a colleague is experiencing boundary difficulties with a client, the authors urge you to seek assistance to resolve the situation.

Boundary Testing by Clients

Clients with a trauma and abuse history are people in great distress; therapy is a confrontational, challenging, and frightening journey. The role of the therapist is to gently and safely guide the client towards that which her defenses have kept at bay. The therapist becomes a threat to the client's defenses and the object of her projections and transference. It is the nature of therapy that clients project unresolved issues onto therapy and the therapist. Testing boundaries is part of the therapy process. Transference with clients manifesting borderline personality characteristics can be challenging. Patience, repetition, and setting firm, fair, and consistent boundaries are required.

Frequently, this client group simultaneously resents but paradoxically craves boundaries to create a sense of safety in which to do the work of therapy. If there is no transference or boundary testing then the real work of therapy has not yet begun. Working with transference requires respect, compassion, and skill on the part of the therapist. Transference and boundary testing are grist for the mill in therapy.

BOUNDARY TESTING BY CLIENTS

- Consistently arriving late for sessions

- Consistently attempting to go over session time

- Regular non-attendance without notice

- Non-payment

- Phone calls outside of prescribed times

- Repeated requests for "special" consideration outside stated therapeutic boundaries

- Asking personal questions about life, family, relationships, history

- Turning up at therapist's house

- Giving expensive or frequent gifts

- Inappropriate touching and/or attempts to initiate sexual contact

- Verbal aggression (beyond expected conflict as part of therapy)

- Threats towards therapist, family, or property

As stated above, boundary testing is to be expected. Understanding the dynamics driving inappropriate behaviour by a client, such as attempts to sexualize the therapeutic relationship, greatly assists in managing the situation sensitively and ethically. The message that the child who has been sexually abused received is that her value or worth was derived from being sexual. "Love," "closeness," and feeling or being "special," were equated with sex.

The magical thinking of the child (the locus of control shift) is that she has power and control in a situation where she is in fact vulnerable and powerless. Therapy is a situation where a feeling of fear, vulnerability, and inequality in power in the relationship is reminiscent of childhood dynamics. In view of this, it is easy to see how the client draws on learned behaviours, relational dynamics, and defenses to negotiate the therapeutic relationship.

Attempts to sexualize the therapeutic relationship can reflect the client's best attempts to relate, and to try to feel safe by controlling the therapist through sex. Paradoxically, attempts to "seduce" the therapist may also be seen as a test for the therapist. How safe are you? How much can I trust you? Past experience has proven that the people whom she should have been able to trust were the ones she was least able to trust.

Further complicating this complex transference dynamic is the client's experience. The therapist may be the first person she has ever been able to trust and who has proven to be trustworthy. The therapist may be the only person with whom she has shared her most painful and shameful secrets, yet not been judged or rejected. This is a powerful intoxicant for the client. The desire for a safe, nurturing relationship as an adult and the experience of a positive relationship with the therapist, may result in confusing the emotions this arouses with "romantic love."

While the feelings the client has for her therapist are indeed powerful, the relationship is not personal or equal. The client does not know her therapist as a "real" person but as an idealized image of who she imagines him or her to be. A therapist should never take clients' expressions of love at face value. Furthermore, the therapist needs to examine strong feelings engendered by a client (see Chapter 18—The Victim-Rescuer-Perpetrator Triangle).

When a boundary violation occurs, there is commonly an interaction between the client's transference and the therapist's counter-transference. However, the therapist has a responsibility to anticipate, understand, and respond appropriately to what can be difficult, challenging, and at times unreasonable behaviour by clients. No matter how "difficult" the client, the therapist is always responsible for managing boundary violations. The duty of the therapist is always to hold the client's welfare as the primary concern. This remains true even when a client is an apparently willing participant or initiates a boundary violation, such as a sexual relationship.

Setting and Maintaining Boundaries

It is understandable that clients are curious about their therapists. It is a normal part of relating to be interested and to ask questions about another person's life. A client discloses very personal and painful information to her therapist. She shares her fears, her failures, and her triumphs while the therapist's life remains shrouded in mystery. The therapy relationship is a very one-sided relationship. While sharing general aspects of personal experience to illustrate a point in therapy may be helpful at times if used sparingly, disclosure of personal details and history is generally counter-productive, impeding the process of therapy, and giving more scope for transference distortions.

To reduce the potential for misunderstanding regarding client and therapist rights and responsibilities, it is helpful to provide clients with an information sheet outlining the "rules" of your practice. Information that may be helpful to include, follows:

CLIENT INFORMATION SHEET

- Office hours

- Phone calls between sessions

- Fees

- Appointment times and length of session

- Cancellation policy

- Confidentiality

- Expectations of therapy when working with trauma history (informed consent)

> - Focus and use of sessions
>
> - No personal, social, sexual contact between client and therapist
>
> - Policy regarding physical contact if the client is upset
>
> - Behaviour contract if client becomes aggressive, or is known to be on referral

An information sheet is not designed to prevent boundary testing. Rather, it makes your practice as clear and as transparent to the client as possible, which is particularly important for clients with a history of trauma and abuse. An information sheet provides a reference point for discussion and clarification when boundaries are tested and challenged.

Handling Boundary Testing

A therapy session concerning boundaries might include the following conversation:

Client: I know you've explained that you don't give out personal information, but it would really help me to know if you have been sexually abused.

Therapist: I understand your curiosity about that and as you say, I have explained that I don't talk about my personal life or history. But I would be interested to know why you're asking me that question?

Client: Well, my last therapist told me she had been sexually abused and it really helped 'cause I knew for sure then that she understood what I was saying; it helped me to trust her.

Therapist: How did it help you to trust her?

Client: 'Cause she was open and honest. She didn't try to hide stuff and wasn't all secretive like you are.

Therapist: So it feels like I'm being secretive because I don't talk about my personal life?

Client: Yes.

Therapist: And you feel like you could trust your last therapist because she told you that she had been sexually abused?

Client: Yes.

Therapist: How long did you see your last therapist?

Client: About 2 ½ years.

Therapist: Can you remind me why you finished up with her?

Client: I don't know. I got to a certain point and then didn't seem to be getting anywhere. Whenever I talked about a memory and other stuff she would talk about how it had been for her and it wasn't always the same for me. Sometimes it made me feel that what I experienced was wrong.

Therapist: So it wasn't always helpful to know about her experience?

Client: Well no, but mostly it was. I didn't feel such a freak.

Therapist: So having been sexually abused makes you feel like a freak?

Client: Yes.

Therapist: If I told you I had been sexually abused what would that mean to you?

Client: Well, I'd know you'd understand what I was talking about. It'd make me feel safer and that you wouldn't hurt me. It would make me feel that if you dealt with it then maybe I can too. I'd feel less like a freak.

Therapist: And if I told you I hadn't been sexually abused what would it mean to you?

Client: I'm not sure. I mean, I think you could still help me but maybe you wouldn't understand me so well. You wouldn't really know what it was like to go through all that shit.

Therapist: And you think a therapist can be more helpful if they have been through the same thing as the client?

Client: I don't know. Maybe.

Therapist: Another client asked me if I had been sexually abused and when I asked her the same questions I just asked you she had some different thoughts. Would you like to hear how she felt?

Client: OK.

Therapist: Well the other client said that if I was sexually abused she might feel even worse about herself because she saw me as really together and if I had also been abused then she would wonder how come I was so together and her life was such a mess. She also thought that if I had been sexually abused she couldn't be sure that I wasn't projecting my own stuff onto her and putting ideas in her head. But if I hadn't been sexually abused then she thought I might have a clearer perspective. She said she would prefer it if I hadn't been sexually abused.

Client: That's the opposite of how I'd feel—not that I'd be glad you'd been abused.

Therapist: I know what you mean but, yes, two people with the same experience believe they would feel better, safer, and more understood if I answered differently to the same question. Each of you has a completely opposite perception of how you believe it would help or hinder you to know if I had been sexually abused.

Client: Guess you can't please everyone.

Therapist: True. But maybe the point is that it's not helpful to try to please everyone.

Client: Well I can relate to that. I'm sick of other people's expectations of me.

Therapist: Yes, it can be draining. But apart from that, by believing it is important to your healing to know if I was sexually abused both you and the other client are externalizing your sense of safety, power, success, or failure on to what has or hasn't happened to me. If I told you I had or had not been sexually abused I would be colluding with those projections and interfering with your process. I would be trying to solve your internal conflict for you, but by doing so I would become part of the problem.

Client: Oh, I guess I can see that, sort of. But I'd still like to know.

Therapist: It's OK you still want to know but perhaps we can explore more about the conflict underlying your wanting to know.

Client: That sounds like fun; I can hardly wait.

As stated at the beginning of this chapter, there are boundaries that are non-negotiable, boundaries that may vary according to a particular work setting and discretion with particular clients. There are times when a client challenging or testing a boundary needs to be addressed immediately and times when it may be more helpful to "let it go." Discerning the difference is not a science but an art born from insight, compassion, common sense, and experience. The following is a quick reference checklist for negotiating boundary issues:

SETTING AND MAINTAINING BOUNDARIES CHECKLIST

- Be clear on the reasons for each boundary you set.

- Inform new clients of the "rules" of therapy and your practice—preferably give them something in writing.

- Expect boundaries to be tested.

- Be gentle, firm, and consistent when a client tests boundaries.

- Question yourself: am I being overly rigid or too flexible; am I being consistent; do I need to be firmer or more relaxed with boundaries with this client?

- Remember boundaries will trigger conflicts within the client—your role is to guide and reflect, not to take the polar position or try to fix the conflict for the client (this will lead to a dance on the Victim-Rescuer-Perpetrator triangle).

- Clients will also trigger strong feelings in the therapist—these should be explored in case consultation or your personal therapy.

- Ask yourself if you are making a "special exception" or doing something you wouldn't ordinarily do with a client—if you are, this may be a warning that boundaries are being crossed.

- Do you think the client's behaviour is what you would "expect" with this client or the stage of therapy and/or for current issues that are in focus—if not there may be another issue going on for the client that requires exploration.

- Seek additional case consultation if boundary testing escalates or does not abate.

- Apologize if you make a mistake.

As stated earlier, clients have an ambivalent relationship with boundaries in therapy, simultaneously resenting them and feeling that they provide a much needed sense of safety. The therapeutic relationship is perhaps their first experience of consistency, fairness, and of having limits set on their own and another's behaviour.

Ben Ari, A., & Somer, E. (2004). The aftermath of therapist-client sex: Exploited women struggle with the consequences. *Clinical Psychology and Psychotherapy*, 11, 126-136.

Chefetz, R., & Courtois, C. (1993). The erotic and traumatic transference-countertransference matrices. Fiffth Annual Eastern Regional Conference, Alexandria, Virginia, June.

Chu, J. (1998). *Rebuilding shattered lives: The responsible treatment of complex post-traumatic and dissociative disorders*. New York: John Wiley & Sons.

Dalenberg, C. (2000). *Countertransference and the treatment of trauma*. Washington, DC: American Psychological Association.

Gabbard, G., & Wilkinson, S. (1994). *Management of countertransference with borderline patients*. Washington, DC: American Psychiatric Press.

Pearlman, L.A., & Saakvitne, K.W. (1995). *Trauma and the therapist: Countertransference and vicarious traumatization in psychotherapy with incest survivors*. New York: W.W. Norton.

17

"Do You Believe Me?" How to Avoid Becoming Part of the Problem

Working with clients reporting memories of abuse and trauma is a potential minefield for the client and the therapist. The formation of the False Memory Syndrome Foundation (FMSF) in the United States in 1992 led to a political and legal storm across the trauma and abuse field. Many lawsuits resulted against alleged perpetrators and the therapists of alleged victims. Clients faced additional stress and trauma as a consequence of sensationalized media stories about sexual and ritual abuse, child pornography, and sex rings. These stories frequently alleged that high ranking public officials, including politicians, judges, lawyers, police, doctors, teachers, and others with access to children, were among the perpetrators. The predominant position taken by the media, often without any conclusive evidence that a crime had or had not been committed, was that claims by alleged victims were false. Furthermore, according to the media, such memories were the result of suggestion from charlatan therapists and questionable therapy on vulnerable clients. The term *Recovered Memory Therapy [RMT}* was coined by the media. While there is no doubt that there have been cases of questionable therapeutic practices, that have caused harm to clients, alleged perpetrators and the trauma field, to the knowledge of the authors, there is no actual therapy called RMT.

Some clients present reporting continuous recall or partial recall of abuse. Others may seek therapy due to common life experiences, such as unsatisfactory relationships, addictions, generalized depression, or dissatisfaction with life. A major life-changing event, such as a birth, death, marriage, separation, job loss, or a serious accident or illness may be the precursor to entering therapy. While these events can be experienced as traumatic in and of themselves, they may also be the catalyst for dissociated memories to begin to surface.

Clients may have diverse reactions to the veracity of their memories of abuse and this may change throughout the initial phases of therapy, including during the processing of traumatic material. This can occur regardless of whether the memories have always been intact, have been partially conscious, or have surfaced years after the events. Some clients are convinced of the truth and accuracy of their memories. Others are racked with doubt, erring on the side of disbelief. These clients will search for some other cause or reason for the mental images, physical sensations, or intense emotional reactions they experience, including a preference for believing they have a "mental illness" or for some inexplicable reason are simply making it up. Oscillation between belief that memories are real and recanting is common.

At some point during therapy, a client may seek from the therapist, directly or indirectly, validation of her memories. This is the, "Do you believe me?" question. It is a question asked at a time of great confusion, uncertainty, and vulnerability, and out of a need for something or someone to hold onto. Depending on how the therapist answers this question, it can have far-reaching consequences for the client and the progress of therapy. Preempting the question through educating the client about the principle of therapeutic neutrality can avert a great deal of misunderstanding, minimize the potential of the client externalizing her conflicts and ambivalence about memories through polarizing with her therapist, and help keep therapy on track.

This chapter will cover

- The Principle of Therapeutic Neutrality

- "Believing" or "Not Believing" Memories

- "Taking Sides"—Conflicted Feelings Toward the Alleged Perpetrator

- Communicating the Principle of Therapeutic Neutrality

- When It Is Important Not To Be "Neutral"

The Principle of Therapeutic Neutrality

As therapists, we identify ourselves as people with a great capacity for compassion and empathy. Indeed, these are important traits in our work, as well as life in general. This is why the word "neutrality" in reference to therapy can sound counterintuitive. Neutrality seems to conjure a lack of empathy, even indifference. To be non-empathic and indifferent would be damaging to the client and limit the potentials of therapy. The essence of the principle of therapeutic neutrality is *"supporting the client through ambivalence, conflicts, and intense emotions about her memories and alleged perpetrator."*

Transference describes the process whereby a client projects conflicts about himself and significant people in his life, the issues he is in therapy to address, the therapist and therapy process, onto the therapist. Counter-transference describes the therapist's reactions to her client's projections, as well as reactions toward the client's personality, behaviour and the material he brings into therapy. During the course of therapy both client and therapist may have genuine reasons to be upset, angry, or hurt by the other's behaviour. However, it is always the therapist's responsibility to manage these reactions with a clear understanding of the unequal power relationship, and the context, boundaries, and triangle dynamics in operation.

In any therapy situation the possibilities of transference are limitless. The nature of trauma, abuse, and dissociation amplifies the potential for complex transference reactions. It can be almost guaranteed that, in varying degrees, two of the biggest internal conflicts a trauma client will grapple with are the "reality" of his memories and his relationship to the alleged perpetrator. This is true even when a client is high functioning and has a clear understanding of the dynamics of attachment to the perpetrator and the locus of control shift. The ability to understand concepts does not immediately translate into a shift in the emotional "reality" of the client.

To support a client through the painful and confusing process of working with memories and the client's conflicts regarding the alleged perpetrator requires compassion and empathy. It also necessitates an understanding of attachment to the perpetrator, the locus of control shift, the Victim-Rescuer-Perpetrator triangle (see Chapter 18), transference and counter-transference and the complexities of memory. Clients undertaking trauma therapy need to understand and give informed consent to the process (see chapter 15 on Consent, Contracts, and Treatment Goals). This involves educating clients about what they can expect as standard elements of trauma therapy. How to explain to clients the principle of therapeutic neutrality regarding memory and relationships with alleged perpetrators will be discussed later in this chapter.

"Believing" or "Not Believing" Memories

Factors that influence a person's response to memories include the two fundamental issues outlined in Chapters 11 and 12, which are the basis of the Trauma Model, 1) Attachment to the Perpetrator, the client's past and current relationship to the alleged perpetrator(s) and 2) the Locus of Control Shift, using magical thinking to shift responsibility to self in an attempt to gain some power and control in a situation of powerlessness and helplessness. Other factors may include the age the abuse occurred, the duration and severity of the abuse, whether there was any intervention, and support or acknowledgment at the time of the abuse and in their lives currently. Alcohol and drug use can be additional factors, as is, potentially, the client's general level of functioning and stability. A client may recount a memory laden with intense affect, or speak of a sadistic account of abuse as if she were describing what she had for breakfast.

FACTORS INFLUENCNG CLIENT RESPONSES TO MEMORIES OF ABUSE

• Attachment to the Perpetrator

• Locus of Control Shift

• Age and duration of abuse

• Intervention and support

• Level of functioning and stability

Most adults who report a history of abuse do not have independent corroboration, such as police, hospital, or school reports, or verification from a witness. It is for this reason we often refer to the "alleged perpetrator." This term may seem cumbersome, and as if we are casting doubt on clients' reports of abuse. The intention is to assist clinicians to approach clients' uncorroborated reports of abuse with an open mind and avoid the risks of making assumptions about true or false memories.

Taking the position of believing or not believing a client's memories, where there is no corroboration, sets the client up for greater conflict. For example, if the therapist says she believes her client, she takes away the possibility for him to disbelieve, which is an important avenue that he needs left open as he works through painful and conflicting feelings. If the therapist disbelieves the client, he will feel unsupported, not validated, and limited in his ability to explore all the issues he needs to deal with, whatever the truth of his experience may be.

Lacking corroboration, it is possible that the client's memories may not be accurate in part or totality. The client needs to explore what is coming up for him and what it means, for himself. If the therapist takes a position of believing or not believing, this process is hindered.

The memories are a source of great conflict and ambivalence. This is a struggle in which the client needs support to find his way through. The therapist who states a belief or disbelief in her client's memories becomes a player on the Victim-Rescuer-Perpetrator triangle. The client will either feel rescued or victimized by the therapist's position. Whichever the client feels, the therapist has also become the perpetrator.

If the therapist believes and the client recants or it becomes apparent the memories were in part or total not true, then the therapist has contributed to his suffering by encouraging him to believe. If the therapist doesn't believe, she has hurt the client, whether the memories are ever found to be true or not. She has become another person who has let him down and not validated his experiences. Whatever the truth of the memories may be, the therapist who states a belief or disbelief has hindered the client in his own journey of discovery and its potential for healing and growth.

In stating a belief or disbelief in client's memories, the therapist is in fact "suggesting" that abuse did or did not occur. In addition to the conflicts this creates for the client as already outlined, it leaves the therapist open to potential lawsuits by the client and/or his alleged perpetrator.

REASONS TO REMAIN "NEUTRAL" ABOUT UNCORROBORATED REPORTS OF ABUSE

• To minimize the client projecting the conflict of believing or disbelieving onto the therapist

• To not become part of the problem through taking on the polar position in the client's conflict

• To allow the client the space to work through conflict and ambivalence

• To keep off the Victim–Rescuer–Perpetrator triangle

Where there is no corroboration of a client's accusations the therapist can never know what did or did not happen. There will be exceptions, such as a client in a state of psychosis. For example, a client of one of the authors, during a psychotic episode, claimed that she knew that there were tunnels underneath the therapists' office building and that she had seen one of her therapists colleagues exit the building through these tunnels to meet secretly with secret service agents in a nearby coffee shop.

Another client, who was not psychotic at the time, had a memory that she had given birth to piglets. The therapist knew that neither of these events had occurred. However, it is important not to dismiss such claims as delusional and therefore, meaningless. The therapist may choose, depending on his knowledge of the client, to remain "neutral." It may also be equally valid in some instances for the therapist to state that these events didn't occur (in the first instance) or couldn't have occurred (in the second instance). Whichever approach the therapist takes, such material can be explored (once a psychotic episode has subsided) in the same way other memories and issues that are brought to therapy are explored.

Of course, a therapist will form opinions about a client's memories over time. These opinions may or may not be accurate. While it may appear to be supportive and empathic, stating an unequivocal belief or disbelief in memories will typically create more problems. As with many things in life, "never say never." There may be times, with some clients, when stating your beliefs may be helpful to therapy. We recommend that if you think you have such a client and it might be helpful to state your position that you explore this thoroughly with your supervisor or case consultant.

"Taking Sides"—Conflicted Feelings Toward the Alleged Perpetrator(s)

Linked to the delicate issue of believing or not believing a client's memory is managing your client's and your own feelings toward the alleged perpetrator. Ambivalent attachment to the perpetrator is to be expected. The client may mostly express idealized love, outrage, and hate, or seemingly total indifference. It is common for an individual to oscillate among these states. When the client has DID or DDNOS, other parts will hold the polar position to the one that is being expressed, creating additional internal conflicts.

Horror, disgust, anger, and outrage are some of the feelings as therapists we experience when we hear about the atrocities committed against others. These are normal and healthy reactions. When we are working with clients we need to monitor these reactions in sessions. We are not suggesting that it is inappropriate to show or express any feelings in front of clients. It can be validating and a pivotal point in therapy for a client to witness another human being—their therapist—expressing sadness and anger on their behalf. It is the timing and degree of such expressions that may either help or hinder a client's process.

Conflicted feelings about the perpetrator will be present throughout all stages of therapy, including end stages. Clients generally need a great deal of assistance in learning how to manage and express their feelings in healthy ways. Learning to hold conflicting and intense feelings safely is an integral part of therapy and will be discussed in a later chapter.

It is important that our own feelings toward our client's experiences do not cloud our judgment or pressure clients to take a particular position toward their perpetrator. We have consulted with clients where they have felt their current or a previous therapist was pressuring them to take a particular course of action, such as legal processes, ceasing contact with particular people, making contact with someone, or forgiving their perpetrator. Clients have reported they were getting the message from their therapist, implicitly and at times explicitly, that they should or shouldn't be feeling a particular emotion, such as anger, hate, or love. Clients have expressed feeling they were "wrong" to feel or not feel something. Similarly, we have consulted with therapists who were either pushing too hard in a certain direction or colluding with their client to avoid unpleasant feelings and reactions. In general the process the therapist was trying to initiate may have been correct but the timing was inappropriate for the client.

When the therapist "takes sides" regarding a client's alleged perpetrator, not only is he making a statement about the accuracy of the client's memory, he also becomes a player on the Victim-Rescuer-Perpetrator triangle. The client will either feel rescued or victimized by the therapist's position. As with the memory issue, whichever the client feels, the therapist has also become the perpetrator. When the client gets in touch with the polar position of the therapist she may feel she is "wrong" or "not allowed" to express these feelings. She may fear rejection or disapproval from her therapist and so hide what she is feeling, which will hinder her progress and create further conflicts.

When the therapist takes a one-sided stance toward the alleged perpetrator, it deprives the client of the important process of learning to hold and manage her conflicting feelings, which will eventually lead to a place of resolution. Resolution does not mean "happily ever after," it means the client can sit with whatever feelings she has at any given point in time and make healthy choices about her actions and relationships. When the therapist is overwhelmed by his feelings and they are left unaddressed, they interfere with therapy. It is important to take such feelings and reactions, which are part of the territory, to supervision or personal therapy.

HANDLING CLIENTS' FEELINGS TOWARD THE PERPETRATOR AND NON-PROTECTING PARENT

• Clients typically have strong and ambivalent feelings toward their perpetrator and non-protecting parent.

• It is common for therapists to have strong feelings about a client's perpetrator; these should be processed in supervision or the therapist's own therapy.

• Allow the client to experience and express all feelings: anger, hate, fear, love etc.

• Be careful of explicit or implicit messages regarding contact, no contact, forgiveness, etc.

Communicating the Principle of Therapeutic Neutrality

A client may come into therapy reporting a history of abuse. Further memories may emerge or be recalled for the first time during the course of therapy. At the point your client raises a known or suspected history of abuse, it is important to explain to him what he may expect working with such issues. This includes information about the nature of memory, some of the difficulties he may experience and encounter along the way, and the principle of therapeutic neutrality. An outline of the concepts of attachment to the perpetrator and the locus of control shift can also be useful to help him understand your "neutral" position in relation to his memories and his relationship to his alleged perpetrator.

As well as providing a verbal explanation, it is also helpful to provide handouts and/or an informed consent form (see Chapter 15). As with any psycho-education, timing is key to when and how much information you give in any particular session. These things will depend on your assessment of your client's emotional capacity as well as his current level of functioning.

PROVIDE INFORMATION TO HELP NORMALIZE FEELINGS AND REACTIONS

• Information on memory, traumatic memory, and dissociation

• Informed consent explaining some of the issues that will come up as part of working with a history of trauma and abuse

• Information on Attachment to the Perpetrator and the Locus of Control Shift

---

Therapy is never clear sailing and it generally doesn't run along the neat lines laid out in manuals and books! Other issues come up out of the blue that require attention; the best therapy plans don't necessarily flow smoothly. For clients with a history of abuse, therapy is usually long term and the same ground is covered many times. A client may disclose abuse without your having any idea this is where he was heading, and he may ask if you believe him or ask for your position about his perpetrator before you have had the opportunity to explain the principles behind therapeutic neutrality—so be prepared!

Most clients are eager for any educational material you can give them that can help them understand their experiences. Education about memory often eases the pressure clients place on themselves to believe or disbelieve their memories. Education can assist in developing tolerance for ambivalence and uncertainty. It helps to normalize confusion and fluctuating emotions. It helps to prepare for some of the difficulties clients will encounter along the way.

However, providing information does not mean that clients will necessarily welcome this position in the midst of working with difficult material or grappling with intense feelings toward their perpetrator. These are times when you may expect your client to express anger, frustration, and feeling that you are not supporting or validating him. A "neutral" stance can be misinterpreted as you saying you don't believe. Remember, these are conflicts that your client needs to navigate with your help. Let him know you understand why he is angry, remain emotionally present and empathic, and reinforce to him that you know his distress is real and that something has caused him to feel this way. Your role is to help him work out what the cause of his distress is, for himself. Remember that you are working "as if" his memories are true.

When It Is Important Not To Be "Neutral"

Therapeutic neutrality is a fundamental principle in Trauma Model Therapy. As explained above, therapeutic neutrality does not mean lacking empathy or warmth. Therapeutic neutrality is about *"supporting the client through ambivalence, conflicts, and intense emotions about her memories and alleged perpetrator."* This requires the therapist to be empathically attuned to the struggles and conflicts within the client.

Explaining the principle of therapeutic neutrality to your client allows the therapist to be free to respond compassionately, and validate her client's distress and feelings, without compromising the therapy. By explaining that you are not in a position to believe or disbelieve the reality of memories (where there is no corroboration) but that you can see that something has caused your client to be experiencing such great distress and difficulties, you can proceed while working with memories and material "as if" your client's memories are factual. The client and therapist should remain open to all possibilities.

WHEN NOT TO BE NEUTRAL

• Make clear statements that abuse of any kind is never OK

• Make clear statements that it is never the client's fault he/she was abused

• Follow professional guidelines regarding mandatory reporting

---

> • Express concern if client is in a current abusive situation; explain that working on safety is a priority
>
> • Assess and take appropriate action regarding threats of violence toward others and suicide risk

Equally crucial to humane and ethical therapeutic practice is making clear statements that abuse of any kind—emotional, physical, sexual, or spiritual—and neglect are never OK and are never the fault of the client. This will need to be reiterated throughout therapy as the client works through issues of attachment to the perpetrator and the locus of control shift.

If a client reports knowledge of the abuse of a child occurring in the present, therapists are required to follow their professional guidelines regarding mandatory reporting. If your client is currently in an abusive situation, it is important to state that what is happening to her is not OK, and that you are concerned for her current well being and safety. Working with a client on how to increase her safety is crucial. Clients are rarely ready to immediately exit an abusive relationship or cease contact with a perpetrator who is still abusing them. However, stating concern about her safety, and reminding that this needs to be a primary focus of therapy, is vital.

Therapists need to respond when a client makes threats of violence toward another person that they believe could be acted upon, and when suicide is assessed to be an imminent risk. Seeking supervision or case consultation in such situations is recommended.

Finally, being compassionate and empathic to a client's struggles with the long term and ongoing impact of trauma is central to effective therapy. Similarly, offering encouragement, praise, and humour where appropriate are the golden threads that weave together the intricate and complex tapestry of a strong therapeutic relationship. While knowledge and skill in working with trauma provide the foundation of effective therapy, it is the "relationship" between client and therapist that provides the framework for healing to take place.

Chu, J. (1998). *Rebuilding shattered lives: The responsible treatment of complex post-traumatic and dissociative disorders*. New York: John Wiley & Sons.

Courtois, C.A. (1999). *Recollections of sexual abuse: treatment principles and guidelines. New York: W.W. Norton.*

Courtois, C.A. (2002). *Implications of the memory controversy for clinical practice: An overview of treatment recommendations and guidelines. Journal of Child Sexual Abuse*, 9, 183-210.

Freyd, J. (1996). *Betrayal trauma: The logic of forgetting childhood sexual abuse*. Cambridge, MA: Harvard University Press.

Henry, S., & Halpern, N. (1995). The delayed memory controversy: An overview of considerations for ethical practice. Fourth Annual Conference of the Australian Association of Trauma and Dissociation, Melbourne, September 15-17.

Ross, C.A. (1995). *Stanic ritual abuse: Principles of treatment*. Toronto: University of Toronto Press.

Ross, C.A. (2007). *The trauma model: A solution to the problem of comorbidity in psychiatry*. Richardson, TX: Manitou Communications.

18
The Victim-Rescuer-Perpetrator
Triangle

The Victim-Rescuer-Perpetrator triangle is a complex dynamic that operates within the clients' internal world, external relationships, and within the therapeutic relationship. The formation of the triangle can be traced back to the two survival mechanisms explored earlier, 1) Attachment to the Perpetrator and 2) The Locus of Control Shift. When the client and therapist become entangled in the Victim-Rescuer-Perpetrator triangle there is an interaction between the transference of the client and the counter-transference of the therapist. Unrecognized boundary problems contribute to this dynamic (see Chapters 11, 12, and 16). If the therapist does not identify the Victim-Rescuer-Perpetrator triangle dynamic and step out of the dance, the ensuing struggle between client and therapist can quickly escalate, disrupting the therapeutic alliance and throwing therapy off course.

This chapter will cover

- What is the Victim-Rescuer-Perpetrator Triangle?

- The Connection Between the Victim-Rescuer-Perpetrator Triangle and "Attachment to the Perpetrator"

- The Connection Between the Victim-Rescuer-Perpetrator Triangle and the "Locus of Control Shift"

- The Victim-Rescuer-Perpetrator Triangle Operating Within the Client's Internal System

- The Victim-Rescuer-Perpetrator Triangle Operating Within the Therapeutic Relationship

- The Victim-Rescuer-Perpetrator Triangle and Co-therapy or Multiple Agency Involvement

- How to Quit Being a Player in the Victim-Rescuer-Perpetrator Triangle

What Is the Victim-Rescuer-Perpetrator Triangle?

The construct of the Victim-Rescuer-Perpetrator triangle is simple. When something terrible happens, be it a deliberate act of abuse or an accidental trauma, the recipient of the act becomes the *victim*. The source of the terrible event—an individual, a government or an act of nature—becomes the *perpetrator*. The person who comes to the aid of the victim—be it a family member, a teacher, a rescue worker, a soldier or God—becomes the *rescuer*. The rescuer may be an individual who literally intervenes and rescues the victim in reality, or a fantasy figure in the victim's own mind or internal system.

A child in an abusive and chaotic family lives in this dynamic on a daily basis. He may be beaten (victim) by his father (perpetrator). His mother may try to stop her husband from beating their son or at least tend to his bruises once her husband has left the house (rescuer).

The little boy is confused, hurt, frightened, and angry. He cannot express his anger at his father; he's too frightened of him. He cannot express his anger towards his mother for failing to protect him because she is at least there for him when his father is done. Besides, his father beats her too, so he feels guilty that he can't protect her. Where can he go with all this rage and hate? He can go to school and bully (perpetrator) the new boy in class (victim) who eats funny food and speaks with a strange accent. The teacher sees him punching the new boy in the playground and intervenes (rescuer).

When the boy gets home from school he can hear his mother and father fighting as he walks up the driveway. He can tell they've both been drinking. He hears his mother scream and furniture crashing. He knows his mother has become the monster (perpetrator) and is throwing crockery at his father (victim). He rushes in and tries to calm his mother down (rescuer) and take the knife she is brandishing, fearful she will cut him or his father or that she may fall and hurt herself.

The Connection Between the Victim-Rescuer-Perpetrator Triangle and "Attachment to the Perpetrator"

As discussed in Chapter 11, the child in an abusive family is caught in a double bind. He needs to develop and maintain attachment to his caregivers, while at the same time defending himself emotionally and mentally from those very same people. As can be seen from the above scenario, this boy's relationship with his parents is complex and unpredictable. His attachment to both parents is in a constant state of flux.

This little boy is trapped in a chaotic world. In the course of one day he may play any one of the characters on the Victim–Rescuer–Perpetrator triangle. This relational dynamic becomes fixed and entrenched. The child logic or *magical thinking* he used to maintain his attachments to his parents is a double edged sword. It allowed him as a child to love or hate each parent according to the rules of the Victim-Rescuer-Perpetrator triangle. However, it entraps him in the same destructive relationship dynamics as an adult.

The Connection Between the Victim-Rescuer-Perpetrator Triangle and the "Locus of Control Shift"

The adult survivor of abuse enacting the Victim-Rescuer-Perpetrator triangle is emotionally locked into the child logic of the locus of control shift (described in Chapter 12). The core belief, "I am bad," gives license to play victim *(bad things happen to me because I am bad)* or perpetrator *(I am bad because I do bad things)* or rescuer *(I am all powerful and so if I try hard enough I can make everything right in my world)*.

The adult survivor may predominantly or overtly play one role on the triangle. However, whenever one dynamic is operating, the other two players in the triangle will be lurking not too far away in the shadows. The other players may be the client's partner, family members, friends, colleagues or parts of the internal system. Identifying the dynamics of the triangle operating in his external world is the key to understanding his relationship dynamics. However, identifying and addressing the internal Victim-Rescuer-Perpetrator dynamic is the key to fundamental and lasting change in his relationship to self and others.

The Victim-Rescuer-Perpetrator Triangle Operating Within the Client's Internal System

In the story of the little boy above, we saw him alternate between victim, rescuer, and perpetrator in the course of a single day. It is easy to press an imaginary fast forward button and see how he might perpetuate these roles in his friendships, with his partner, in his parenting style, and in his relationships with his boss and co-workers.

The external world is a reflection or a mirror of the internal world, and vice versa. The external world becomes the stage upon which the conflicts and defenses developed as a child are played. The struggles and challenges clients face in the course of daily life are the internal dramas and painful stories from childhood retold with the same sad ending repeated over and over. The characters in the dramatic tragedy of the Victim-Rescuer-Perpetrator triangle are not only the model upon which adult external relationships are based but have become the driving forces operating within the psyche.

In the internal system of DID these dynamics are easily identifiable. The victim is reflected in child alters who hold painful and terrifying experiences. These victim experiences are expressed through the *host* who may be subjected to switching against his wishes, seemingly out of his control (the host is the victim of switching). However, it is an alter personality who gets cut or burnt as punishment for telling, and who is therefore the real victim. This unwitting alter is suddenly pushed out front to cope with a situation that others inside don't want to deal with. Being the victim of the cutting puts this alter in the role of rescuer at the same time because, as a result of the self-mutilation, the other parts don't have to deal with the feelings they are trying to avoid.

The perpetrator is reflected in the alter who punishes child parts for crying or telling secrets. This part survived by aligning with the perpetrator of his abuse, claiming to have enjoyed the abuse and enjoying hurting others, including both "people" on the inside and people in the external world.

The rescuer is reflected in alters described as *inner self helpers*. These are parts of the system that commonly look after hurt and frightened alters. They attempt to solve problems in the client's internal and external world. These parts of the system are the first to align with therapy and the therapist. These alters often have a great deal of knowledge and understanding of the internal system and offer insight and guidance in regard to proceeding with therapy, forewarning about potential problems.

In the client with DDNOS, the players in the triangle may not have names or be so clearly defined but the essence of the victim, rescuer, and perpetrator is nonetheless operating.

The Victim-Rescuer-Perpetrator Triangle Operating Within the Therapeutic Relationship

It should come as no surprise that the dynamic of the Victim-Rescuer-Perpetrator triangle will inevitably come to visit therapy. However, it can sneak in through the back door and before you know it, client and therapist are bouncing from one point on the triangle to the next, locked in an endless dance and bringing therapy to a virtual standstill.

The Victim-Rescuer-Perpetrator triangle dynamic in therapy results from a collision between transference, counter-transference, and boundaries. The catalysts may be as many and varied as the issues that are brought into the room. However, in all cases the therapist has moved away from a stance of therapeutic neutrality and become *part of the problem* (see Chapter 16).

The therapy relationship is not an equal relationship. No matter how ethical, compassionate, and skilled the therapist is, the power balance is always unequal. This inequality reminds the client of past unequal relationships in which he was abused. The client will be acutely sensitized to real or imagined acts of perpetration by the therapist and triggered to feelings of powerlessness and victimization. At times, a client may become the unintentional victim of the therapist's perpetrating behaviour. Some of the less serious behaviours are previously listed in the table of boundary transgressions in Chapter 16. Other unintentional but pain-causing blunders are described in the following table.

UNINTENTIONAL VICTIMIZATION OF THE CLIENT BY THE THERAPIST

- Pushing a client to do work he is not ready to do

- Insensitive comments

- Ill-timed use of humour

- Disclosure of therapist's trauma history

- Not maintaining therapeutic neutrality in relation to memories and feelings about a client's alleged perpetrator(s)

Also, as discussed in the boundaries chapter (Chapter 16), a client may be victimized by severe boundary transgressions.

SERIOUS VICTIMIZATION OF THE CLIENT BY THE THERAPIST

- Therapeutic strategies that illicit regressive behaviour and foster dependency

- Extreme counter-transference reactions (punitive, belittling, hostile, deliberately eliciting guilt)

- Involvement in each other's lives and families

- Multiple roles such as therapist, supervisor, co-therapist, friend

- Being party to hostile confrontations with alleged perpetrators

- Inappropriate touching, including but not limited to, a sexual relationship

---

When the therapist steps into the client's transference projections she has immediately taken up a position on the triangle, either as victim, rescuer, or perpetrator. However, the triangle is not static. The positions of client and therapist will soon shift. When the therapist accepts the rescuer role and takes on the client's transference that she is the only person who understands, who can be trusted, and who can save her from killing herself, she has made a serious error and transgressed a boundary. In one therapy, this manifested as the therapist going to the client's house in the middle of the night.

The same dynamic is at play when a therapist takes a position of wholeheartedly "believing" her client's unverified memories, or when the therapist becomes involved in hostile confrontations with alleged or verified perpetrator(s) (see Chapter 17). The therapist may be re-enacting her own childhood desire to be rescued, but in doing so has become an unwitting perpetrator and *part of the problem*.

The client may feel rescued, safe, and special for a while. At a subconscious level, however, the client knows that her therapist has let her down. Her therapist can be manipulated and so is unsafe. The client will understandably become angry and hostile towards the therapist. The client then takes the perpetrator position and victimizes the therapist.

The therapist may be working ethically and skillfully but still be victimized by a client's transference. Commonly, this can take the form of anger projected onto the therapist about the client's perpetrator, non-offending parent, or her life in general. The anger may be directed at anything to do with therapy and the therapist: boundaries, fees, not being available when the client wanted to talk on the phone, going on leave, wearing a particular color, getting pregnant, etc.

As discussed in Chapter 16, transference is grist for the mill. However, when the therapist acts out counter-transference reactions and takes a position on the triangle, therapy has ceased. Instead both client and therapist become key players in each other's internal and unresolved conflicts.

The Victim-Rescuer-Perpetrator Triangle and Co-therapy or Multiple Agency Involvement

The authors' view is that the most effective approach with the dissociative client is psychotherapy with one primary clinician. Some clients benefit from adjunctive support from other professionals, such as a case manager, psychiatrist, or general practitioner to manage any medications or participation in a therapy group.

The inherent structure of dissociation is internal separateness and dividedness maintained by amnesic barriers. The person with DID has myriad internal conflicts and issues with trust and boundaries. Developing a therapeutic alliance is understandably a monumental challenge for those who have experienced the trauma of betrayal by the people closest to them, or by others in positions of power and trust. Internal disconnection and conflicts are mirrored in external relationships. Different parts of the system have different relationships with the same people, and hold different feelings and perceptions about past and current relationships. This is true for the client's relationship with the therapist.

When there is more than one therapist and service involved, the internal dividedness and ambivalence is often spread across the professionals involved in different aspects of care. Difficulties arise when different parts of the system develop different relationships with each professional, resulting in no one therapist or support service getting the whole picture. The client does not do this to be difficult, but through fear. The magical thinking behind such a strategy is that if no one therapist has the whole picture then the client can remain safe. The cost of this defense is a fragmented and dissociated therapy that provides limited benefits and potentially results in more harm than good.

To provide a cohesive and unified approach to therapy, communication between all professionals involved is crucial. Problems arise when therapists employ different methods to manage situations such as self-injury and suicidal ideation, or when one therapist is undertaking trauma work without the other's knowledge. This scenario quickly results in the client and each therapist or agency taking a position on the Victim-Rescuer-Perpetrator triangle. The ensuing dance involves any number of variations, as the client plays the therapists off against each other. For instance, the "good" rescuing therapist unwittingly colludes with the client against the "bad" perpetrating therapist (a re-enactment of the non-offending parent and the offending parent). Who plays the "good" therapist and who plays the "bad" therapist will change depending on the transference projected at any given time.

How To Resist Becoming a Player in the Victim-Rescuer-Perpetrator Triangle

The Victim-Rescuer-Perpetrator triangle is not the sole creation or problem of the client. Research shows that many health professionals have a history of trauma. The desire to enter the "helping" professions often stems from such a history. At best, this can create a therapist who, having dealt with her own history, is highly attuned to the experiences, needs, and issues of clients. At worst, it unleashes a well-intentioned therapist who attempts to heal herself through rescuing her client but inevitably becomes part of the problem. However, a trauma history is not the only reason a therapist may find himself caught up in the VRP triangle dynamic.

The desire to be saved is a normal fantasy for a child and it is understandable to wish for this as an adult. However, a therapist can never, nor should try to, save the client or compensate for the hurt and trauma from childhood. Even the most skilled, ethical, and compassionate therapist will fail her client in numerous ways on numerous occasions. Therapist failings are grist for the mill in therapy. Handled with care they can often lead to strengthening of the therapeutic alliance, assisting the client to develop more realistic expectations of the therapist and relationships in general.

Educating clients about attachment to the perpetrator and the locus of control shift allows them to gain a clearer understanding of their defenses and how they operate in the present. It provides the key to opening the door to the hidden pain that these defenses protect. Explaining the position of therapeutic neutrality allows clients to begin to own their transference and the inner conflicts behind their projections. Finally, maintaining clear, consistent boundaries with compassion provides a safe space for the client to embark on the painful journey of healing.

Ross, C.A. (2007). *The trauma model: A solution to the problem of comorbidity in psychiatry.*
        Richardson, TX: Manitou Communications.

19

Understanding the Function of "Negative" Symptoms and Behaviour

Within Trauma Model Therapy, all symptoms, addictions, thoughts, and behaviours have a function, a meaning, and a context. They all fit into an individual person's life story, which in turn fits into a particular culture, language, and history. Therapy focuses primarily on the internal and external functions of symptoms in the present and recent past—recent means weeks, months, and years, but not decades.

The motto governing this aspect of therapy is: *the problem is not the problem*.

The function of "positive" symptoms and behaviours is usually either self-evident or not a clinical problem. Exceptions include mania. Humour, empathy, altruism, and similar high level defenses can be reinforced and encouraged, but don't need to be fixed. Any of these can be harnessed as avoidance strategies, but none are as problematic on as regular a basis as "negative" emotions, symptoms, and behaviour. These include the addictions, rage, and verbal and physical abuse.

In this chapter we cover

- The Problem Is Not the Problem

- Mood State Regulation

- Treatment Techniques

The Problem Is Not the Problem

In family systems work, a family comes to the clinic certain what the problem is: a teenaged child is stealing from stores. The family wants the child fixed. A biological psychiatrist might order a series of EEG, blood chemistry, and brain MRI studies and, even with normal results, might inform the parents that the problem is a sub-threshold epileptiform discharge in the child's non-dominant temporal-parietal lobe. The treatment might be an anticonvulsant or an antidepressant. The parents will be glad that they have no responsibility for the problem and are not at fault.

A stereotypical psychoanalyst, on the other hand, might agree that the problem is inside the child, but instead of locating it in the child's brain, the therapist would inform the parents that there are unresolved pre-oedipal conflicts in the child's id. Both these clinicians locate the problem inside the child, and both treatment plans involve fixing the problem inside the individual child. The two clinicians view the problem as the problem. The family and society are off the hook.

A family therapist, in contrast, would see the child as the identified patient or symptom bearer in the family, and would assume that the child's behaviour provides the family a solution to an unacknowledged family system problem. The intervention could be marital therapy for the couple, who are drifting closer to divorce, and who function with joint passion as a couple only when dealing with the child's "bad" behaviour. The function of the behaviour is to prevent the parents from drifting further apart. The systems therapist knows that the problem is not the problem.

This principle is applied to every symptom, behaviour, addiction, diagnosis, defense, and behaviour, whether it be cutting, sex addiction, depression, taking the victim role, not being responsible because "someone else" took control of the body, flashbacks, or auditory hallucinations. Everything is assumed to be a meaningful, functional, but maladaptive coping strategy. The goal of therapy is to help the person learn how to solve the problem in a more fluid, flexible, healthy fashion. The problem—for instance, grief over a lost childhood—will not go away with recovery, but the pain will reduce in intensity, it will not dominate life on a daily basis, and the unhealthy coping strategies will no longer be required. Once the problem in the background is solved, the presenting problem melts away—the person can let go of the drug because the problem solved by the drug can now be solved without it.

Mood State Regulation

The basic function of all symptoms and unhealthy behaviours is mood state regulation. Bad feelings, bad conflicts, and bad external situations build up precipitously. Various coping strategies are used with partial and temporary benefit. Eventually, however, the feelings have been too bad for too long and it is time to cut, burn, drink, beat your wife, act out sexually, or "leave" for a few days while "someone else" takes over.

People never get addicted to drugs that don't work. Throwing up in the toilet is an extremely effective way to get rid of calories. Shooting heroin relieves pain immediately. Going away inside provides real respite for the host personality. But when the client sobers up, or returns, he is back at square one, therefore the drug must be taken again and again. The relief obtained reinforces the addiction. It may be that genuine chemical withdrawal can occur in the brain even when the "drug" is a behaviour, like sex addiction. If this is the case, the behaviour may stimulate the release of dopamine or some other rewarding neurotransmitter, and it would follow that there must be withdrawal due to the drop in neurotransmitter levels that occurs when the behaviour stops. This doesn't have to be true biologically for the treatment model to work, but it is, at a minimum, a therapeutically useful analogy.

The addicted person, then, isn't just an *addict*. Rather, the person is a smart consumer making an intelligent choice at the supermarket of coping strategies: the macaroni in aisle two doesn't provide much of a rush, but the opiates in aisle three certainly do. The person knows from experience what works, and chooses the drug because it offers relief. The addictive behaviour is self-soothing, kind, and based on self-love—the drug would be an unqualified blessing if it were not for its side effects and social costs.

The so-called "addict" is a traumatized person who was never taught or modeled healthy coping strategies, and who has much more conflict and painful feelings to deal with than the average person. The addiction is driven not by a core biological defect in the individual, but by a mixture of too few healthy coping strategies and too much pain. This model of addictions is taught to the client as part of the work.

Treatment Techniques

It seems counter-intuitive to tell a rape survivor that her flashbacks are not the problem. It took more than a decade of work in the field before I figured out how *the problem is not the problem* applies even to the symptoms of PTSD. PTSD could be thought of as *bipolar trauma disorder*. The up pole includes the hyperarousal, fear, terror, and anxiety symptoms such as hypervigilance, scanning, increased startle response, and flashbacks. The down pole is represented by numbness, social withdrawal, and avoidance.

PTSD involves a cyclical failure of shut-down. When images, feelings, and physiological arousal are stuffed in the abdomen and chest, the PTSD is *gone*. Then the suppression fails and the positive or up symptoms emerge. Pressure is relieved deep in the volcano, addictions are activated, and the symptoms are suppressed again until the next trigger activates them. The triggers are avoided through agoraphobic withdrawal, and the perimeter of the person's life space shrinks to a smaller and smaller size. If the life space becomes small enough, and far enough removed from the madding crowd, then it becomes manageable and safe. The cost of the strategy is to be lonely, isolated, and depressed.

It is thought that flashbacks in the few weeks following a traumatic event, may be the psyche's attempts to process and heal from an overwhelming event. When a person is diagnosed with PTSD the flashbacks have become a debilitating symptom of unresolved trauma. The active symptoms of PTSD serve three functions: 1) an avoidance strategy, 2) a memorial to the trauma, and 3) omens. Sometimes it is better to hide in the hyper-arousal and fear than to fall into the underlying powerlessness, helplessness, and grief. The active PTSD can be the lesser of two evils. The active symptoms drive and justify the addictive behaviours. In some clients they may also reinforce secondary gain or the patient role.

Also, the addictions can take on a life of their own—one might say that the person becomes addicted to his addiction. Initially, alcohol was abused as a form of self-medication for PTSD, but eventually the person may get drunk even when the up pole of the PTSD is not active. The addiction then becomes a global avoidance strategy, not just a way of dealing with the PTSD. In behavioural language, this process is called *generalization*.

One must always remember that avoidance is a wonderful thing. None of us could survive without it. Avoidance becomes a symptom or a diagnosis when it is pervasive, inflexible, too intense or unhealthy, or, often, all of the above. The core function of all "negative" symptoms and behaviours is survival. Paradoxically, more people die from their survival strategies than from feeling the feelings they are avoiding through their addictions. Treatment is required when, on balance, the survival strategies are more of a threat to survival than they are protective. This includes literal biological survival, but also survival at emotional, intellectual, spiritual, and interpersonal levels.

A person can hold onto the symptoms of PTSD as her memorial to the trauma. She has been told by her perpetrators for years to "let it go, get past it, get on with your life, and stop living in the past." What the perpetrators are actually telling her is to deny, minimize, blow off, and disavow the abuse and the harm it caused. Minimization of the impact of the abuse is a milder variant of denying that it ever took place. In order to rebel against the perpetrators, and in order to honor her suffering, the client holds onto her symptoms very hard. She believes that if she gets better, she will betray herself and agree with her perpetrators.

This is an understandable cognitive error, but it needs to be corrected. Holding onto the symptoms means staying in the dance, allowing the perpetrators to dominate and control one's psyche, and being their property—*damaged goods*—forever. Staying stuck in the symptoms means the perpetrators win. Getting well, and letting go of the symptoms, means walking away, throwing off the shackles, and no longer being defined by the words, deeds, and beliefs of the perpetrators.

Omens are beliefs that arise in the mind of the traumatized magical child. The term was coined by the child psychiatrist, Lenore Terr (1992), in her book, *Too Scared To Cry*. She interviewed children in Chowchilla, California who had been on their school bus the day the bus was commandeered at gunpoint by two men. The men forced the driver to drive to a gravel pit where they buried the bus under several feet of gravel with the driver and children inside. They told the passengers that if anyone dug out, one of the gunmen would be there to kill them.

After many hours buried in the bus, the driver and the children dug themselves out—the two gunmen were gone and everyone was OK. Lenore Terr then followed the children for years and listened to their magical solutions to the powerlessnes, helplessness, and unpredictability of their abduction.

A child might say, "You know, Dr. Terr, the newspaper boy leaves the paper on the same side of the sidewalk every day. That day, he left it on the other side. I should have noticed that something was wrong. I shouldn't have gotten on the bus."

A second child might say, "You know, Dr. Terr, every day all year Mary sat on the same seat on the bus. That day she was in a different seat. I should have noticed something was wrong. I shouldn't have gotten on the bus."

This is the locus of control shift. The child was not actually powerless and helpless—she really was in control of the situation, except that she failed to be sufficiently vigilant, at least in her own magical beliefs. These overlooked clues to the impending trauma are called *omens*.

How does one acquire an inventory of omens that one missed prior to a traumatic event? By reviewing the tape of the event; this is called a *flashback*. But it is no good reviewing the tape just once. What if some omens were missed? Better check another one hundred times.

Finally, thankfully, one can be reasonably confident that the list of omens is complete. Now, finally, one can relax. But not quite. What good is a list of omens unless one is hypervigilant for them in the present and future? In order to detect and escape future trauma, one must have PTSD—one must be hyperaroused, hypervigilant, and scanning for danger at all times. The up or positive symptoms of PTSD thus serve a protective function by helping the child avoid future trauma.

The problem with the strategy is that it has no objective predictive value. It is all magical thinking. The control, power, and mastery over future trauma are an illusion, as is the self-blame for failing to prevent the past trauma. In fact, the trauma was unpredictable and unavoidable, and similar inescapable trauma might occur in the future.

Others besides children rely on omens to cope with trauma. Adult victims of date rape often review the mental tapes over and over for years, scanning for rape-prevention clues. They blame themselves for not spotting the perpetrator inside the apparently healthy male, for getting in the car, for going to the bar, or for wearing the wrong dress.

Omens are different from objective risk analysis. If a woman concludes after a sexual assault that she should not be alone half-intoxicated in a crack neighborhood after midnight, that is a realistic risk assessment that can lead to behaviours that in turn will objectively reduce the risk of future assaults. Checking to see where the newspaper is cannot protect anyone from future abductions by strangers at gunpoint.

The symptoms of PTSD are not simply symptoms of a stuck brain, "biology," or a neurotransmitter imbalance. They have a function; the underlying errors in core beliefs can be corrected in therapy, resulting in symptom reduction.

A conversation in therapy might go as follows:

Therapist: What would happen if your PTSD symptoms just stopped, went away for good?

Client: That would be wonderful. Then I could start living again.

Therapist: If it would be so good to let go of your symptoms, why are you holding onto them so tight?

Client: What? You think I want to have PTSD?

Therapist: That's how it looks to me. You seem to be actively afraid to let go of your PTSD.

Client: So it's my fault I was raped?

Therapist: No. It was 100% the perpetrator's fault. There was nothing you could have done to predict it or avoid it. It's not that I'm blaming you—it's you who are blaming you. I'm disagreeing with you on that.

Client: Well, I shouldn't have gone to that bar.

Therapist: How many times have you been to that bar or similar bars in your life?

Client: I don't know; counting college, hundreds of times, I guess.

Therapist: How many times have you been raped since you started college?

Client: Once.

Therapist: So you get raped some small fraction of 1% of the time when you go to bars. What was different about that night compared to the hundreds of other nights where nothing bad happened?

Client: I got raped.

Therapist: I understand that. But up till the point in time when the rape happened, what was different about that night?

Client: Nothing, I guess; but I should have known.

Therapist: Should have known what?

Client: That he was going to rape me.

Therapist: Let's imagine you and I could travel back in time to before the rape happened and watch while all the events of that day unfolded. What specifically could we have observed that would have told us a rape was coming?

Client: I don't know.

Therapist: Exactly: you don't know. That's my point. Hindsight is perfect, but prior to the rape you didn't know it was going to happen, and there was no way you could know. It was unpredictable. He was waiting in the dark. He was a stranger.

Client: I still should have done something.

Therapist: Like what? Not based on hindsight, but based on the information you actually had available at the time, how were you supposed to know?

Client: I guess I wasn't. I see what you mean. At the time there was no way for me to know.

Therapist: Right. Your self-blame tells me that you are holding yourself responsible for something that was completely out of your control. That's the locus of control shift, that we talked about earlier. The problem is not that you had the power and control, but failed to exercise it. The problem is that you had no power and control. You couldn't predict the rape, and you couldn't have stopped it.

Client: I should have fought harder.

Therapist: Maybe you could have. But maybe if you had fought harder, he would have escalated his violence and killed you. Maybe not fighting was a smart strategy.

Client: You really mean it's not my fault, don't you?

Therapist: Yes, I do. And if you let go of the self-blame, then you can start to let go of the hyperarousal, hypervigilance, scanning, and avoidance. None of those things are really protecting you from future trauma. They are just a heavy burden you carry, which you can set down. You can't avoid past trauma, and you can't avoid unpredictable trauma in the future either.

Client: So I'm helpless then?

Therapist: You are helpless in some ways. You can't prevent hurricanes. Neither can anyone else. The symptoms of PTSD can't control things like that—they just don't work for avoiding unpredictable trauma. If you let go of them, you will be just as safe, in fact maybe safer, because you will have more energy to focus on realistic self-protection. Does that make sense to you?

Client: I'm starting to get it.

Negative, undesirable symptoms and behaviours often do not seem to serve any purpose. On closer inspection, however, they do. Because the symptoms are active defense mechanisms, they are treatable with psychotherapy. There is a choice behind them, even if it is not conscious; the person chooses to feel powerful and in control, chooses to search for omens, and therefore commits herself to the symptoms of PTSD. By interrupting the process upstream of the symptoms, the survivor gains control of the uncontrollable. The symptoms are usually experienced as involuntary—it is true that they are experienced this way, but it is not true that they are actually involuntary. If they were, there would be no point in psychotherapy and no possibility of recovery.

20
Understanding and Transforming Self-Injury

Self-injury is one of the negative behaviours identified in Chapter 19. As with other negative symptoms and behaviours, self-injury is a solution to another problem. It is such a serious and pervasive behaviour among clients with an abuse history that it deserves its own chapter.

The type, severity, and reason for self-injury can vary from episode to episode. In clients with DID and DDNOS the type and reason for self-injury are frequently particular to different parts of the system. Self-injury is different from suicidal ideation, but can be present simultaneously.

As with other negative symptoms and behaviours, self-injury is harmful to the physical, emotional, psychological, and spiritual well-being of the individual. However, it serves as a solution to an internal conflict or experience. Understanding the purpose and meaning of self-injurious behaviour is crucial to transforming the behaviour and finding healthier solutions to the underlying conflicts.

This chapter will cover

- Functions of Self-injury
- Common Types of Self-injury
- Self-injury Versus Suicidality
- Self-injury and the Victim–Rescuer–Perpetrator Triangle
- Asking About Self-injury
- Contracts and Self-injury
- Developing Alternative Strategies

Functions of Self-injury

Clients report many reasons for self-injurious behaviour. In the Table below are some of the more common reasons for self-injury.

FUNCTIONS OF SELF-INJURY

• Trance logic (hurt myself before someone else hurts me, therefore I'm in control; or, to let the badness out)

• Tension reduction

• To feel real and connected

• To compensate for feelings of emptiness

• To prevent suicide

• To alter states of consciousness

- To control/punish self or another part of the system

- To get help without telling

- Safe expression of affect

- Distraction from overwhelming affect or other physical pain

- Re-enactment of abuse

- Conditioning or training to self-injure

- Contact with perpetrators or anniversary of significant events

- Iatrogenic—pursuing memory work too fast or too soon—anger at therapist

- Secondary gain—sexual arousal/need for some kind of attention or acknowledgment

As seen in the above table, self-injury offers a solution to a wide range of internal conflicts and experiences, yet it is often misunderstood as primarily attention seeking, "bad borderline," or acting out behaviour. However, self-injury is generally carried out in secrecy and is associated with intense feelings of shame and self-loathing. It is generally perceived by the client as being outside her control. Many clients are amnesic to acts of self-injury.

Common Types of Self-Injury

Survivors of abuse often develop some form of self-injurious behaviour from a very young age. Self-soothing through violent rocking as a toddler may develop into head banging, and escalate into more sophisticated forms of affect regulation, such as cutting and burning, as an adolescent. By the time an adult enters therapy, self-injury is a long standing and entrenched behaviour that has worked effectively and efficiently to manage and regulate intolerable internal conflicts and experiences.

Below are some of the most common types of self-injury.

COMMON TYPES OF SELF-INJURY

- Cutting

- Burning

- Scratching or picking skin

- Pulling out hair

- Head banging or hitting body

- Swallowing toxic substances or sharp objects

- Pinching

- Biting

- Substance abuse

- Over- or under-eating

Many types of objects are used to cause injury, including razor blades, knives, hair brushes, scouring pads, kitchen utensils, knitting needles, matches, cigarettes, pins, broken glass, scissors, tweezers, etc.

Cutting and burning the body are the most commonly reported behaviours. Injury may be inflicted on any part of the body, including arms, breasts, abdomen, thighs, feet, and genitals. The injury may be superficial scratches through to deep cuts and burns that require medical attention. Serious injury that does not receive medical attention may result in further injury through infection.

Self-injury Versus Suicidality

Self-injury and suicidality are usually different in source and purpose. In fact, self-injury is commonly employed as a strategy to avoid suicide. The act of cutting can reduce tension, distract from overwhelming feelings, and create a feeling of being real and connected enough to steer away from suicidal ideation or behaviour.

However, self-injury and suicidality frequently co-exist. When working with severely traumatized and dissociative clients it is prudent to assume that there is a high risk of self-injury and suicidal ideation. Both require ongoing monitoring and assessment during therapy, as the risk level of both can fluctuate dramatically and be determined by internal or external triggers.

Another possibility to consider with a DID client is if an apparent suicide attempt may in fact be an attempted internal homicide. One part of the system may be trying to "kill off" another part of the system. In these instances, there is usually a lack of understanding by the homicidal part that killing off one part of the system means the body, and all other parts, including the homicidal part, would also be killed.

A client may have one or more parts of the system that self-injure, and one or more other parts that are genuinely suicidal. Self-injurious behaviour while harmful and dangerous is usually not life threatening.

Self-injury and the Victim–Rescuer–Perpetrator Triangle

In chapter 19 we explored the connection between negative symptoms and behaviours and the Victim–Rescuer-Perpetrator Triangle. Regardless of the reason driving a part of the system to hurt the body, self-injury is self-victimization. The internal Victim–Rescuer–Perpetrator dynamic is being activated.

One part of the system is motivated to self-injure to alleviate some form of internal conflict and distress. This part perceives herself as the rescuer. Alternatively, the motivation may be to punish for telling secrets. In this instance the punishing part is enacting the perpetrator. Regardless of the motivation, self-injury always creates distress for other parts of the system and the body, who become the victim. In reality all parts of the system are victimized by self-injury. However, the part(s) who engage in the activity will not initially recognize this.

What is the relationship between self-injury and the external Victim–Rescuer–Perpetrator triangle dynamic operating in the therapeutic relationship? An example of this is contained in the following scenario:

The host part presents to the therapist in great distress about self-injury for which she has no memory. She feels overwhelmed, ashamed, and out of control. The host is feeling the emotions of the victim.

The therapist becomes distressed by the severity of the injury and by the client's sense of powerlessness. The therapist aligns with the host, and becomes the rescuer.

The therapist explores the client's internal system to find the "culprit" of the self-injury, and chastises this part for the distress caused to the host and damage to the body. The therapist has now switched to the perpetrator. The triangle has been activated in therapy.

The positions on the triangle then begin to shift. The part responsible for the injury feels angry, misunderstood, and unrecognized for her best efforts to manage some internal distress. She feels alienated from the therapist. This part feels like a victim of the host and the therapist.

Another part of the system can see that the situation is escalating and fears the consequences, so prompts a switch—rescuer.

The part pushed out to handle the situation has learned that the best way to keep scary people at bay is to rage and yell—perpetrator.

The therapist feels unsafe with the client—victim.

There are endless possibilities as to how the triangle can be enacted as a consequence of a) not understanding that *the problem*, self-injuring, *is not the problem* but a communication about an internal conflict and b) aligning with one part of the system against another.

Aligning with, and offering support to all parts, including those who self-injure, is the most effective approach. The reasons why they engage in self-injury need to be heard, understood, and validated. At the same time, the part who is causing the injury requires help to understand that while it has been an effective strategy over a long period of time, continuing it is detrimental. Self-injury reinforces internal conflicts, mirrors the external perpetrators' behaviour, and contributes to the client remaining stuck in abuse dynamics.

Through aligning with parts of the system that self-injure, while being firm that the behaviour is not OK, leverage is created. All parts of the system begin to feel they are being heard and understood.

In time, this creates a willingness to explore alternative strategies to manage overwhelming internal states and conflicts.

Asking About Self-injury

As discussed earlier, self-injury is an act that is typically carried out in secret and with a great deal of shame and self-loathing. Questioning about self-injury in the early stages of assessment may not result in disclosure; however it is still important to ask. By asking during the assessment stage the client is given permission to disclose if she wishes. If she is not ready to disclose, the seed has been sown that it is an issue that you are willing and able to assist with.

It is important to frame the question in a way that minimizes the potential for the client to feel judged or shamed. Let the client know that you understand that self-injury serves to alleviate some form of distress and internal conflict.

ASKING ABOUT SELF-INJURY

"Have you in the past, or do you currently, do things that hurt your body?"

"Would you be willing to help me understand how hurting helps you and try to find other ways to deal with your distress?"

Once trust and a therapeutic alliance have been established many clients will be open and honest about self-injury. For others, it may take a very long time to be able to tell their shameful secret. If a client's general level of functioning does not appear to be improving at a rate that you might expect, or is deteriorating, one of the possibilities to explore may be hidden self-injuring. It is also important to consider other reasons for a lack of improvement or deterioration, such as a current abusive relationship, contact with past abusers, and pursuing memory work too early or too fast.

A non-judgmental approach and reframing the behaviour as functional empowers the client to find alternative solutions to inner conflicts. It also assists in decreasing the possibility of the behaviour remaining hidden.

Contracts and Self-injury

Contracts, agreements, and goal setting can be very helpful tools in therapy. However, a great deal of care needs to be taken about using contracts around self-injury. Asking a client to contract to stop self-injury, or accepting a client's suggestion to make such an agreement, may result in suppressing the behaviour and underlying conflicts, leading to the possibility of setting up a more dangerous level of harm.

If the function of self-injury has been to prevent suicide, a contract not to self harm may send suicidal ideation underground for a while but may result in the tension becoming unbearable and increase the risk of suicide. Furthermore, contracts that are not very clearly worded, or are overly rigid, or goals set unrealistically high for the client's current capabilities, may set her up to fail. This will damage the client's self-confidence and the therapeutic alliance (either by the client's having to report "failure" or by her withholding important information).

Contracting about how the client will work to change the behaviour, rather than focusing on the behaviour itself, may be helpful for some clients but not for others. While self-injury is essential to address, the authors suggest that contracting be carefully considered and discussed with the client as to the possible benefits and pitfalls.

In the event a client requests to contract around self-injury and/or suicidal ideation, this is a clear communication that she is feeling unsafe within herself. This necessitates thorough exploration as to what is going on internally and in the client's external world. There may be issues that have not have been previously disclosed or the therapist may have misjudged the distress the client has been experiencing.

In the event that a client attempts or succeeds in injuring herself in front of the therapist or on the therapist's premises, the therapist has an obligation to both herself and the client to stipulate that such behaviour is unacceptable. Such a situation places the therapist in a double bind: terminate the session to set clear boundaries and limitations on what is and isn't acceptable versus concern for the client's safety when she leaves the session. In some instances, mobilizing an external intervention (such as hospitalization), may be necessary to keep the client safe, as well as preserve the rights and needs of the therapist, and others in the building. This models boundaries and places responsibility for containing the behaviour with the client rather than the therapist.

In such circumstances the therapist may elect to continue or not continue therapy with the client. This may be a case by case assessment, which would consider all aspects of the therapy and therapeutic alliance leading up to the behaviour in session. In the event the therapist chooses to terminate therapy, there is a responsibility to assist the client to find another therapist.

While limit setting is required in such a situation, it is also important to explore with the client whether attempts to show injuries or inflict them in front of the therapist are an attempt at projective identification (to get the therapist to feel and express the client's feelings), or are a test to see if the therapist will re-enact triangle dynamics.

Developing Alternative Strategies

To develop alternatives there needs to be an understanding of the function of self-injuring. The first step is to invite the client to explore the meaning of her self-injuring behaviour.

EXPLORATORY QUESTIONS

- When do you self-injure?

- How often do you self-injure?

- What was happening internally or externally leading up to self-injury?

- What were you thinking, feeling, aware of during the self-injury?

- What was happening right after the injury?

Some clients may be very aware of how, when, and why self-injury happens. Others may initially have no insight. Some clients may be amnesic for the self-injury. The client may report suddenly "coming to" and finding herself bleeding, or holding a razor or empty pill bottle, with no recollection of events leading up to the event, or of the event itself.

Dissociative clients frequently have a distorted perception of and connection with their bodies. Suggesting to the client that she count the marks on her body (at home, not in your office) or to draw an outline of her body indicating where the cuts, bruises, and other injuries are located, can have a profound impact on the client's perception and awareness of the extent and seriousness of her injuries.

The clients' self-assessment of her self-injury assists in the following ways:

SELF-ASSESSMENT OF SELF-INJURIOUS BEHAVIOUR ASSISTS IN:

- Owning the behaviour

- Understanding that self-injury is functional but it is time to find safer ways to help

- Acknowledging the impact self-injury has on the whole person, physically and

  emotionally

Chapter 27 emphasizes the importance of internal communication. In essence, internal communication is the key to all aspects of the therapy process. Communication between parts of the system about the function and the impact of self-injury develops a collaborative approach to reducing the frequency and degree of the self-injury. If the client is successful in this task it provides a valuable experience of containment and managing crisis situations. This experience is empowering and ego-strengthening.

Finding a substitute for the behaviour can, in the short-term, express the need for self-injury while at the same time reducing the harm inflicted. This creates physical safety and the emotional and psychological space to address the underlying conflicts that self-injury is attempting to resolve.

FUNCTIONAL ALTERNATIVE BEHAVIOURS

- Show there is pain inside: Draw or write about the pain.

- Release endorphins: Do a physical workout.

- Feel something: Place an ice cube or heat pack on the body.

- Punish self or another part: Dialogue about the conflict.

- Reduce tension: Perform relaxation techniques or exercise.

- Express anger and rage: Write, verbalize, draw, do physical anger exercise.

- Distract from painful feelings: Use self-soothing and distancing techniques.

Chapter 30, *The Healing Power of Feeling: Working with Anger and Grief,* will outline specific strategies to explore and process the conflicts that self-injury and other negative symptoms and behaviours express.

Briere, J. (1993). Understanding tension-reduction behaviors in adult survivors. Fifth Annual Eastern Regional Conference, Alexandria, Virginia, June.

Briere, J., & Scott, C. (2006). *Principles of trauma therapy: A guide to symptoms, evaluation and treatment.* Newbury Park, CA: Sage Publications.

Calof, D. (1995). Chronic self-injury in adult survivors of childhood abuse: Developmental process of anger in relation to self-injuury (Part I). *Treating Abuse Today,* 5, 11-17, 31-36.

Calof, D. (1995). Chronic self-injury in adult survivors of childhood abuse: Sources, morivations and functions of self-injury (Part II). *Treating Abuse Today,* 5, 61-67.

Calof, D. (1997). Chronic self-injury in adult survivors of childhood abuse: Developmental process of anger in relation to self-injury (Part II). *Treating Abuse Today,* 7,

Gil, E., & Calof, D. (1993). Understanding and responding to self-injury. Fifth Annual Eastern Regional Conference, Alexandria, Virginia, June.

van der Hart, O., Nijenhuis, E.R.S., & Steele, K. (2006). *The haunted self: Structural dissociation and the treatment of chronic traumatization.* New York: W.W. Norton.

21
Just Say "No" to Drugs: Addiction Is the Opposite of Desensitization

We apply the addictions model in a very broad fashion. On the one hand, referring to all defenses, coping strategies, and ways of acting out as *addictions* is a metaphor, and possibly an overextension of the term. On the other hand, many behaviours such as self-mutilation probably activate endorphins and other neurotransmitters, and result in a biological high that is just as real as an opiate high. Often, the brain might not be able to tell the difference between the dopamine rush caused by certain street drugs, by fast driving, and by other thrill-seeking behaviour. So the metaphor is not simply a metaphor.

In this chapter we cover

- The Definition of Addiction

- The Definition of Desensitization

- Just Say "No" to Drugs

- Treatment Techniques for Desensitization

The Definition of Addiction

In any addiction, the problem is *here*. Here is where the client is now, which means intolerable feelings, conflicts, or life situations. The purpose of all addictions is to take one from *here* to *over there*. Over there is anywhere in the universe except here: stoned, wasted, thrilled, distracted, or passed out. All addictions, then, are avoidance strategies. They are basically vehicles that take you from *here* to *over there*.

We treat all symptoms, addictions, unhealthy behaviours, and diagnoses as avoidance strategies, therefore we apply the addictions model to everything. This includes depression, auditory hallucinations, throwing up your food, amnesia, the patient role, and everything else encountered in treatment. If the addictions model doesn't apply in a given case, or to a given problem, then we modify our approach. But the opening assumption is that everything has the same effect as a drug.

If a person is admitted to the hospital in an anticholinergic delirium due to an overdose, we certainly don't initiate psychotherapy while the person is delirious. This is an example of a problem that can't be treated under the heading of *"Just say 'no' to drugs."* The treatment for the delirium is time, medical support, and possibly medications. Once the person is out of the delirium, though, the addictions model will certainly apply.

Similarly, chronic severe drug and alcohol abuse can cause brain damage. The brain damage itself may not be treatable with psychotherapy, although the brain's capacity for self-repair is just beginning to be understood. But the brain damage wasn't there when the substance abuse started—it is an effect of the abuse, not the underlying cause. Therefore the addictions model still applies, even if the substances have added a dimension of physical damage and dependency.

Our focus is not primarily on the particular vehicle a client drives to get from here to over there. We are more interested in *what* is being avoided than in *how* it is being avoided. Treatment is about learning how to tolerate the intolerable without acting out. This does not mean, however, that we ignore the addictions.

If one client has an eating disorder but no alcohol problem, then we will talk with her about food more than we talk about alcohol. If a second client has an alcohol problem but no eating disorder, we will talk with him about alcohol more than about food. The content of the therapy conversation includes the content of the addictions, but the content does not determine the structure, tasks, or goals of treatment.

This is analogous to desensitization of simple phobias. If one person has a snake phobia, then the therapeutic conversation deals with snakes more than spiders. The inverse is true for the person with a spider phobia. In both cases, however, the work of therapy is basically the same: one must learn the vocabulary of behaviour therapy, construct a desensitization hierarchy, and learn to tolerate the intolerable. This is done in a series of steps that is determined by the treatment model, not by the content of the phobia.

The Definition of Desensitization

Desensitization is the opposite of addiction. Desensitization is when you turn around and face the thing you have been avoiding, in a deliberate, planned fashion. Desensitization can be done in one of two fashions: flooding or systematic desensitization. In workshops, I may illustrate the perils of flooding with the following story:

> *The Trauma Model is a general model of mental health problems and addictions. At our hospital in Dallas, we want to be ready to treat any problem that presents itself. Since there are a lot of snakes in Texas, I wanted to be ready to treat a snake phobia, should anyone be admitted with a snake phobia.*
>
> *So one day I went out and dug a pit on the hospital grounds. Then I collected up a couple of hundred snakes and threw them in the pit. I fed them and checked on them till finally someone was admitted with a snake phobia.*
>
> *I said to this person, "How would you like to go for a walk on the grounds?"*
>
> *She agreed, so we went out walking. When we got near the snake pit, I suddenly pushed her in. Then I looked at my watch, and noticed it was time for lunch. After lunch I went to a meeting, then several hours later I remembered the patient in the snake pit and went back to check on her.*
>
> *"Hi! How you doing?"*
>
> *No response.*
>
> *"It's me, Dr. Ross. How are you doing?"*

> *Still no response, so, being careful not to get too close to the edge, I peeked into the pit and saw the woman in a frozen, catatonic state at the bottom of the pit. After trying this approach six or seven times with the same result, I decided that flooding is not the way to go.*

This vignette is generally regarded as amusing, until it is pointed out that in the 1980's and into the 1990's, trauma therapy often consisted of flooding. This was done under the heading of *memory work*. The outcome was regression, dependency, more crises, more acting out, more self-mutilation, more hospital admissions, and more memories. The solution was to do yet more memory work.

The correct approach is systematic desensitization, not flooding. We break the steps down to the smallest steps necessary, and we take as long as it takes. This is important because it keeps a focus on containment, pacing, stabilization, and function outside therapy.

Systematic desensitization has two components: going into the feelings, and backing out. In trauma therapy, the phobic stimulus is mostly internal, in the form of unresolved feelings and conflicts, so exposure is to the feelings, not to external objects. The principles are the same as behavioural treatment of simple phobias, but the phobic stimuli are internal and more complex.

In a structured, planned fashion, often in experiential therapy groups (see Chapter 31), we mobilize the feelings and get them up and running. We simultaneously work with the person to keep herself grounded, with her adult thinking cap on. Because of the containment, support, and structure of the treatment, the person is able to feel her feelings more intensely, and longer, than she thought possible—without acting out. This is a revolutionary experience.

Prior to the desensitization, the person was looking at the feelings through the eyes of the magical child. She believed they were as huge, threatening, and overwhelming as they actually were in childhood, and she predicted that catastrophe would ensue from feeling them. But when she experiences the feelings while keeping her adult cognition up and running, and then backs out and settles down without acting out, she learns an important set of lessons: *the feelings are not as huge as I thought; I have more mastery than I gave myself credit for; this process is do-able and I could survive it; I now have realistic hope based on my own experience; since the feelings are more manageable than I thought, I can contemplate saying "no" to my addictions; and, since there is light at the end of the tunnel, I don't have to kill myself.*

It is the power of the experience that drives the changes in cognitions and core beliefs.

Also, since it is now possible to go into the feelings this far, the next time it might be possible to go a little further, so the process continues. This process of approaching ever closer to the phobic stimulus, while not dying or going insane, is what we usually think of as *desensitization*.

The other half of the process is equally if not more important, however: backing out of the feelings and settling down. This is the work of affect management and skills building. The power of the experiential therapies is that the avoided feelings—grief, rage, fear, emptiness—are mobilized and felt, intensely. Once the feelings are activated, a problem arises—what now? Now the person actually has to back out of them, de-escalate and re-stabilize. This isn't just an intellectual exercise because the feelings are actually present.

By mobilizing the feelings, the exercise becomes a real-life simulation in the laboratory of therapy.

Since it resembles the real world situation, the learning in therapy should generalize more effectively. Simultaneously, backing out of the feelings successfully results in further desensitization due to the experience of mastery, and makes greater risk in the next session more feasible. The culmination of the exercise is therapeutic and positive feedback between the feelings and the cognitions.

Treatment Techniques for Desensitization

The first step in desensitization is creating a structure, teaching the vocabulary, and explaining the model. This transforms the task of feeling the feelings from an impossible catastrophe into a feasible project, which is itself a desensitization. Part of the power of therapy is that it makes sense, is broken down into defined steps and tasks, and yields actual experiences of incremental hope and mastery.

The opposite is also true: ineffective treatment models can drive a person downward into despair and hopelessness, especially when the person attributes the lack of progress to her own hopelessness, rather than to the ineffectiveness of the treatment model.

Discussion of the rationale for systematic desensitization might go like this:

Therapist: I want to explain how this works a little more. It's like when you fall off a horse: are you going to let your fear master you, or are you going to master your fear and get back on the horse? In your case, we are going to work on your fear of your feelings, but we're going to do it step by step.
Client: If I feel my feelings I'll kill myself. That or get drunk every day.
Therapist: That's why we're going to break it down into tiny steps, as tiny as they have to be. The ultimate goal is to feel your feelings and stay safe.
Client: Sounds impossible to me.
Therapist: Well, let's give it a try. You have a problem with anger, right? What is it you are angry about?
Client: Lots of shit.
Therapist: Like what? Give me an example.
Client: Like the fact that my father beat the crap out of me the whole time I was growing up.
Therapist: And how did that make you feel?
Client: Scared.
Therapist: What else?
Client: I've got so much rage inside me I might blow up.
Therapist: Do you feel any of that rage right now?
Client: Yeah.
Therapist: Where?
Client: Here, in my stomach.
Therapist: If you were to assign a colour to your rage, what color would it be?
Client: It's black.
Therapist: And how big is it? How much space does it take up?
Client: It's about the size of my two fists put together.
Therapist: OK, so that's good to know. You know quite a bit about your anger—where it's located, what colour it is, what size it is. And we've talked before about what triggers the anger, resulting in your flying into a rage. This is our basic map of your rage problem. We know where it came from, where it is now, and what triggers it. This makes it a manageable problem, something we can get a grip on.
Client: But I don't know what to do about it; I just blow up.
Therapist: How many times have you had a rage attack in the check-out line at the supermarket?

Client: None.

Therapist: How about while watching cartoons on TV?

Client: None. What's your point?

Therapist: My point is that your rage attacks aren't random. They occur in a context on predictable occasions. They are understandable. This means you can get a handle on them.

Client: I'm glad you believe that.

Therapist: I do believe it, based on experience with other people who have done the work. This is realistically possible for you.

Client: I don't know, it just seems too huge. If I let it out, I might kill someone.

Therapist: Well, first, that proves that you are basically a decent person. That's why you are concerned about letting your rage out. If you were a person with no conscience, you wouldn't care who got hurt or killed. So that's good to know.

Client: That's a good way to look at it.

Therapist: And second, let's look at why you are angry. You are angry because bad things would happen to you that would make anyone angry. Your anger is normal and healthy. It is your fear you will be violent that is the problem.

Client: That doesn't make it any easier to handle.

Therapist: True, but it's important to understand that your anger is normal, healthy, legitimate, and there for a good reason. You aren't just an angry maniac for no reason. The question is, how to handle it, and that's what needs work. The anger itself is just a feeling.

Client: So it's normal to fly into rages and get out of control?

Therapist: No, not at all. But it's normal to be angry when you've been abused and betrayed—I'm talking about the feeling, not the behaviour.

Client: OK, so the problem is not how I feel, it's my behaviour.

Therapist: Right. And that we can work on.

Client: So I'm not basically weird or defective?

Therapist: Right. One more thing: how angry are you right now on a scale of zero to ten?

Client: One

Therapist: How angry were you a few minutes ago when you were describing the colour, size, and location of your anger?

Client: Four.

Therapist: Congratulations, then! You've just done a piece of desensitization. You took your anger up to a four, felt it, then brought it back down to one. And you did it without getting aggressive, without acting out, without going insane, in fact, you were under perfect control the whole time.

Client: Yeah, but that wasn't rage.

Therapist: I know, but it was 40% of rage. If you can do 40, you can do 50, if you can do 50 you can do 60. But one step at a time, remember?

Client: OK, that's starting to make sense.

This vignette included techniques of education, reframing, normalizing, correction of cognitive errors, building a treatment alliance, guided imagery, desensitization, and validation.

When the person begins to get lost in the feelings, particularly anger, and is escalating too far up the scale too fast, the therapist has to apply the brakes. This is called grounding or containment. The interventions are usually direct, practical, and straightforward. The therapist can instruct the client to stand up, look around (to break the auto-hypnotic stare), shuffle her feet, rub her hands, or perform some other physical action. The therapist can remind the client of the location, date, and safety of the present. It can be helpful for the therapist to identify herself by name and state her role and profession.

The therapist can also switch topics suddenly by asking the person about his dog, his fishing trip, his favorite football team, or some other topic that carries very different feelings.

If such interventions don't work, a more directive tone of voice can be used. The person can be instructed to focus and ground. Then statements can be made about consequences such as ending the session immediately or calling in other professionals to maintain safety. Ultimately, the therapist can state that she is going to leave the room or call the police if the client doesn't get grounded; if that doesn't work, then one of those things may need to be done.

If such measures are required it reflects the steps have not been small enough and the therapist has misjudged the client's current capacity to hold such intense feelings. It is not therapeutic to get lost in rage or terror. Within therapy sessions, such episodes are avoidable and unnecessary. They are not part and parcel of recovery, and they have no benefit to anyone. The same is true of extreme terror, reliving trauma as if it is happening in the present, and getting lost in prolonged trance states.

All of these behaviours are avoidance strategies and can be treated with an addictions approach, a review of the commitment to recovery, and limit setting. However, this work requires careful assessment of the client's readiness and capacity to undertake the work.

Additional techniques for desensitization are included in subsequent chapters, and can include the "what if cascade," developing internal safe places, focusing on adaptation in the present, various experiential therapies, medications and in some cases, inpatient treatment. Chapter 30 covers specific strategies and techniques for working with feelings. All of these techniques can be included under the headings of pacing, containment, affect management, grounding, and skills building. This is so because all the different techniques are intertwined and overlap with each other, and because desensitization involves the two phases of work: going into the feelings, and backing out again.

SPECIFIC TREATMENT TECHNIQUES

22
Resistance: Normalizing and Working with Defenses

Validation and normalization are used throughout Trauma Model Therapy. They aren't just "words of encouragement," rather they are fundamental to the Trauma Model (Ross, 2007). The working assumption is that the person is not fundamentally abnormal or defective. The motto is: *there but for the grace of God, go I*. The person is assumed to be exhibiting a normal reaction to the trauma, abuse, neglect, and tragedy to which he has been exposed. Within the normal range, a given individual may be a little more or a little less resilient, a little more or a little less prone to mental health problems, but very few people are genetically doomed to acquire specific DSM diagnoses, no matter what happens to them. This viewpoint is stated in a way that leads to many specific, testable, scientific predictions within the Trauma Model.

Validation of defenses is called *aligning with the resistance* in some schools of family therapy. It is a type of judo move—instead of working against the defenses to eradicate them, one emphasizes their positive functions and the choice element involved. The energy driving the symptoms and addictions is then directed toward more positive, flexible, and adaptive coping strategies.

In this chapter we cover

- The Definition of Resistance

- The Therapist's Attitude Toward Defenses

- Examples of Treatment Strategies

- The Problem of Host Resistance

The Definition of Resistance

Resistance is often thought to be entirely negative—the more resistance, the less progress and the more severe the problems. Although this can be true, the opposite is more important in recovery. If all resistance was taken away, the person would melt down, commit suicide, or become catatonic. Getting through life without defenses and resistance is impossible. It's all a matter of degree and flexibility. Some resistance is good; rigid, extreme, inflexible resistance is not.

Resistance is exactly what the word says: resisting, pushing down, blocking out, avoiding, or ignoring intolerable feelings and conflicts. Originally, with Freud, the idea was that the ego resists emergence of material from the id, but resistance is a general systems term as well: the cell wall of a bacteria resists leakage of excess material from inside the cell to the outside world; resistors are used in electrical circuits; and so on. One can talk about resistance within any school of psychotherapy.

A therapist might explain resistance to a DID client as follows:

Client: Maybe I'm just resistant.
Therapist: I hope you are. Resistance has kept you alive all these years.

Client: What do you mean? I thought resistance was bad.

Therapist: It can be, if it's extreme and inflexible. But think about it for a minute—why do you have DID?

Client: Because my parents were assholes.

Therapist: Right, but why didn't you just cope with all that without developing DID?

Client: It was too much.

Therapist: Exactly. The whole purpose of DID is to have resistance. Creating alters was your mind's way of pushing all the terror, grief, and guilt away, so you could function and survive. If you hadn't *resisted*, what would have happened?

Client: I probably would have killed myself.

Therapist: Good thing you were resistant, then.

The Therapist's Attitude Toward Defenses

Defenses are classically categorized as *mature* and *primitive*. This is not a problem in theory, but it can become a problem in practice when "primitive" is used to express and rationalize a hostile, condescending, belittling, or demeaning counter-transference. The implication—the disavowed, double-bound, covert message—is that the patient is *primitive* while the mental health professional is *mature*. A counter-therapeutic "us versus them" mentality then develops that is similar to that of the genetically defective patient versus genetically normal psychiatrist.

The same conversation could ensue concerning *denial*:

Client: I must be in denial.

Therapist: I hope you are. I wouldn't want to try to get through the day without any denial.

Client: What do you mean? I thought denial was bad.

Therapist: It can be, if it's extreme and inflexible. But if you didn't have any denial—you the average person, I mean—you'd be so overwhelmed with problems and conflicts you couldn't function. Imagine a mother who lost a child to leukemia. She has to be in denial about how she feels a lot of the time for years in order to take care of her other children.

Client: I never looked at it that way before.

Therapist: On the other hand, if she completely suppressed all her grief, never cried at the funeral, never talked with the other children about their feelings, and told everyone in the family to "get on with life," that wouldn't work. She'd get depressed, the other kids couldn't get any support from her for their grief, and so on. It would set up a vicious cycle.

Client: Sounds like my family.

Therapist: So two things don't work: too much denial and too little denial.

Client: OK, I get it.

The therapist works on reframing resistance in a number of different ways, including didactic education; modeling flexible thinking and attitudes; pointing out the dysfunctional aspects of defenses; normalizing and validating defenses; examining the cost-benefit of various defenses in their current forms; and working on a serious commitment to recovery from the unhealthy defenses.

Examples of Treatment Strategies

Normalizing and validation can be applied to all symptoms, behaviours, and defenses. An example of a general explanation of the normality of defenses follows:

Therapist: It isn't normal to be bleeding with broken bones sticking out through your skin. But if you've been in a multi-car wreck on the freeway, it can be a perfectly normal reaction to what has happened.

Client: I'm not bleeding.

Therapist: Not physically, but remember, this is an analogy I'm making. It isn't normal to have all your mental health problems, but it's normal for what you've gone through. Do you see what I'm saying?

Client: Sort of.

Therapist: What about it doesn't make sense to you?

Client: I don't see how you can say I'm normal—I'm really messed up.

Therapist. True. Why are you messed up?

Client: Because of what . . . oh, I get it.

Therapist: Good. Explain it to me.

Client: It's not normal to have broken bones, but it's normal if you've been hurt badly.

Therapist: Right, and there's a big difference. In one way of looking at it, you're messed up because there's something *fundamentally* wrong with you—bad genes, bad chemicals, weak character, whatever. In the other way of looking at it, there's nothing basically wrong with you; you're messed up the way anyone would be if they went through what you've gone through.

Client: How do you know I don't have bad genes?

Therapist: I don't, but that's putting it the wrong way around.

Client: How do you mean?

Therapist: Do you know for a scientific fact that there is something wrong with you genetically?

Client: No.

Therapist: Neither do I. Since neither of us—nor anyone else on the planet—knows you have bad genes, why assume you do? That's a very negative belief to have about yourself. Believing you are genetically defective and abnormal can't make you feel good about yourself.

Client: That's for sure. It makes me feel like a freak.

Therapist: So why not assume you are basically normal, and your problems are understandable fallout from what you've experienced?

Client: Sounds nice, but I don't believe it.

Therapist: I know—that's because you're holding on tight to the locus of control shift.

Client: Oh, that.

Therapist: The abnormal genes model gives you a rationalization for hating yourself, which gives you a rationalization for treating yourself badly, which reinforces feeling badly about yourself, which reinforces feeling hopeless and suicidal, which reinforces treating yourself badly. Round and round it goes.

Client: Huh. So I'm perfectly normal then.

Therapist: 100%. But let's look at an example of an unhealthy coping strategy you use. Choose one.

Client: Why?

Therapist: Explaining the overview, like I've just been doing, is good but then we have to put it into action and work on something specific.

Client: OK, how about throwing up my food.

Therapist: Why do you throw up your food?

Client: To get rid of it.

Therapist: Why do you want to get rid of your food?

Client: So I don't get fat.

Therapist: Why don't you want to get fat?

Client: What is this, kindergarten?

Therapist: No, second grade. Why don't you want to get fat?

Client: Does anybody?

Therapist: Anybody isn't here today. You are here today, so I'm asking you.

Client: Then I'd be gross and ugly like my dad.

Therapist: And how would that feel?

Client: Gross. Bad. Sick.

Therapist: Would anyone in their right mind want to feel that way?

Client: No.

Therapist: Do you want to feel that way?

Client: No.

Therapist: So you're in your right mind, then. That's good to know. You're describing a completely normal wish not to feel feelings like that. Why do you feel so horrible about the idea of being like your dad?

Client: Because he was a pervert.

Therapist: Right, so you are having the normal feelings anyone would have if they had a dad like that, and a normal wish not to have those feelings.

Client: OK, but it's not normal to throw up in the toilet every day.

Therapist: It is if you're on chemo.

Client: That's different.

Therapist: True, but the point is, there are some situations where anyone would throw up in the toilet every day. You were never taught healthy eating. Your parents never modeled it. Your mom freaked out if you gained three pounds. Your dad molested you and your sister, and your mom didn't do anything even when she saw it happening, which she admitted when we met with her. So how surprising is it that a person from your background has bulimia, especially when we add all the pressure on women to be thin in our culture?

Client: So it's OK to keep throwing up?

Therapist: Depends on whether you're OK with it or not. If you are, you'll continue. If you're not, we can work on it.

Client: Let me guess . . . it's a choice.

Therapist: You didn't choose to get into this mess, but you can choose to get out of it.

Client: OK, I choose. Are we done?

Therapist: Yes, you're fully recovered now.

Client: That was easy. Thanks.

Therapist: You're welcome. Anything else?

Client: If I choose to stop purging that doesn't help much. I don't know how to stop.

Therapist: You'll never learn if you don't decide to learn. Deciding is the first step, but it's a long walk down the road.

A core principle of recovery is: *you didn't choose to be a victim, but you can choose not to be a victim any longer.* Normalizing and validating defenses does not provide an excuse for bad behaviour. It leads to taking responsibility, growing, and healing. If you are simply a victim of bad genes and bad chemicals, there isn't much you can do except take medication. A fundamentally normal person can get to work on a program of realistic, attainable change by building on a solid genetic foundation.

The Problem of Host Resistance

The host personality is the part who is out front and in control most of the time. There is usually a single host personality throughout the person's lifetime, but it is possible for there to be a series of hosts, and sometimes there is a committee of parts that jointly takes care of the host executive functions. For simplicity, it's easier to talk about a single host personality, but the same principles apply no matter what the structure of the system.

Host resistance is often subtle and difficult to spot. It can take many forms. Like resistance in general, host resistance is a protective survival strategy, but it becomes a problem when it is excessive, rigid, and inflexible.

The host may claim to be "the real person," and believe that the parts are "my alters" or "the alters." This is a form of apartheid with first-class and second-class citizens. It may be gratifying for the host, but no other parts feel good about it. They either agree and have low self-esteem, or disagree and are in conflict with the host. Overcoming host resistance is the first step in forming a treatment alliance with persecutor parts.

A conversation about host resistance might go as follows:

Therapist: So you're the real person and the other parts are just parts.
Client: Right.
Therapist: And you want to get integrated, right?
Client: Right.
Therapist: What does integration mean to you?
Client: It means I don't have parts anymore. There's just me.
Therapist: And where would the parts be?
Client: They'd be gone; they wouldn't exist anymore.
Therapist: Where would they have gone to?
Client: I don't know, they just wouldn't be here anymore.
Therapist: I understand that, but it seems from what you're saying, and what you've said previously, that your idea of integration is basically getting rid of parts.
Client: That's what I want. Then I won't hear voices anymore and I won't have to deal with them anymore. They cause me a lot of trouble.
Therapist: I have a name for that kind of integration.
Client: What's that?
Therapist: I call it *integration by firing squad*. Your idea of integration is getting rid of parts. They see that as you killing them off, so, not surprisingly, they are against integration. Since they're against integration they also have to be against you and against therapy.
Client: That's their problem.
Therapist: But it becomes your problem when they act out against you and do stuff when you are blanked out.
Client: But if I was integrated, that wouldn't happen anymore.
Therapist: True, but your attitude toward integration is preventing you from getting integrated. Imagine if my plan of therapy was getting rid of you. Would you want to do therapy?
Client: No, but I'm the real person. This is my body.
Therapist: Actually, the real person is all the parts added together. You're one of the parts just like all the others. Your job is to be out front and be "the person," but that is just one of the jobs in your system. Other jobs are just as real and just as important.
Client: You mean I'm not real either? I'm just a part?
Therapist: You're making an error of categories: You've got yourself divided into the real person, you, versus the unreal parts, everyone else. In fact, all the parts are real parts of a real person. You are all part of the whole. Integration is not about getting rid of parts; it's about accepting, joining, and blending. Integration works in the opposite direction of getting rid of parts—it's about bringing the

parts closer, not pushing them further away.

Client: But if I accept them I'll feel all their pain.

Therapist: True. That's why you have host resistance. But trying to get rid of the parts isn't working—it just makes them feel more rejected, hurt, and angry, so then they counter-attack and try to get rid of you.

Client: Oh.

Therapist: How did it feel when you were a kid and your mother either neglected you, pretended you didn't exist, hurt you, or tried to get rid of you?

Client: Bad.

Therapist: So how do you think your parts feel when you treat them that way?

Client: Lousy.

Therapist: How else would you expect them to feel?

Client: So when I try to get rid of my parts, I'm treating them like my parents treated me?

Therapist: Yup.

Client: I'm abusing them?

Therapist: Yup.

Client: I never looked at it that way.

Therapist: Now that you're looking at it that way, what do you think?

Client: I think I'd better change how I treat my parts.

Therapist: Are you getting any reaction from inside when you say that?

Client: Some parts are cheering.

Therapist: You'd better follow through on what you're saying, then, or they'll be really disappointed.

Client: I will.

Therapist: Do you believe you when you say that?

Client: Kind of.

Therapist: Right. I bet your parts are skeptical too—because they're smart. They know you might not follow through. You'll have to build up a track record with them before they really buy that you're going to treat them differently, for real, and consistently.

Client: I know.

In this vignette, the therapist was simultaneously working on the VRP triangle. The host had been feeling like a victim of the parts but, in fact, had been perpetrating on them. This illustrates how the different principles, techniques, and strategies of Trauma Model Therapy are all intertwined with each other—working on host resistance is automatically also working on the VRP triangle.

The host personality often takes the victim role, sets the other parts in the persecutor role, and wants the therapist to be the rescuer. When the therapist agrees to become the rescuer, the passive victim role of the host, and the evil enemy roles of the other parts, are reinforced. A series of feedback loops are set up so that more rescuing creates more host victim-hood, which creates more acting out by the parts, which then requires more rescuing by the therapist. A therapist might approach the problem of host resistance in the following manner:

Therapist: So you want me to work with your parts to get them to stop threatening you?

Client: Yeah.

Therapist: In fact, you want me to work with your parts to get them to go away and leave you alone.

Client: Double yeah.

Therapist: How do you think I could do that? Could I get a pair of tweezers and reach in and grab them? Maybe vacuum them out? If I wanted to grab your parts and throw them away, how would I do that?

Client: I don't know. You're the therapist—aren't you supposed to know?

Therapist: The point is twofold: 1) even if I wanted to, there is no way for me to get rid of your parts. So getting rid of your parts is not a feasible plan. 2) not only is it not feasible, it's not desirable. These are parts of you who are holding your feelings, conflicts, and memories for you so that you won't be totally overwhelmed.

Client: Then why are they trying to kill me?

Therapist: Because you're trying to kill them. Why is it OK for you to want to get rid of them, but not OK for them to want to get rid of you? Your attitude seems a little unfair.

Client: Hmmm.

Therapist: You can't expect them to ease up on you if you don't ease up on them. You're the host. You could set an example. For instance, you want me to work with your parts to get them to stop cutting on you, but you aren't willing to stop cutting yourself. Your words say, "Stop," but your actions say, "Go." Your parts are listening to your actions not your words.

Client: So I'm putting them in a double bind.

Therapist: Yes, you are. How did it feel when your mother put you in endless double binds? And another thing, your parts are like subcontractors. You're the lead contractor and you've contracted out most of the self-mutilation to them. They do it for you because that's their job. You get the benefits— bad feelings gone—but you don't have to take responsibility for the behaviour because "someone else" did it. That's your out, but you're not fooling your alters. They know how you operate.

Client: Great. I guess they don't trust me very much.

Therapist: Would you trust you?

Client: No, I guess not.

Therapist: Well, then.

Client: But I want to get better.

Therapist: I believe that. But in order to get better, you're going to have to say "no" to self-mutilation and be consistent with that for quite a while. You have to build up a track record with your parts before they're going to buy it. Till then, I expect them to be skeptical because they're smart.

Client: My parts are smart? How do you know that?

Therapist: Because they live in your brain.

Client: Oh. Thanks, I guess.

Host resistance can take the form of the host bemoaning the fact that the parts won't cooperate. The host claims that she journals, tries to talk internally, and is prepared to listen at any time. But when the parts do share anything, the host decompensates and becomes suicidal. It is another double bind. For things to change, the host has to see and take responsibility for her double-bind communication pattern. Then she has to say "no" to the drug of decompensation and begin building a plan for her own systematic desensitization.

The parts are not the problem. They are a solution to a problem the host, and the whole person, can't solve without them. Insisting on the host's taking responsibility for her internal communication pattern is the same as getting a non-DID person to take adult responsibility for her behaviour. The psychological structure is different, but the basic tasks, goals, and techniques are the same.

Skepticism about DID is driven in part by a common incorrect belief, namely that people with DID are not responsible for the behaviour of their parts. When the client believes this, it is the problem of host resistance. When the therapist believes it, it is a counter-transference distortion. When an extreme skeptic believes it, it is a straw man argument. All parties are making the same cognitive error.

Consider the inverse: if people with DID were twice as responsible for their behaviour (i.e., if they got twice the jail sentence for the same crime), would skeptics then be in favour of the diagnosis? That would be the reciprocal cognitive error. If the rules of the social system were flipped so that people without DID were not held responsible for their behaviour, people with DID might then fake not having it. Would the skeptic then "diagnose" DID in every accused criminal who claimed not to have it?

In Trauma Model Therapy, people with DID are held to the same moral, ethical, behavioural, and legal standards as everyone else. Although this might seem excessively tough, it is the only way to get to recovery. Not holding the person to this standard fosters dependency, regression, addiction, and acting out. It is not kind, therapeutic, or helpful to enable a person with DID in that way.

23
Talking Through to the Voices

Talking through to the voices is a technique that can be used whenever there are auditory hallucinations. The diagnosis can be DID, DDNOS, schizophrenia, schizoaffective disorder, psychotic depression, or psychosis NOS. The Trauma Model (Ross, 2007; 2004) predicts that voices have certain characteristics in the dissociative subtype of schizophrenia compared to the subtypes recognized in DSM-IV-TR (catatonic, paranoid, and undifferentiated).

In dissociative schizrenia, the voices are more structured, clear, coherent, and interactive with each other and the therapist. Conversely, in non-dissociative schizophrenias, the voices tend to be narrower in range, rigid, stereotyped, and unresponsive to questions by the therapist. If the voices can be engaged in a therapeutic conversation, then the techniques in this chapter can be used irrespective of diagnosis. We say this because two thirds of people with DID meet structured interview criteria for schizophrenia or schizoaffective disorder. Although the relationship between dissociation and psychosis is multifaceted and complex, much of the time the two overlap or are indistinguishable.

This chapter covers

- Reasons to Talk to the Voices

- Reasons Not to Talk to the Voices

- The Structural Model of Dissociation

- The Relationship Between Therapist, Client, and Symptoms

- Techniques for Talking Through to the Voices

Reasons to Talk to the Voices

If the diagnosis is DID, then talking to the voices follows automatically and is supported by the relevant literature. When the diagnosis is schizophrenia, however, the same technique is controversial, or even prohibited by many clinicians. Why should one talk to the voices if the diagnosis is schizophrenia? There are several reasons.

First, if the individual has dissociative schizophrenia, then the disorder may be indistinguishable from DID, and all that differs is the diagnostic label. One purpose of the dissociative subtype of schizophrenia is to open up the possibility of an environmentally caused form of schizophrenia treatable with psychotherapy. Why not, then, simply diagnose DID? One answer is political: many clinicians simply will not diagnose or treat DID. In order for the individual to get trauma-based psychotherapy, if the diagnosis is schizophrenia, there must be a dissociative subtype of schizophrenia—otherwise the technique of talking to the voices will likely not be used.

The complexities and controversies surrounding whether to diagnose DID, dissociative schizophrenia, neither, or both, are discussed elsewhere (Ross, 2004). We will not go into them further here.

Another reason to try talking to the voices is failure to respond to conventional treatment. A large number of people with schizophrenia and schizoaffective disorder do not respond to medications. The ethical burden and political barriers to talking to the voices are reduced when conventional treatment has not worked.

The main reason to talk to the voices is a practical one. The technique often works, even when used sparingly as an adjunctive intervention. The purpose of much of the theory is to remove roadblocks to the technique. Since this book is a treatment manual, we prefer to de-emphasize theory.

Reasons Not to Talk to the Voices

There are several reasons not to talk to the voices. The technique may alarm the patient, reinforce delusional thinking, reify the voices, stimulate regression, or distract from more important treatment tasks and goals—in theory. In practice, we have not encountered serious versions of these reactions in our own work. However, they are more likely to occur with inexperienced clinicians unfamiliar with the psychotherapy of DID. In such a case, professional ethics require that the therapist refer the client to an experienced clinician who is able to provide the appropriate therapy.

Talking to the voices should not be the first intervention until basic safety, containment, education, and other tasks of the initial phase have been completed—at least partially if not fully. If a verbal contract to use the technique cannot be established, then it should not be used.

Otherwise, talking to the voices is just one more technique in the armamentarium. Extreme opinions regarding the technique are not warranted, whether they be positive or negative. Once the clinician is familiar and comfortable with the technique, the reasons for extreme caution evaporate, and the standard precautions applicable to any intervention apply.

The Structural Model of Dissociation

For talking to the voices to make sense, there must be a structural model of dissociation in place (van der Hart, Nijenhuis & Steele, 2006). In our view, the structural model applies to a broad range of disorders including DID, PTSD, obsessive-compulsive disorder (OCD), and dissociative schizophrenia. In order to understand the model, remember the four meanings of dissociation discussed in Chapter 1; structural dissociation does not imply that the intrapsychic defense mechanism of dissociation is necessarily operating.

In principle, structural dissociation could result from a defective gene, complications of labour and delivery, intrauterine infections, psychological trauma, or any of many causes. In practice, it is usually due to trauma, but this need not be so in all cases. In a given case of OCD, for instance, there may be no severe psychological trauma, but structural dissociation may still be in place.

By definition, OCD consists of the executive self experiencing obsessions and compulsions that intrude from outside. The intrusions are experienced as ego-alien, and are resisted until the anxiety level becomes too high; compliance with the intrusion temporarily reduces the anxiety.

In the standard OCD literature, one never asks the location or source of the intrusions. This question simply doesn't arise. It seems to us, however, that the question should be asked. If OCD is present, there is only one logical possibility: For the intrusions to be experienced as ego-alien, they must be originating in a disowned, disavowed, disconnected—that is, a dissociated—sector of the psyche. There cannot be intrusion without structural dissociation.

This is generally true, whether the intrusions are Schneiderian symptoms in schizophrenia, compulsions in OCD, flashbacks in PTSD, or similar phenomena in DID.

The inverse of intrusion is withdrawal. This corresponds to numbing in PTSD, negative symptoms in schizophrenia, some of the Schneiderian symptoms such as thought withdrawal, negative hallucinations, conversion symptoms such as motor paralysis in DID, and so on. In this class of symptoms, affect, memory, information, motor function, identity, or other psychic components are withdrawn from the executive self by an active psychological process. They are not simply absent; they have been withdrawn, are stored elsewhere, and can be recovered.

Within the structural model, the voices are not products of a genetic defect. They are dissociated aspects of the self that need to be integrated back into the executive identity. The goal of treatment is not to cancel the voices; it is to accept, welcome, and blend them back into the host self.

From the perspective of the structural model, suppressing the voices behaviourally or pharmacologically reinforces the dissociation. If a person with OCD responds to antidepressants, the obsessions and compulsions are not gone: They are walled off more completely so that they can no longer intrude. In some cases, at a practical level, this may be the best outcome that can be achieved. Ideally, however, the underlying conflicts should be resolved; the disavowed impulses, thoughts, and feelings acknowledged and owned; and the psyche integrated.

The Relationship Between Therapist, Client, and Symptoms

For talking to the voices to make sense, there is another requirement: The classical relationship between doctor (or therapist), patient (or client), and symptom, cannot apply. In family medicine, a patient may come to the office complaining of a sore knee. The doctor asks the patient questions about the knee, and then works with the patient to fix the problem. The doctor does not ask the knee for its opinion.

In our model of therapy, however, the voices are not simply symptoms with which the patient is afflicted. The voices are just as much *the patient* as the patient is—they are disowned, disavowed aspects of the self. There is a need for a treatment alliance with the voices, and to engage the voices in therapy, just as much as—and no less than—one needs to form a working treatment alliance with the executive self who hears the voices. Further, in Trauma Model therapy, the therapist may well ask a client with a hurting knee, "If your knee could talk, what would it say about the pain it's in".

Trying to cancel or suppress the voices can have a number of negative consequences. It can reinforce the passive victim stance of the executive self; reinforce denial, avoidance, and dissociation; stigmatize the person as fundamentally defective and abnormal; result in the loss of feelings, history, life narrative, identity, and sense of personal agency; triage the person to medication rather than psychotherapy; and reinforce an identity of being psychotic, or mentally ill.

It is true that the person has a psychological disturbance, but the two models differ fundamentally. In conventional biological psychiatry, the person is genetically defective, has a permanently damaged brain, is likely to deteriorate, cannot gain control of her symptoms herself, must take medication for life, and has no context, life narrative, or meaning for her symptoms. Within the Trauma Model, however, the person can unlearn her symptoms, achieve self-mastery and integration, and exit from the mental health system. In the biological disease model, remission is possible, but not recovery.

Techniques for Talking Through to the Voices

Techniques for talking to the voices are described in the dissociative disorders literature but not in the contemporary literature on psychosis. One of our goals is to integrate these two literatures. An initial engagement in talking to the voices might go as follows:

Therapist: I'd like to try something that we do some of the time in treatment. I'd like to try asking your voices a few questions.
Client: Are you nuts?
Therapist: No, and neither are you. This may seem a bit odd, but it's a technique that is oftentimes very helpful.
Client: Wait 'til I tell everyone my shrink wants to talk to my voices.
Therapist: Well, it depends on how you think of the voices. If you think of the voices as symptoms of brain disease, then talking to your voices would be like talking to your lungs or your liver. It certainly wouldn't make sense. But if your voices are your own thoughts and feelings that you've pushed away, if they're more like your own conscience talking to you, then it makes sense to try to understand their viewpoint. Really, it's just another form of conversation between me and you, and you and yourself.
Client: I still think it's weird.
Therapist: That's fine. If we try it and you get used to it, it might seem less weird later. Or we might try it, it doesn't work, and we just carry on. Nothing ventured, nothing gained.
Client: If I see pink elephants, are you going to try to talk to them too?
Therapist: No.
Client: Why not?
Therapist: Because I don't know their language.
Client: You really are nuts.
Therapist: Thank you. OK, can we give it a try?
Client: You're the professional.
Therapist: OK, then. Well, what I'd like to do is see if the voices can hear me and are listening to the conversation. Let's start with the angry male voice that is always putting you down. What I'm going to do is ask that voice a question. Voice, if you can hear me, I'd like you to answer inside Mary's head and tell me if you heard me. Then Mary will tell me what you said.
Client: I still say this is weird.
Therapist: I understand that. OK, Voice, can you hear me and understand what I'm saying?

At this point, Mary may pause, appear to be introspective, or may even look a little tranced out momentarily. She may appear to be listening to someone, or she may not have any particular expression.

Client: The voice said, "Yeah, what do you want?"
Therapist: Well, I'm glad we can talk. I'd like to get to know you a little and understand your point of view a little better. Are you the angry male voice that Mary hears criticizing her?
Client: The voice says, "Yeah, that's me."
Therapist: I'd like to ask you a few questions about that. Why are you so angry at Mary?
Client: I can't repeat that.
Therapist: Oh. Can you give me a rough translation?

Client: The voice says I'm bad.
Therapist: What did Mary do that is so bad?
Client: She let the abuse happen.
Therapist: Really? How old was Mary when she let the abuse happen?
Client: Four.
Therapist: Four. Huh. What do you think she should have done to stop it at age four?
Client: She should have told someone.

The client has just switched. The voice is now in executive control and is talking directly to the therapist. This happens fairly often after four or five or six questions. Often there is no abrupt switch behaviourally. Rather there is a subtle shift in facial expression and manner, which might not otherwise be remarkable, except for the fact that Mary is now speaking about herself in the third person. The therapist does not have to acknowledge the switch at this point, but may do so now or later.

Therapist: Who could she have told?
Client: I don't know. Someone.
Therapist: But that was the problem—who to tell? Who was it who was abusing you?
Client: I wasn't abused.
Therapist: Oh, who was it who was abusing Mary?
Client: Her father.
Therapist: So there was no point in telling her father; he already knew about it. What about telling her mother?
Client: That bitch was so out of it, she didn't even know.
Therapist: And how would her mother have reacted if Mary told her about the abuse?
Client: Mary was too chicken and too goody-goody to tell anyone.
Therapist: I understand that, but what if she had told her mother?
Client: The mother wouldn't have believed her.
Therapist: And would Mary have gotten in trouble?
Client: Yeah. The mother would have told the father, and the father would have beaten the crap out of her.
Therapist: So Mary was protecting herself from a beating by not telling, then.
Client: I guess so.
Therapist: Why didn't you tell anyone?
Client: It wasn't my problem.
Therapist: If it wasn't your problem, why are you so angry at Mary?
Client: What do you mean?
Therapist: I mean, if you weren't abused and it wasn't your problem, why do you have any feelings about it at all? Why are you angry? If you didn't care, you wouldn't be angry.
Client: I don't give a shit about her, or her abuse, or anything about her.
Therapist: I see. Well, let me ask you something else then . . .

At this point the client shifts her body position, looks bewildered, and stares at the therapist. She was switched back to her executive self. This hasn't happened at random—the conversation has become too threatening for the voice, who has actively retreated into the interior. Mary has re-emerged to fill the vacuum left by the departure of the voice.

Therapist: Are you with me?
Client: Huh? What were we talking about?
Therapist: Mary?

Client: Yeah.

Therapist: I was just checking to see if you are with me. You looked a little spaced out there for a minute.

Client: What happened?

Therapist: What's the last thing you remember?

Client: You were asking the voice some questions.

Therapist: What was the last thing I asked?

Client: You asked me to translate some nasty things the voice said inside.

Therapist: And what do you remember next after that?

Client: Feeling foggy and you were calling my name.

Therapist: OK, well it looks like you spaced out for a little while. While you were gone, the voice answered a few more questions, then you were back.

Client: How could the voice be talking if I'm not there?

Therapist: That happens sometimes.

Client: Great, so now I'm possessed. Did my head spin around?

Therapist: No, you did levitate up to the ceiling though.

Client: I figured.

Therapist: Actually, nothing out of the ordinary happened, you just answered a few questions.

Client: But I wasn't there.

Therapist: Well, you were and you weren't. You, Mary, were gone, and your voice was here talking to me. But it was the same body and overall the same person. It's just another part of you that you're disconnected from. Remember, I said the voice is kind of like your conscience talking to you? Well, it turns out your conscience can talk to me too, instead of just answering through you. That happens sometimes.

Client: I'm definitely weird.

Therapist: I understand that it might feel psychotic, but actually you're perfectly sane. This isn't psychosis, it's something we call dissociation. It's pretty common in people with your diagnosis.

Client: My psychiatrist never said anything about this before.

Therapist: Well, I'll talk to him about it. We'll put our heads together and figure out where to go from here.

Client: OK. I hope you guys know what you're doing.

Therapist: We do. Don't worry about it. I'll explain everything as we go along. I'd like to check and see if the voice wants to say anything at this point. I mean inside your head, and you could pass it on to me.

Client: OK.

Therapist: Voice, do you have any comments you want to make?

Client: I didn't hear anything.

Therapist: In that case, Voice, thanks for saying hello. I look forward to talking to you again. Now, Mary, tell me what happened with the interview at the rehab program.

In this vignette, the therapist repeatedly used normalization, a "no big deal" approach, and a general tone and manner meant to de-escalate any catastrophization. There was humour, education, the beginning of a challenge to the voice's locus of control shift, initial engagement of the voice in the treatment process, some practice at both talking through and talking directly to the voice, simple reassurance, and a reminder of the dependability and unity of the treatment team.

The therapist has not challenged the voice's departure, knowing that being too aggressive, insistent, or confrontational at this point would interfere with building a treatment alliance.

In another case, the attempt to talk to the voices might go differently:

Therapist: OK then. Well, what I'd like to do is see if the voices can hear me and are listening to the conversation. Let's start with the angry male voice that is always putting you down. What I'm going to do is ask that voice a question. Voice, if you can hear me, I'd like you to answer inside Mary's head and tell me if you heard me. Then Mary will tell me what you said.
Client: I still say this is weird.
Therapist: I understand that. OK, Voice, can you hear me and understand what I'm saying?
Client: I don't hear anything.
Therapist: OK, well let me ask again. Voice, I don't want to bother you or take up too much of your time, but I'm wondering if you can hear me. I'm not trying to get you to talk about anything in particular, I'm just wondering if you can hear me.
Client: Nothing.
Therapist: Hmm. Well, sometimes this technique just doesn't work. When I ask to talk to the voice, do you sense anything at all inside?
Client: Like what?
Therapist: Anything . . . any kind of reaction at all.
Client: You mean like someone crying?
Therapist: That, or anything. Why did you ask about crying?
Client: Because the voice didn't talk, but I could hear a little girl crying.
Therapist: Oh, well, if my asking to talk to the voice is causing any upset inside, I'm sorry about that. Maybe it would be better if I didn't push on this right now.
Client: I heard something.
Therapist: What was that?
Client: A voice said, "No kidding."
Therapist: Well, I'll pay attention to that. That sounds like enough for now. Maybe we can try again another session. Any other messages or comments for me before we stop?
Client: I don't hear anything.
Therapist: Well, let's talk about something else then.

On other occasions, the person may not hear any words, but may report a feeling such as agitation, fear, anger, or hostility intruding into awareness from somewhere inside. This is possible evidence of an emotional reaction by one of the voices, but it could just be a feeling in the usual sense. The therapist should file the information for future reference and exploration.

At other times the person may report sensing an internal presence but no words. All such phenomena are forms of internal communication between self and self, no matter how dissociated the internal structure. Also, information can be communicated as thoughts, *knowing* or intuition: the person may get a strong sense of the voice being afraid to talk, for instance. This is a hint, but only a hint. It is equally important not to overinterpret it, and not to underinterpret it.

Subsequent to unsuccessful attempts to engage the voices in conversation, one can try the same thing a few more times. There is no point in trying unsuccessfully ten or fifteen times, but a few attempts are warranted. If nothing at all happens, it is important not to regard this as failure.

Therapist: Well, we gave that a try. For you it might not be a technique we can use. That's no big deal. There are lots of other ways we can work. If any of the voices do want to communicate with me in the future, the door is open. If they don't, that's fine too. I'll keep working with you either way.
Client: I didn't think I was that messed up.

Therapist: Like I said, this has nothing to do with being psychotic. Some people who are psychotic hear voices, but some don't. Same thing the other way around: some people who hear voices are psychotic, and some aren't. In your case, you clearly aren't psychotic. Your thought processes are logical and intact, what you say makes sense, and a lot of your symptoms are quite understandable. You have a lot of internal conflict and distress, and at times you are very upset emotionally, but you're not psychotic. There is a big difference between being disturbed and being psychotic.

Client: I'm glad you believe that. I still feel concerned about it.

Therapist: I know. What I'm saying is, just because you *feel* psychotic, doesn't mean you *are* psychotic. It's like a person with a really severe elevator phobia. She's on the second floor of a building, the down elevator door opens, and she is so flooded with fear and anxiety, there is no way to get on the elevator. Is the elevator really that dangerous? No. But does the person really feel overwhelming, paralyzing fear? Yes. Is her heart rate up? Yes. Are her adrenal glands pumping out adrenalin furiously? Yes.

Client: That makes sense. I'm starting to get it.

Therapist: Good. So what do you want to work on now?

Once a therapeutic conversation is established with the voices, one can negotiate with them as if they are separate "people" who live in various rooms in the same house as the executive self. Let's say the voice is threatening to kill the person. The therapist might ask as follows:

Therapist: So the voice threatens to kill you. How could it do that?

Client: By stabbing me.

Therapist: How could a voice in your head get hold of a knife and stab you?

Client: What do you mean?

Therapist: Well, what is the voice?

Client: What do you mean?

Therapist: If you wanted to stab another person with a knife, and there was a knife on the table, how would you do that?

Client: I'd pick up the knife and stab him. Why are you asking this?

Therapist: I'll get to that in a second. What would you use to pick up the knife?

Client: My hand, of course.

Therapist: Right. And does the voice have hands?

Client: No, it's just a voice in my head.

Therapist: So how could the voice pick up a knife and stab you if it doesn't have any hands.

Client: Well, I guess it couldn't. But it would bug me so much, and threaten and threaten and never let up, until I stabbed myself.

Therapist: Oh, OK, so the problem isn't that the voice might stab you, it's that *you* might stab you.

Client: But I couldn't help it. The voice won't shut up.

Therapist: I understand that; I'm just trying to clarify the problem, which is that you might stab yourself to get the voice off your case. That's a different problem than the voice stabbing you, so we have to look for a different solution. Why do you think the voice wants you to stab yourself?

Client: I have no idea.

Therapist: No idea at all?

Client: No.

Therapist: If you were to take a wild guess, what would your guess be?

Client: I wouldn't.

Therapist: I realize that, but what if you did?

Client: I said I wouldn't.

Therapist: OK, I'm clear on that. But just hypothetically, let's say you did make a guess—just to get me off your back.

Client: Great. Well, I'd say it's to stop me from talking about the abuse.

Therapist: Why would you make that guess?

Client: Because the threats always get worse when I talk or journal about the abuse.

Therapist: OK, let me ask the voice about that. Voice, is that right, do you not want her talking about the abuse?

Client: The voice said, "That's right, genius."

Therapist: Well, thanks for the compliment. Why is it important for her not to talk about the abuse?

Client: Because it's no one else's business.

Therapist: I see. Whose rule is that, that it's no one else's business?

Client: The voice says it's his rule.

Therapist: I got that, but my question is, where did you get that rule from?

Client: Her father.

Therapist: Oh, so the voice got the rule from your father. The voice apparently thinks it's very important to follow Dad's rules then.

Client: It was; otherwise we really got it.

Therapist: So the voice is trying to protect you from extra punishment by your dad, then?

Client: I guess.

Therapist: Well, that's good to know. Really, the voice isn't your enemy, it's trying to protect you. The way the voice is going about it is unpleasant and upsetting for you, but the intention is good. Would you agree?

Client: If you put it that way, yeah, I guess.

Therapist: Well, I have another question for the voice, then. Voice, if I try to get Jennifer to talk and journal less about the abuse, would you agree to back off on the threats for a while? Not forever, just for a while?

Client: The voice said "It's about time someone got her to shut up."

Therapist: I'll take that as a "yes"—good. So, Voice, this is how it works: Not only do I not want to get rid of you, in fact I want you to participate more in therapy. I figure you know a lot about what's going on inside, and you could provide me a lot of good advice and guidance, since I'm pretty much in the dark about a lot of what goes on in there.

Client: So now the voices get to be in charge?

Therapist: No, that would be swinging the pendulum too far the other way. What I'm talking about is discussing, listening, negotiating, and trying to understand the voices' points of view. The person who needs to be in charge is you as a *whole person*. This process of internal consultation, communication, and cooperation is how to get there. If you could form a working team inside, maybe the civil war that's been going on could stop eventually.

Client: That would be good.

Therapist: OK, then. No more trying to get rid of the voices. They're not the enemy.

Client: OK, OK.

Therapist: Good. You've made a lot of progress already. There's lots more to do, but these are steps in the right direction.

The therapist has validated, aligned with, and praised, accurately, both "the client" and the Voice. The therapist is modeling the style of communication with the voices that the client needs to learn. Although structural dissociation is in place, and even though one works with the separate self structures as separate units at a microcosmic level, at the macrocosmic level, everything is directed toward self-soothing, affect management, self-worth and self-respect. You can't love yourself if you hate the dissociated parts of yourself.

24
Developing Internal Safe Places

Internal safe places are important structures for self-soothing. Safe places can calm and de-escalate traumatized child parts; this reduces the need for addictions and punitive internal behaviour towards child parts. Safe places can take any form but they are typically rooms, gardens, beaches or country settings. The central paradox of DID applies to safe places: They are not literally real, but they are psychologically real. It is important not to get lost in the details of the inner landscape, which can be very elaborate at times.

Developing internal safe places involves transformation of the existing landscape and "construction" of new quarters. This was illustrated in the chapter on increasing internal communication and cooperation.

This chapter covers

- The Rationale for Internal Safe Places

- Building Internal Safe Places

The Rationale for Internal Safe Places

Safe places are not ends in themselves. Usually, they no longer exist post-integration because there are no separate parts left to live in them. They are an interim self-soothing and containment strategy that makes use of the intense, vivid, inner world of people with DID and DDNOS. The ability to construct a subjectively real, visually distinct inner world can be related to the ability to imagine Middle Earth, a science fiction world, the characters in a play, or, indeed, any new creation in the arts and sciences. The ability to create safe places is a gift.

That said, the vivid inner world is also a two-edged sword. It can become a place to hide from responsibility and the outside world. It can be used as a drug. People can get lost in the glamour and excitement of the inner cast of characters, their secrets, dalliances, disputes, and friendships. Really, there is nothing glamorous about an abused, neglected child retreating into fantasy.

People with DID and DDNOS can become intensely absorbed in expressive therapy tasks and tasks in the inner world. Great progress can be made by using safe places effectively.

Building Internal Safe Places

It is important to leave the construction of safe places, or any other navigation in the inner landscape, under the control of the client. The therapist consults and makes suggestions but the client carries out the tasks. Too much control or hypnotic guidance by the therapist can foster dependency and regression. Formal hypnotic inductions, elaborate relaxation procedures or other special rituals are not required. The therapist can be practical and matter-of-fact in manner and can use a regular tone of voice.

The conversation could go as follows:

Therapist: You seem to be feeling a lot of anxiety. What are you anxious about?
Client: I don't know.
Therapist: Does anybody else inside you know?
Client: I don't know.
Therapist: Well, look inside and see if you can tell where the anxiety is coming from.
Client: The children.
Therapist: How do you know that?
Client: I can feel it.
Therapist: Can you see them?
Client: No, they're in their room.
Therapist: Is anyone in there with them?
Client: No.
Therapist: Is it dark in there?
Client: Yes.
Therapist: How about getting them some light?
Client: Why?
Therapist: Scared children don't want to be alone in the dark.
Client: That makes sense.
Therapist: Could you go into their room and ask them what's the matter?
Client: I don't go in there.
Therapist: Why not?
Client: It's not my room.
Therapist: True, but you're the adult. Are you checking on what's going on with the children in your own house?
Client: I'm not in charge.
Therapist: Who is?
Client: No one.
Therapist: No wonder the kids feel frightened, then. Are you willing to help them or not?
Client: I guess.
Therapist: What are you willing to do for them?
Client: I don't know what they want.
Therapist: Could you ask them?
Client: I guess so.
Therapist: Go ahead.
Client: Now?
Therapist: Yes. Ask the children what they would like in their room.
Client: They said, "Books and a TV."
Therapist: Anything else?
Client: I don't know. They didn't say.
Therapist: And you, the adult in the house, are powerless to find out?
Client: No.
Therapist: Find out, then. Unless the plan is to continue ignoring the children like you have been. That plan doesn't seem to have been working.
Client: No, it hasn't.
Therapist: Would the kids like you to read to them?
Client: They said, "Yes."
Therapist: Good. So don't forget.

Client: I won't. They seem happy.

Therapist: Not surprising. They've been waiting a long time.

Client: Yeah, I've really done a bad job with them.

Therapist: You were never taught how to nurture yourself. From now, moving forward, you can either beat yourself up for that, or start treating the children like you deserved to be treated as a child.

Client: I'm tired of beating myself up.

Therapist: Good. Time to stop, then.

The details vary from case to case, and from situation to situation within the same case, but the principles of safe places are simple, therefore exhaustive examples are not necessary. Creating safe places is a variation on imagining you are walking on the beach while you are sitting in a dentist's chair. It is also related to visualization exercises used in sports psychology, and to strategies recommended by motivational speakers.

25
Orienting Parts of the System to the Body and the Present

Especially in DID, and less so in DDNOS, parts literally may not know that they are in the same body. They may give the date as 1972, 1983, or some other time in the past. In the 1980's and into the 1990's, orienting the parts to the body and the present tended to be left until later on in the therapy. The idea was that trust had to be built, a therapeutic relationship formed, and memories processed first. Gradually it became apparent that there are many benefits to doing the orientation earlier in treatment.

This chapter will cover

- Rationale for Orienting Parts Early in Therapy

- Clues That Parts Are Not Oriented

- Techniques for Orientation

A Rationale for Orienting Parts to the Body and the Present Early in Therapy

Core components of PTSD include hyperarousal, flashbacks, and floods of traumatic feelings and sensations in response to minor triggers in the present, such as hearing a car backfire. I usually use the example of the Vietnam vet who is in his backyard ten years after the war, cooking on his barbecue. A news helicopter flies overhead and the vet, a former Navy Seal, dives under a hedge and starts hallucinating a combat scene.

What do we conclude? That the Navy Seal is a *hysteric*, weak, or trying to get attention? No, we conclude that he has PTSD and is being triggered. He is having a reaction that is way out of proportion to the present, but it is not out of proportion to the reality of the past. The problem is that the vet is transferring his reaction to the past onto the present, where it is out of proportion to the current threat.

This is the problem in PTSD: The person is stuck in fight-or-flight mode. In DID cases, there is a very convenient way to get a handle on this problem. In a non-DID vet, you can't just point out that it is 2009 and expect the triggering to stop. The vet already knows that.

In DID, however, child, adolescent, and other alters often literally believe it is 1972 or 1983. They are in high alert mode, ready to scramble the jets and launch the nukes at any moment. They are responding to the present as if it is the present of 1972; the abuse just happened yesterday, it is going to happen again tomorrow, and the secrets must be kept at all costs. The alters will do whatever it takes—threaten death, self-mutilate, make the host catatonic—these strategies are justified by the threat assessment.

If the terror-alert parts are oriented to the body and the present, and brought into the current year, and if they really comprehend that they are much safer now, then they de-escalate automatically. The level of hyperarousal drops down, everyone can listen more carefully, and the desperate countermeasures do not need to be activated. One can then work on other treatment tasks and goals in non-emergency mode.

Orienting the parts to the body has an additional benefit. Often, one part is threatening, trying to kill, or cutting or burning another part, without realizing that there is only one body. The part thinks that the host's body is bleeding while his body is unaffected. If the part realizes that he is bleeding, too, a thorough reevaluation of the cost-benefit of the behaviour is required. Additionally, the body is bigger, stronger, and older now, and is better able to defend itself, so the level of terror alert can be reduced for that reason as well.

Clues That Parts Are Not Oriented

Whenever there are surges of strong affect or physiological sensation of unknown origin, early in therapy, the odds are high that they are coming from parts who are stuck in the past. Internal alarm reactions, physical scrambling of parts in the internal landscape, sudden disconnections of the internal world from the host or the therapist, angry or threatening postures by parts, rigid adherence to the family rules from childhood, and extreme loyalty to the perpetrators, are all clues that parts may be locked in the past.

Sometimes a part may understand cognitively that the year is 2009, but still operate emotionally as if it is 1983. One should point this out, and then begin the work of desensitization. If there are parts locked in dungeons, underground tunnels, or other dismal locations, it is likely that they are stuck in the past, as are the parts responsible for containing, threatening, and punishing them. This is also true for parts living in rooms, buildings, or locations that are copies of actual external locations from childhood.

Anytime there is a belief in *programming* or *programmed parts*, the cognitive processes are being dominated by magical thinking, and parts are probably not oriented to the body and the present. This is true no matter what the historical reality of the programming, and the interventions are the same no matter what assumption the therapist makes about the reality of the programming. In the absence of conclusive independent proof one way or the other, the stance of therapeutic neutrality about the objective, historical reality of the memories is the ethical approach to take, unless there is an overriding duty to warn.

Techniques for Orienting Parts

A conversation designed to orient parts to the body and the present might go as follows:

Therapist: Sorry, I didn't catch your name.
Client: Susie.
Therapist: Nice to meet you, Susie. Do you know who I am?
Client: You're the doctor man.
Therapist: Right. I work with Susan to help her feel better.
Client: Do you give needles?
Therapist: No, I just talk. Nothing scary happens here.
Client: Oh. Would you like to talk to somebody else?
Therapist: Sure. Is there someone else who wants to talk to me?
Client: I think so.

At this point the client switches to an adolescent identity responsible for much of the self-mutilation.

Client: What do you want?
Therapist: I thought you wanted to talk to me.
Client: Whatever.
Therapist: Have we spoken before?
Client: Yeah, once.
Therapist: I thought so. What's your name again?
Client: You know who I am.
Therapist: Well, I'm guessing you're Suzanne.
Client: You guessed right. Don't try to get me to stop cutting her. She deserves it.
Therapist: I see. Before we get into that, I'd like to ask you a couple of questions, if you don't mind.
Client: Go for it.
Therapist: What would you say the date is today?
Client: I don't know; I don't keep track of things like that.
Therapist: Well, what would be your best guess?
Client: I don't know. June 3, 1982. Why?
Therapist: I thought that might be the case. I'm going to try to explain something to you that may sound really unbelievable. It's actually May 9, 2009.
Client: Yeah, right.
Therapist: There a couple of reasons I'm talking to you about this. If you really understand that it's 2009, things would be better for you. Here in 2009 you're no longer living at home and you're no longer being abused. Things are much calmer and safer for you in 2009. I don't expect you to believe this right away, though.
Client: That's the only thing you've said so far that makes any sense.
Therapist: That's better than nothing making sense. By the way, how old are you?
Client: Fourteen.
Therapist: And how old is Susan?
Client: Old.
Therapist: Right. She's 39 years old. So you're 14 and it's 1982, so you were born in 1968, then.
Client: If you say so.
Therapist: And where is Susan right now?
Client: I don't know. She left.
Therapist: Is she here in this room?

Suzanne looks around, then replies:

Client: No. She must have gone out.
Therapist: So that means that you and Susan are physically separate people. She can physically leave the room, but you and your body are still here. Is that right?
Client: Yeah.
Therapist: OK. I'd like you to do one thing for me now. Could you raise your right hand in the air?

Unperturbed, Suzanne raises her right hand in front of her face.

Therapist: Does that look like a 14-year old girl's hand to you?
Client: No.
Therapist: Whose ring is that?
Client: Hers.

Therapist: And how did Susan's ring get on your finger?

Client: I don't know. She must have lost it. I must have found it and put it on.

Therapist: But look at your hand again. Does that look like your 14-year old hand?

Client: No. You're confusing me.

Therapist: Well, let me explain what I think is going on. There are two worlds, the inside world and the outside world. In the inside world, where you live most of the time, you are 14 and you have a separate 14-year old body. But here in the outside world, there's only one body, that you share with Susan. You aren't a separate person from Susan; you're actually part of her and you live inside her mind.

Client: Yeah, right.

Therapist: I don't expect you to believe me right away, but if you check it out for yourself, you'll see that what I'm saying is true. You live inside Susan's body in 2009. That's why she's 39 now, because it's 2009. While you've been in the inside world, you haven't always paid attention, and you haven't noticed that a lot of years have gone by: 1982, 1983, 1984, year by year until now it's 2009. Now, in 2009, when you come to the surface of the body to talk to me, you use Susan's 39-year old body to talk to me. That's why when you raise your right hand, it's Susan's 39-year old hand that goes up.

Client: I'm not 39. I'm not old.

Therapist: I understand that, and in the inside world that's true. But not in the outside world; in the outside world you share one body with Susan. What I'd like you to do is look out through her eyes once in a while and check it out for yourself. Like when she's watching TV, if the news comes on, look at what the date is; if you're at the supermarket, check out the magazines and newspapers. Look at the cars, and hair styles, and clothes—you'll see they're different from what you knew in 1982.

Client: I don't believe you.

Therapist: I don't expect you to believe me. What I'm suggesting you could try is checking it out for yourself. Then you can decide whether you believe your own experience. One more thing—when was the last time you cut on Susan?

Client: I don't know. A few days ago.

Therapist: Where did you cut her?

Client: Her left arm. She deserved it.

Therapist: Yeah, you said. And when you cut her, did that have any effect on your arm?

Client: No, I wouldn't cut on myself. I don't want scars.

Therapist: Would you mind looking at your left arm and telling me what you see?

Client: That's her arm, not my arm.

Therapist: Would you mind raising your left arm?

Client: Is this a trick?

Therapist: No. I'm trying to help you understand what's really going on.

Client: I don't want to talk anymore.

Therapist: That's fine. We can talk more later. But I really would like you to look out through Susan's eyes and see for yourself. Could you do that?

Client: OK. Bye.

Therapist: Bye.

It is vital to remember that the defenses are protecting the person from overwhelming feelings and conflicts. One should not push on them too hard or too fast. It's tough to find out that you are 25 years older than you want to be, especially if you are a middle-aged woman rather than an adolescent male. Adolescent males are often mortified to learn that they have no male genitalia in the outside world. Often, they genuinely do not know that their experience of receptive homosexual anal intercourse is an illusion, and that they have actually been having heterosexual vaginal intercourse. The news needs to be delivered directly and honestly, but with tact and sensitivity.

In a later session, the therapist might be able to explain more to Suzanne about the benefits of arriving in the present:

Therapist: So what I'm suggesting is this: Life is a lot better in 2009. Instead of being trapped in abuse and neglect, you live with Susan, her husband, and her children.
Client: Her kids are cool.
Therapist: Susan explained that you play with them quite a bit.
Client: They don't know it's me. They think their mother has a lot of different moods.
Therapist: Well, here's something to consider; if you agree to stop cutting on Susan, I'll work with her to let you share in the family life more. You can practice being close by, and participating from the background more, and she can work on including you more. I'll work with her on that—it's a tradeoff—more involvement and time for you in exchange for no cutting. What do you say?
Client: Can I do what I want sometimes?
Therapist: Sure, as long as it's not unhealthy or dangerous.
Client: I knew you'd say that.
Therapist: You know, Susan needs to loosen up a bit and have more fun—maybe you could help her with that. If you got more involved in her life, there could be benefits to you—like you could share in the love she gets from her children.
Client: I'm not sleeping with her nerd husband.
Therapist: That's fine. I agree with that. It's inappropriate for a 14 year old to be having sex. That's between Susan and her husband.

This comment by Suzanne puts some future therapy work on the agenda. When Susan becomes more integrated, she will have more of Suzanne's characteristics, which include spunk, adventurousness, irreverence, independence, and intolerance for hypocrisy. This will put a strain on her marriage because her "nerd" husband has adjusted to years with an inhibited wife who seldom steps out of her dutiful domestic routine. He may like some of the changes and increased functioning that will be the by-product of greater integration but he may find an increase in independence and assertiveness difficult to adjust to. These are tasks for the late stage of therapy.

In this later work, Susan's resistance to integration could be as much or more about the adjustments she will have to make in the present and future, as it is about her past trauma. She likely fears that her husband won't love her if he sees who she really is, and she may fear also that she will leave him if she gets too well. These concerns are generic to recovery, whether one has DID or not, and they illustrate the rule that most of DID therapy is not about the DID. Most of the work is about the human being, not about the dissociative disorder.

26
Forming a Working Alliance with Persecutor Parts of the System

Forming a working alliance with persecutor parts of the system is important when there is a dissociated psychological structure in place, as there is in DDNOS and DID. The same techniques can be used when there are hostile or negative voices and the diagnosis is schizophrenia or schizoaffective disorder. In that case, the work may be done by talking through, rather than direct communication with the voices while they are in executive control. It is a prediction of the Trauma Model that 25%-40% of people who meet DSM and structured interview criteria for schizophrenia have a dissociative subtype of schizophrenia (Ross, 2004; 2007). People with dissociative schizophrenia can be treated with Trauma Model Therapy just as effectively as people with DID.

People with DID or DDNOS, and people with dissociative schizophrenia, are by and large the same people. Either diagnostic label can be applied, depending on the preference of the clinician. If the diagnosis is schizophrenia, the clinician will usually be more comfortable talking through to the voices rather than asking for a switch of executive control, but this is due to the comfort level and counter-transference of the clinician, not the reality of the client. A full discussion of the relationship between DID and schizophrenia can be found in *Schizophrenia: Innovations in Diagnosis and Treatment* (Ross, 2004).

In this chapter we cover

- Characteristics of Persecutor Parts

- Functions of Persecutor Parts

- Techniques for Forming a Working Alliance with Persecutor Parts

Characteristics of Persecutor Parts

Persecutor parts were present in 85% of cases of multiple personality disorder in large case series published in the late 1980's—no large surveys have been done since. There is no reason to think that the percentage has changed since 1989. Persecutor parts are angry, hostile, critical, punishing, controlling, and abusive. They may verbally command suicide, abuse child parts internally, mutilate the host personality's body (which they often believe is separate from their own body), overdose, or punish other parts by giving them flashbacks. They may starve other parts, or carry out any number of unhealthy behaviours internally or externally.

Persecutor parts may appear as children but more commonly seem adolescent or adult. They may be introjects of the parents; both the persecutor and the host may believe that the persecutor is literally the parent. Even if the persecutor has a name and identity other than one of the parents, he or she is often modeled on an abusive, critical, rejecting, or neglectful parent. A child persecutor may initially be disguised as a monster, mythical creature, or other entity. This identity may be very frightening and intimidating to other child parts and even to the host. There may be more than one persecutor part, but typically one or a few parts carry out most of this role.

The persecutors were often kind, soothing protectors when originally formed in childhood. Often, they transformed into persecutors in late childhood or adolescence in response to deepening self-blame and self-hatred. Basically, they are still protectors because they are part of the overall defensive system, but they are protecting through angry, self-destructive, thoughts and behaviours.

Persecutors often blame, hate, and punish other parts for causing the childhood abuse, not stopping it, or not earning love from the parents. They may be focused on failure to prevent a specific assault or event, or on the overall pattern of childhood. Often, they blame other parts but not themselves, at least overtly. They may also feel ashamed and guilty about their failure to protect the other parts successfully.

Persecutors often hold healthy aspects of the person's anger, resentment, and assertiveness. As a result, they often see the host personality as a wimp or weakling, which then justifies further punishment of the host and the body. A persecutor can become a key component of recovery, once a treatment alliance is formed with him or her.

Functions of Persecutor Parts

As for all parts, the description and function of persecutors is intertwined. One persecutor job is to hold and contain the anger so that the host does not feel it or express it. The child was often punished severely for any display of anger, tears, or distress. The host personality often has an *anger* phobia while the persecutor has a *niceness* phobia, so to speak.

The persecutor almost always holds the most energized, angry aspects of the locus of control shift. The persecutor hates the host so that the host does not have to hate herself quite as much. The persecutor occupies the perpetrator position on the Victim-Rescuer-Perpetrator triangle: through abuse of other parts, the persecutor creates an illusion of power, control, and mastery, and helps reduce the tendency of the client-as-a-whole to play the victim role.

The protector parts fill the role of rescuer in the internal system, while the victim role is commonly played by the host and child parts. All three points of the triangle are part of the geometry, and all three must be engaged in therapy.

Persecutors often hold much of the loyalty to the perpetrators. Whereas child parts may idealize one or both parents and cling to the good parent, the persecutors identify with and remain loyal to the bad parents. The persecutor often views the parental abuse and neglect as necessary and justified.

The persecutor is often both the enemy and the friend of the host. When the host carries out a behaviour, the host can get the benefit of it but disavow any responsibility for the "bad" actions. At other times, the host may let the persecutor out to handle an aggressive boyfriend, a controlling boss, or any other conflicted or threatening situation. The host may simultaneously hate the persecutor while assigning her situations to take care of—the host usually is in denial of how she actively vacates executive control so that the persecutor can take over and take care of business. Instead she sees herself as the passive victim of the persecutor taking over. This is a form of host resistance, not a fact about how the system works.

Techniques for Forming a Working Alliance with Persecutor Parts

The first step in forming an alliance with persecutor parts is to work on changing the beliefs and attitude of the host personality (the part who is out front and in control most of the time). This was reviewed in Chapter 22, on resistance. Assuming that sufficient work has been done on host resistance, the next step is to work directly with the parts, which can be done with them in executive control or by talking through to them.

A conversation with a persecutor part might go as follows:

Therapist: So your job is to take her back to the cult.
Client: Right.
Therapist: How did that get to be your job?
Client: I was programmed for it. That's my job.
Therapist: Do you have any interest in changing jobs?
Client: No.
Therapist: Hypothetically, what would happen if you said to yourself, "That's it, I'm done with this cult stuff. I'm not going back."
Client: I'd never say that.
Therapist: I know; it's just a hypothetical.
Client: What does that mean?
Therapist: *Hypothetically* means *just imagine it for a minute, even though it's not real.*
Client: That's dumb. I want to be in the cult.
Therapist: Why?
Client: That's my job.
Therapist: You keep saying that, but how did that get to be your job?
Client: I was trained for it.
Therapist: Who trained you?
Client: Satan.
Therapist: Was it Satan himself or did he work through someone's body?
Client: It was Satan
Therapist: With bat wings and a forked tail.
Client: No, it was Satan but he was in her father. He worked through her father.
Therapist: I see.
Client: We all serve Satan.
Therapist: What's the benefit of that to you?
Client: What do you mean?
Therapist: I mean, what do you get from serving Satan? Why do you like it?
Client: It's my job.
Therapist: Right. What would happen if you decided to change jobs?
Client: I wouldn't.
Therapist: I know, but if you did for some reason, what would happen?
Client: They'd kill me.
Therapist: Who?
Client: The cult.
Therapist: So if you stopped obeying Satan, your father would kill you?
Client: He's not my father.
Therapist: So if you stopped obeying Satan, her father would kill you?
Client: It would be Satan, not her father.

Therapist: Do you like her father?

Client: I don't care about him. He is just a vessel for Satan.

Therapist: So you wouldn't mind disobeying her father; you don't care what he thinks?

Client: I don't care about him.

Therapist: What if Satan never was inside her father, and it was just her father lying to you to scare you and get power over you?

Client: I'm not scared of anything.

Therapist: Seems like you're scared of Satan.

Client: That's different.

Therapist: Different how?

Client: I want to serve him; I want to be with him forever.

Therapist: But if you don't follow the rules and Satan gets pissed at you, you might get in serious trouble, huh?

Client: I wouldn't do that.

Therapist: How does Satan like you talking about this in therapy?

Client: He isn't afraid of you.

Therapist: That's good. Is there any chance I could talk to Satan directly?

Client: He doesn't talk to humans. He doesn't come down here.

Therapist: But he talks to you.

Client: That's different. I serve him.

Therapist: Satan isn't chicken, is he? I mean, if he's scared to talk in therapy, I understand.

Client: He isn't scared of anybody.

Therapist: What about God; is he scared of Him?

Client: No.

Therapist: So is Satan going to talk to me or not?

At this point the client switches.

Client: What do you want?

Therapist: Are you Satan?

Client: Yes.

Therapist: Thanks for coming to talk with me.

Client: What do you want?

Therapist: I understand you live inside her father's body.

Client: That's right.

Therapist: But then how are you inside her body right now, using it to talk to me?

Client: What do you mean?

Therapist: By the way, what year would you say it is right now?

Client: I'm not interested in years.

Therapist: OK, but if you were to say what year it is, what year would you say?

Client: 1979.

Therapist: And right now you live inside her father's body here on earth?

Client: Right.

Therapist: Did you know it's 2009 and her father died in 1984?

Client: Huh?

Therapist: You can't be in her father's body on earth right now because her father has been dead for years. In fact, you live inside her body here in 2009. That's why you're using her body to talk to me right now.

Client: I can use any body I want.

Therapist: I understand. But I'd like you to think about something. Maybe you're not the real Satan. Maybe you're a part of her named Satan who lives inside her body. Maybe her father tricked you into thinking you were the real Satan.

Client: I'm going now.

Therapist: OK. Bye. Thanks for talking with me. I hope I can talk to you again sometime.

The client switches back to the previous persecutor personality.

Therapist: Is that you, Damien?

Client: Yes.

Therapist: Were you listening while I was talking with Satan?

Client: Yes.

Therapist: What did you think?

Client: He was scared of you.

Therapist: I'm sorry I scared him. But if he was the real Satan, he wouldn't be scared of me, would he? Did you notice he still thinks it's 1979?

Client: Yeah.

Therapist: You know what? I think Satan is really a scared child part of you who took on the identity of Satan in order to feel strong and in order to please her father. I think it took a lot of guts for him to come out and talk with me.

Client: He says he is going to take over control of your body too.

Therapist: That doesn't bother me at all because I know that, really, that can't happen. Really, the Satan inside you doesn't have that kind of power.

Client: He thinks he does.

Therapist: That's OK, but we know better. It's going to be really sad for him when he realizes that her father is dead. He really wanted to be important to her father, didn't he?

Client: He is important. He's Satan.

Therapist: So you have been saying. You know, if he would ever like to change names, that would be fine. Maybe he's getting tired of being Satan.

Client: Maybe.

Therapist: I'll tell you what. I know that she wants to get rid of you and Satan. How about if I work with her to get her to change her attitude? If she would start to be nicer to you, maybe you wouldn't have to scare her with bad memories so much.

Client: That's how we control her.

Therapist: I know, but if she would work with you instead of against you, maybe you could ease back on the memories.

Client: Maybe. Satan says he'll think about it.

Therapist: Good. That's all I'm asking for right now, that you think about it. Nice talking to both you and Satan. Thanks for helping me to understand the two of you better.

Client: Bye.

Therapist: Later, alligator.

Client: I'm not an alligator.

Therapist: Good, 'cause I don't have a swamp for you to swim in here in my office.

Client: You should get one.

Therapist: I'll look into it.

Client: Bye. I'm going now.

Therapist: OK, I'll talk to Mary some more in that case.

The historical reality of the memories, as always, was irrelevant to this therapeutic conversation.

The persecutor alters flood the host with memories for the same reasons, whether the memories are historically accurate or internally generated. The therapist maintains therapeutic neutrality. Much later in the therapy, in the pre-integration or post-integration stages, the client might decide that the cult never existed in outside reality, or she might not change her mind about that. That is the client's to decide, not the therapist's. At this stage of therapy, questioning the reality of the cult would shame the persecutors and destroy the small alliance built with them to that point.

Orienting the parts to the body and the present is a major component of reframing them, forming a treatment alliance with them, and transforming them into protectors. The basic treatment technique is to treat them with dignity and respect, to listen empathically to their point of view, and to represent their legitimate interests in negotiations with the host personality.

Another client might have similar persecutors loyal to the father but no cult elements to her story:

Therapist: So you're the one who cuts on her. Why do you do that?
Client: To shut her up.
Therapist: Why do you want to shut her up?
Client: She's not supposed to talk about what happened.
Therapist: Says who?
Client: Those are the rules.
Therapist: I get that, but where did the rules come from?
Client: Her family.
Therapist: And you think it's important to obey the family rules?
Client: She should smarten up.
Therapist: What might happen if you break the rules and get caught?
Client: Bad things.
Therapist: I know. She told me about that. So you're really trying to protect her from herself. That's very kind of you.
Client: It's for her own good.
Therapist: I see that. But I see that you're not just this evil person who cuts her for no reason. You're trying to protect her. How about if I explain that to her so she understands better?
Client: I don't care.
Therapist: Do you care if I explain that to her?
Client: No. Just don't try to get her to talk about stuff she's not supposed to talk about.
Therapist: OK, I won't. I'll make you a deal: how about if I check with you regularly to see if we are talking about things that are all right to talk about? In fact, why don't you listen in carefully during therapy? Then if you think we are going in the wrong direction, you can just come out and let me know.
Client: You'd listen to what I think?
Therapist: Absolutely. You know a lot more about what's going on inside than I do. I'm kind of like a bull stumbling around in a china shop. You could be a big help to me by pointing out my mistakes before they happen.
Client: Nobody ever wanted to talk to me before.
Therapist: Probably because no one understood your role and how you're trying to keep her out of trouble.
Client: Could you explain that to Her Highness?
Therapist: I'd be glad to.
Client: You're not as stupid as I thought.
Therapist: Thanks. I'm working on it.

Client: That's all. I'm going now.
Therapist: OK, see you next session.

Switches do not happen at random, in life or in therapy. Persecutors often depart abruptly when their cover is about to be blown, or when they are about to get in trouble with other persecutors higher up in the chain of command. They do this not because they are bad, uncooperative, or resistant, but because they are frightened, traumatized, magical children stuck in a terrifying past reality. The key to working with them is to think of them as scared children.

27
Increasing Internal Communication and Cooperation

Increasing internal communication and cooperation is a major task in the therapy of DID and DDNOS. It is both a goal in and of itself, and a by-product of the other work. Sometimes one works directly on internal communication and cooperation, while other times this is achieved through focusing on other targets and goals. Resolving conflicted, ambivalent attachment to the perpetrator involves communication among parts, but also resolution of conflict within individual parts. Much of the work on attachment is done with the host in executive control, without addressing the parts directly. The parts participate in the process through leakage and generalization, and by actively listening in.

In this chapter we cover

- The Reasons for Increasing Internal Communication and Cooperation

- Treatment Techniques

The Reasons for Increasing Internal Communication and Cooperation

The problem with DID or DDNOS is the degree of conflict, antagonism, and civil war in the internal system. The analogy of a computer is useful. The plan is not to get rid of parts or build new ones. All the necessary chips and circuits are already in place. But if short circuits occur between different regions of the board, information doesn't flow freely throughout the system. This results in parts of the system being unaware of each other and working at cross purposes. The idea is to repair the short circuits so the board functions normally.

Some clients believe it is creative or desirable to have DID as long as the system is co-conscious and working together. Our perspective is this is like having a little bit of cancer. Nobody has definitive follow-up data, but experience to date indicates that people who stop at the functional DDNOS level can relapse back into full, dysfunctional DID if they experience severe trauma in the future. The fully integrated person is less likely to relapse. Further, a desire to maintain dissociative defenses reflects a level of internal conflict and/or trauma that is being avoided and a choice to remain in the victim position.

Plus, if therapists are going to bill insurance companies for treatment of diagnoses listed in the DSM, they have committed themselves to defining DID and DDNOS as mental disorders. It can't be desirable to have a disorder that requires treatment; or, alternatively, it is contradictory to bill an insurance company for treatment of a disorder that isn't really a disorder, but instead is an acceptable choice. It is inconsistent to have it both ways at once.

Really, no therapist is against internal communication and cooperation. The disagreement is about the final 10% of the journey of integration, not the first 90%. Internal communication and cooperation bring the person closer to health. The more parts are oriented to the body and the present, sharing information and problem solving, the better the overall functioning and healing of the person.

Treatment Techniques

Every component of therapy is in one way or another, directly or indirectly, designed to increase internal communication and cooperation. Here I will illustrate a few techniques for direct practice of internal communication. The therapist is talking to the host personality:

Therapist: So when Sally comes out, where do you go?
Client: I don't know, I'm just gone . . . far away.
Therapist: Are you awake or asleep?
Client: Usually I'm asleep; sometimes I'm there in the dark, awake, but not hearing or seeing what's going on.
Therapist: And when you're out, where is Sally?
Client: In her room.
Therapist: When she's in her room, can she hear what we are saying?
Client: No.
Therapist: Would you be willing to practice co-consciousness a little right now? We wouldn't talk about anything big at all.
Client: I don't know how to do that.
Therapist: It's not that hard once you get the hang of it. For the first step, I will call Sally out. But when she comes out, I'd like you to stay nearby and listen, instead of going far away like you usually do. Would that be OK?
Client: I can try.
Therapist: OK. Sally. Sally, could you come out? Sally, I'd like to talk with you.
Client: Hi.
Therapist: Hi, Sally. Were you listening when I was talking to Susan just now?
Client: No, I was in my room.
Therapist: I thought so. Well, you know how Susan usually goes far away when you are out?
Client: I don't think she likes me. She thinks I'm bad.
Therapist: Actually, she doesn't know much about you. But I bet if she got to know you, you guys would be able to work out your differences.
Client: Really?
Therapist: Yeah, you're nice. You're fun. So here's what I'd like to do: When I was talking to Susan I asked her to stay close by inside and listen when you came out. I'd like you to stay out while I ask her a few questions—she'll answer on the inside, and you'll tell me what she said. Is that all right?
Client: Yes.
Therapist: Good. Susan, remember, I want you to be awake and listening inside like we talked about. I'd like you to be close by but don't come all the way out. Sally will still be out front. Susan, are you there and listening?
Client: She said, "Yes."
Therapist: Susan, do you have anything you'd like to say to Sally?
Client: She said she wants to get to know me. Maybe she doesn't hate me.
Therapist: Maybe not. Susan, Sally has been thinking that the reason you haven't been talking to her is, you don't like her. Is that right?
Client: She said, "No."
Therapist: What is the reason?
Client: She didn't know how.
Therapist: Well, now that she does, maybe you guys could start talking. Would you be willing to do that?
Client: Yes.

Therapist: Excellent! OK, now I'd like Susan to come out and, Sally, I want you to go back inside but not too far. I'd like you to stay close by and listening, like Susan is right now. So you'd just trade places. Could you do that?

Client: I'm here.

Therapist: Susan?

Client: Yes, it's me.

Therapist: Can you check and see if Sally is close by?

Client: She is. I can feel her.

Therapist: Could you ask her a question?

Client: What should I ask?

Therapist: Anything. It doesn't matter.

At this point the client looks tranced out for thirty seconds. She then regains her focus.

Client: I asked her what she likes to do and she said, "Watch TV."

Therapist: Would you be willing to watch TV with her?

Client: I guess.

Therapist: You guess? That doesn't sound very enthusiastic.

Client: No, I could . . . I will.

Therapist: I bet she would appreciate that. One other thing, though: When Sally is in her room and you're out front, it seems as if you have no way of communicating with her. Is that correct?

Client: Yes.

Therapist: Sounds like the inside house needs an intercom system

Client: What do you mean?

Therapist: I think you should install an intercom throughout the house, with an on-off switch inside every room. Then everyone can communicate with each other when they want, but they can also turn the switch off if they want.

Client: I don't know how to do that.

Therapist: You just do it. Remember, this is a world you have created using your mind. You can change it if you want. It's your world. You just have to decide, just like you decided to be close by when Sally was out. Then it will happen.

Client: I didn't know I could do that.

Therapist: You can. So what are you going to do?

Client: Wait a minute . . . OK, it's in.

Therapist: How much did that cost you in materials and labor?

Client: It's free.

Therapist: Good deal. Inside home renovations are a lot cheaper than outside ones. Would you be willing to walk around in the house a bit and get to know the people in it a little better?

Client: I'm not going in the basement.

Therapist: Why not?

Client: Too dark and scary.

Therapist: OK, we'll leave that for a while. Where is Sally now?

Client: She went back to her room.

Therapist: Can you try using the intercom?

Client: She can hear me. She said, "Hi."

Therapist: You're pretty handy.

Client: I guess so.

Therapist: Well, good. You learned some new skills today that will help a lot in the future. That's what inter-personality communication and cooperation is all about.

The client can carry out any number of tasks in the inside world that are designed to increase co-consciousness. It is useful to practice internal communication on neutral topics initially, and then proceed to more charged and conflicted topics. All efforts to listen to the voices, talk to the voices, journal with other parts, pay attention to feelings and impulses that intrude from elsewhere in the mind, or interact with others in the internal landscape are exercises in increased communication and cooperation.

The host personality can write messages to other parts in journals and they may write their responses later. The host may have amnesia for the entries written by other parts, or may be conscious but experience them as automatic writing. The therapy can be compared to a labour negotiation or mediation exercise in which the mediator—the therapist—shuttles back and forth between the parties modeling good communication skills. The goal is for the therapist to assist the communication, then step out of the loop so that the parts communicate with each other.

It is not a good idea to spend extended periods of time in therapy having conversations with other parts for which the host has amnesia. This fosters dependence on the therapist and reinforces the idea that the amnesia cannot be overcome. Intra-session amnesia cannot be reduced to zero for the entirety of therapy, but it should not be amplified or enabled. Rather than doing extensive work with other parts behind an amnesia barrier, the therapist should ask why the amnesia is still necessary in the present, and should work on reducing it. If this is done in a stepwise fashion consistent with paced desensitization, flooding will not occur.

28
Focusing on Adaptation in the Present

Over the years, we have learned to maintain a focus on adaptation in the present. This is a matter of balance. In order to live better in the present, one must deal with the past; on the other hand, in order to face the past, one must focus on improving life in the present. A therapy can be out of balance in either direction—too much focus on the past, or too much focus on the present. Trauma therapists tend to err in the direction of the past, whereas mental health professionals who do not work within a trauma model tend to focus too much on the present.

As a client, one can hide in the past to avoid the present, or hide in the present to avoid the past. Both forms of avoidance can be over-utilized at different stages of therapy. Overall, recovery involves a focus on all three dimensions of time: past, present, and future. Much of the motivation for recovery comes from the hope of imagining and then building a better future.

In this chapter, we will cover

- Focusing on Adaptation in the Present

- Balancing Past, Present, and Future

- Future-oriented Treatment Techniques

Focusing on Adaptation in the Present

The past informs and influences our perception and experience of the present. The client with a history of abuse and trauma finds himself stuck in memories, beliefs, and behaviours that originated in past experiences. Simply dwelling on the past is not helpful or healing. Ignoring and avoiding the impact of the past on the present is also not helpful or healing.

Life is always lived in the present; all change occurs in the present. In therapy, *the present* does not mean a single instant of time—it means the present circumstances, the recent past, and the recent future, *what is going on now*.

Signs that there is an insufficient focus on adaptation in the present can include many different problems. Each of these problems can have other causes, or multiple simultaneous causes. The signs of insufficient focus on adaptation in the present are red flags. The therapist can utilize these cues to consider the possibility that the client is hiding in the past, to avoid more pressing or painful conflicts in the present.

SIGNS OF INSUFFICIENT FOCUS ON ADAPTATION IN THE PRESENT

• Little or no progress in recovery

• Symptoms getting worse, especially PTSD and dissociative symptoms

• Endless crises or double binds

• Increasing dependency on the therapist or institution

• Increasing resistance to hospital discharge

• Client repeatedly diverts the therapy to past trauma

• Client uses past trauma as an excuse for continuing current self-destructive behaviour and relationships

• Client actively refuses to talk about current conflicts, trauma, or abuse

• Therapist notices that she (the therapist) is vague about current circumstances

• Client states a primary goal of "memory work," "working on the abuse," or something similar

---

In the hospital setting, inpatients may be admitted in crisis, flooded with flashbacks and feelings, while experiencing escalation in self-harm, addictions, and acting out. Often, the primary problem is in the present—the symptoms are being driven by abuse, neglect, loneliness, or fear in the present, rather than by the past. Doing *memory work* in this scenario reinforces the symptoms and the avoidance. It can lead to interminable admissions, with escalation in symptoms prior to any attempt at discharge.

A similar pattern can occur in outpatient work, at a more muted and less intense level. The signs of an insufficient focus on the present are basically deterioration, escalation of symptoms, and failure of progress. There is often a secret that needs to be told, which may be ongoing victimization, addiction, or entanglement in a toxic relationship. Not uncommonly, an enmeshed relationship with a parent is a factor: the client may focus on the "bad" behaviour of that parent in the past, to avoid dealing with enmeshment and conflicted attachment in the present. The problem is not so much that the parent was bad in the past; rather it is the unrealistic wish that the parent will be good in the future.

As in all aspects of therapy, unresolved, conflicted, and ambivalent attachment is often at the root of insufficient focus on the present.

Often, the best intervention is simply bringing up the possibility that something not talked about is going on in the present. The therapist can state this as a hypothesis to be explored, rather than as a fact or certainty. An intervention might go as follows:

Therapist: You seem stuck. Your symptoms have gotten worse and you haven't made the usual amount of progress recently. Any idea why that might be?

Client: Nope.

Therapist: Well, often there's an elephant in the room that isn't being talked about. Is there anything going on that you haven't told me about?

Client: Maybe.

Therapist: Like what?

Client: I've been cutting again.

Therapist: Oh, I'm sorry to hear that. Why have you started cutting again?

Client: To make the flashbacks go away.

Therapist: Have your flashbacks gotten worse recently?

Client: Yeah.

Therapist: When did that start—the flashbacks getting worse?

Client: About a month ago.

Therapist: And when did you start cutting again?

Client: About three weeks ago.

Therapist: Did something happen before the flashbacks got worse?

Client: Yeah.

Therapist: What?

Client: I don't want to talk about it.

Therapist: And how well does not talking about things work for you?

Client: OK, OK.

Therapist: So. What happened?

Client: I said I don't want to talk about it.

Therapist: That's an option, all right. But if you won't talk about whatever it is, how do you expect me to help with the flashbacks, and how do you expect to stop cutting?

Client: I need to do more memory work on the abuse by my dad.

Therapist: The abuse when you were a kid?

Client: Yeah.

Therapist: I'm suggesting this is maybe not the priority right now. I'm working on the theory that you want to focus on the past in order to avoid talking about something more important, something that happened a month or so ago.

Client: So being abused by my dad isn't important?

Therapist: Nice try. It's your choice. Past or present, past or present?

Client: My boyfriend had sex with my best friend.

Therapist: When?

Client: A month ago.

Therapist: OK, now we can work on that. It can't be a coincidence that the flashbacks started getting worse right after that. What are the flashbacks about?

Client: The sexual abuse by my dad.

Therapist: To answer your previous question—of course we need to work on that more at some point, but right now I think the betrayal by your boyfriend is a higher priority.

Client: You're probably right.

Therapist: How did you find out about it?

Client: She told me.

From here, the therapy would focus on the betrayal by both the boyfriend and the best friend, a re-evaluation of both relationships, and a renewed commitment to no self-mutilation. The flashbacks of sexual abuse by the father are being reinforced by their function as an avoidance tactic; once this function is removed, their utility as defenses will vanish, and they will begin to ease off. Additionally, focusing on the betrayal by the boyfriend shifts the theme to loss and grief, and away from the active symptoms of PTSD. Processing the current trauma will also generalize to past betrayals by the father, thereby further reducing the flashbacks of sexual abuse by father.

It is always true that symptoms and behaviours have a context and a function in the present. They are not simply defenses against the past that have persisted into the present; rather, they have been molded and harnessed as defenses against conflicts in the present. The therapy needs to focus on both their origins and their current functions. This is true of all defenses, including *inside people*.

Balancing Past, Present, and Future

Balancing past, present, and future is a challenge for everyone, not just for trauma survivors. It is a general principle of healthy living. In the present, one learns from the past in order to build a better future. This is true of both individuals and societies. Like an individual, a culture can be excessively focused on the past, or handicapped by historical amnesia.

The main requirement is simply for the therapist to keep this balancing act consciously in mind, and to review it continuously.

Future-Oriented Treatment Techniques

Historically, over the last quarter of a century, trauma therapies have erred in the direction of too much focus on the past. The antidote to this error is a set of future-oriented treatment techniques and, more importantly, maintaining a general future orientation. This can be done through an ongoing review of life and treatment goals divided into short, medium, and long-term time frames.

A therapy session might involve the following interchange:

Therapist: What is your overall goal in therapy?
Client: I want to be well.
Therapist: That's an excellent goal, but the problem is, you can't really work on a global, overall goal like "being well." To get there, you have to boil things down to a specific set of goals and tasks. Being well is the outcome of working successfully on these specific tasks and goals.
Client: Like what, for instance?
Therapist: Well, let's look at that. In five years I would like you to be working at a supermarket in Vladivostok.
Client: Where's that?
Therapist: Russia.
Client: But I don't want to move to Russia.
Therapist: Oh, so this is about your goals then, not my goals?
Client: OK, I get it.
Therapist: So, where would you like to be five years from now, if everything worked out? I'm not asking you to be realistic. I mean what are your wishes, hopes, and dreams, even if they're not totally realistic?
Client: What's the use of having dreams? They always get ruined anyway.
Therapist: No dreams, no future. No future, no recovery. Do you think it's better to chase your dreams and only get halfway there, or to stay in the swamp in a funk?
Client: Boy, you're brutal.

Therapist: Thanks. So?

Client: I'd like to be selling my art and showing it in galleries.

Therapist: That's a cool goal. What's standing in the way of getting there?

Client: How do you mean?

Therapist: I mean, what are the roadblocks between you and your goal? What do you have to change in order to get to where you want to be?

Client: I have to get over this depression.

Therapist: What are you depressed about?

Client: Everything.

Therapist: "Everything" is too global—you can't work on "everything." Is there anything you are not depressed about? Let's just stay with your painting. Anything about it you're not depressed about?

Client: No.

Therapist: Oh, so you have no talent and you've never produced a single painting in your life?

Client: No, I have talent, but none of my stuff has ever been shown.

Therapist: How many galleries have you talked to?

Client: None.

Therapist: Gee, I wonder why you work isn't being shown?

Client: I'm too depressed to call anyone.

Therapist: Well, that's a chicken-and-egg problem. Are you depressed because you're not calling, or not calling because you're depressed?

Client: Probably both.

Therapist: I agree. So, how many paintings do you have, already completed, that are good enough for a portfolio?

Client: A few.

Therapist: How many is a few?

Client: About ten.

Therapist: Ten! I thought you were going to say two or three. That's a good example of your negative, failure-oriented mind set—*a few*. A few means *not enough* and not enough means *I can't call a gallery*, which puts you right back in the swamp.

Client: True.

Therapist: How many do you need for a portfolio, to take to a gallery?

Client: Probably about fifteen.

Therapist: Probably about fifteen? So, it could be two thousand, but it's probably about fifteen?

Client: Geez! What is this, the Inquisition?

Therapist: I prefer to call it therapy. But you're pointing the compass toward failure again—you need a specific number of paintings so you have a defined goal to work toward.

Client: Fifteen.

Therapist: How long does it take to produce one painting?

Client: I haven't painted in months.

Therapist: That's not my question. Did you brush your teeth today?

Client: What are you now, my dentist? Yes, I did.

Therapist: Good. So you can operate a brush. It looks to me like the main thing standing in the way is you telling yourself you can't get started. Can you make a commitment to bring one new, gallery-level painting to your session next week?

Client: I could.

Therapist: You could, but are you going to?

Client: I can commit to that.

Therapist: Good. I'll hold you to it. So you could get five paintings done in five weeks?

Client: Give me a break.

Therapist: You've been giving yourself a break for too long, and it's depressing for you. As well, I'm assigning you the task of bringing the names, addresses, and contact info for ten galleries you could approach about exhibiting.
Client: Next session?
Therapist: Yep.

The overall strategy is to imagine a meaningful, rewarding future, then create a detailed, sequenced, operational road map for how to get there. There is always joy in accomplishment, whether it be a single tomato plant yielding edible tomatoes or an exhibition at a major gallery followed by a number of sales.

A general principle of the cognitive-behavioural treatment of depression, on the behavioural side, is to create a series of attainable goals, starting as small as necessary. A bleak, empty future is a cardinal feature of both PTSD and depression, but the experience of success and mastery is a powerful antidote to hopelessness.

29
The "What If" Cascade

The *"what if" cascade* is named after the biochemical cascades one studies in medical school. If the body wants to make adrenalin, for instance, it starts with a precursor molecule; an enzyme converts the precursor molecule into a second molecule, then a second enzyme converts that molecule into a third molecule, and so on. There can be many steps in a single cascade, and some cascades have multiple side-branches.

The "what if" cascade is a series of "what if" questions. It is a *cognitive cascade*. The purpose of the technique is to move behind the defenses to the core issue being avoided. This technique requires just six easy steps. There is nothing easy for the survivor about doing the work, but the repeated "what if" questions allow the therapist to identify the underlying feelings and conflicts, rather than getting stuck in the defenses.

Therapy is about learning how to deal with what is being defended against, not about the defenses as such. This is true even though the mental health field is currently structured according to supposedly separate categories of defense—eating disorders, substance abuse, personality disorders, etc.—each category with its set of journals, section of the DSM, experts, conferences, and therapy methods. According to the Trauma Model (Ross, 2007), the distinctions between these categories are mostly artificial and of limited relevance to the goals, tasks, and strategies of therapy.

This chapter covers

- The "What If" Cascade

The "What If" Cascade

The idea of the "what if" cascade is straightforward, so we will illustrate it through therapy vignettes rather than talking about it at length. The therapist poses a series of hypothetical questions:

Therapist: What do you want to work on today?
Client: My cutting.
Therapist: OK. Why do you cut on yourself?
Client: It makes me feel better.
Therapist: What would happen if you stopped cutting?
Client: That would be great.
Therapist: If it would be great, why don't you just stop then?
Client: What do you mean?
Therapist: Well, if stopping cutting would be *great*, and if that's what you want to do, then why don't you just go ahead and stop? What's standing in the way of just stopping?
Client: I don't know how to stop.
Therapist: There's really nothing to know. You just have to decide whether you want to get serious about saying "No," to cutting. It's like any addiction.
Client: You make it sound so easy.
Therapist: It isn't easy; it's very hard. If it was easy for people to say "No" to their addictions, I'd be out of business pretty quickly. Anyway, we need to back up a step. You say you don't know how

to stop cutting, but that's the second step in the process. The first step is deciding whether you're going to get serious about stopping. That's where you're at, the deciding step. If you make a serious commitment to abstinence from cutting, then we can start working on how to maintain sobriety.

Client: Oh.

Therapist: I'm assuming that there are very good reasons why you cut. I want to understand those reasons more clearly. So I'm going to ask you a hypothetical question to try to get there. Speaking hypothetically, what would happen if you just didn't cut anymore, starting right now.

Client: I'd feel great. I'd have hope then

Therapist: But if it felt so great to quit, you would have quit already. You said that cutting makes you feel better. If you didn't cut, what would happen to the feelings you get rid of temporarily by cutting?

Client: They'd build up.

Therapist: Then what would happen?

Client: Then I'd cut.

Therapist: Right, but what if you didn't cut? Remember, this is a hypothetical.

Client: Then I'd feel really bad and it wouldn't go away.

Therapist: And if you felt really bad and it didn't go away, what would happen then?

Client: I'd have to get drunk.

Therapist: What if you said "No" to alcohol and drugs, and didn't use anything?

Client: You mean if the feelings didn't go away?

Therapist: Yeah.

Client: I'd have to kill myself.

Therapist: OK, so cutting is actually a suicide prevention technique, then?

Client: I guess so, yeah, if you put it that way.

Therapist: What if you didn't act out in any way at all, didn't cut, drink, kill yourself, or use any other unhealthy behaviour?

Client: Then I'd get lost in the feelings forever.

Therapist: And if you got lost in the feelings forever, then what would happen?

Client: What do you mean?

Therapist: Well, for instance, would you ever eat again, or go outside? What would you do for the rest of your life if you got lost in the feelings forever?

Client: I'd be locked in some mental hospital forever.

Therapist: OK, so you'd go catatonic. What if I define catatonia as another drug, another addiction? What if you said "No" to catatonia?

Client: You make it sound so easy. Just say "No" and poof!—you're cured.

Therapist: Uh uh. When you say "No" for real, that's when the really hard work begins, remember?

Client: Well, then I'd feel really bad forever and I couldn't stand it.

Therapist: And if you couldn't stand it, what would happen?

Client: I'd kill myself.

Therapist: But we agreed that in this hypothetical you wouldn't act out in any way.

Client: Well, I'd have to feel the feelings, then.

Therapist: Right, so the worst thing that would happen if you stopped all your addictions and all your acting out, is you would feel your feelings.

Client: I guess so.

Therapist: Well that's good to know, because you're over-estimating how big a catastrophe that would be. You've got *feeling your feelings* defined as an absolutely intolerable catastrophe. But they're just feelings.

Client: I know, but I can't stand my feelings. They hurt too much.

Therapist: Well, if that's true, if you really can't stand your feelings, then the situation is hopeless and you might as well keep on cutting.

Client: So cutting is OK?

Therapist: It depends. It's OK if you say it's OK. But if you want a different life, then you have to make a different choice. What's blocking you at the moment is your belief that stopping cutting is impossible because the feelings are intolerable. You're giving your feelings too much power and you're not giving yourself enough credit for toughness, courage, and survival skills.

Client: That's probably true.

The therapist would then explain how the feelings in fact won't last forever, but will peak in intensity and then ease off over a limited, tolerable period of time.

Another session might go as follows:

Therapist: So you want to stop throwing up your food?

Client: Yeah, that's why I'm here. I'm sick of being bulimic.

Therapist: Don't wrap your entire identity up in *being bulimic*—there are many more dimensions to you than just being bulimic.

Client: Like what?

Therapist: Do you speak English?

Client: Yes, obviously.

Therapist: OK, so you're a person who speaks English and throws up her food. Do you read, go to movies, exercise, travel, shop for clothes?

Client: OK, I get it.

Therapist: Are you someone's daughter, someone's friend, someone's ex-girlfriend, someone's owner? I'm thinking of someone who's very hairy and eats from a bowl on the floor.

Client: Do you ever give up?

Therapist: Not on you. No. So why don't you stop throwing up then?

Client: I can't help it; it just happens.

Therapist: It's out of your control, then?

Client: Yeah.

Therapist: When was the last time you threw up in the checkout line at the supermarket?

Client: I'd never do that.

Therapist: At school during a lecture?

Client: Never.

Therapist: How about while making out with your boyfriend?

Client: Gross!

Therapist: Gross for sure. So the point is, throwing up doesn't occur at random. It never happens in public. It happens in private, almost always in the toilet. When was the last time you threw up on your TV?

Client: I'm not crazy.

Therapist: I agree. And you're not out of control, either. That's my point. You throw up for a reason and you do so in a planned, controlled fashion. If that wasn't true, you would throw up in public, or anywhere, because it would be out of control and random.

Client: Well, that's true.

Therapist: So, speaking hypothetically, what would happen if you didn't throw up your food at all, ever?

Client: I'd get fat.

Therapist: And what would happen if you got fat?

Client: I'd look like a pig.

Therapist: Really! How long is your tail?

Client: You know what I mean.

Therapist: I do, but words carry a lot of feelings and pictures along with them. If you paint a picture of a pig wallowing in the mud, bad feelings go along with imagining you'd look like that. What if you told yourself you'd be attractive but slightly overweight instead?

Client: But I wouldn't be attractive.

Therapist: OK, let's go with that. What if you looked like a pig?

Client: Then nobody would like me.

Therapist: Nobody like who? John Smith in Idaho?

Client: Who's he?

Therapist: I have no idea. But you said *nobody* would like you—that means nobody on the whole planet. Is there somebody in particular who wouldn't like you?

Client: My boyfriend.

Therapist: And if your boyfriend didn't like you, what would happen?

Client: He'd dump me.

Therapist: And what would happen if your boyfriend dumped you?

Client: What do you mean, what would happen? I'd be alone.

Therapist: And what would happen if you were alone?

Client: I'd feel lonely. I'd hate myself.

Therapist: Why?

Client: Because I'd be a loser, a fat ugly loser.

Therapist: And what would happen if you were a fat ugly loser?

Client: I'd be alone forever. Except for my mother—she'd still nag me to lose weight.

Therapist: How would it feel to be alone forever?

Client: Horrible, of course.

Therapist: OK, so it's a series of steps. Your core belief seems to be that unless you are a perfect weight, no one will be interested in you, you'll be alone forever, and that will be intolerable.

Client: Basically, yeah.

Therapist: Is your dog psychotic?

Client: No. Now what are you talking about?

Therapist: Does your dog love you?

Client: Yes.

Therapist: Why, if he's not delusional or psychotic?

Client: Because I feed him and play with him and I'm nice to him.

Therapist: So from your dog's perspective, you're a pretty cool owner?

Client: Yeah, I am.

Therapist: Did you know there's very little difference between dogs and boyfriends?

Client: Dogs are more dependable.

Therapist: That's true. But maybe there's a guy somewhere who could see the qualities your dog sees in you.

Client: Where, in Idaho?

Therapist: Actually, the problem isn't how guys see you, it's how you see you. It sounds like your dog has a more accurate perception of you than you do.

Client: Great. So my dog is smarter than me.

Therapist: In that regard, yes, he is. I think you're addicted to a very negative picture of yourself.

At this point the therapist could shift to an exploration of the locus of control shift. A third session might go this way:

Therapist: What would happen if the flashbacks just stopped?

Client: Then I could have a life.

Therapist: But if the flashbacks stopped, what would happen to your sex life?

Client: Finally I could give my husband what he wants.

Therapist: Do you want to give your husband what he wants?

Client: No, I think sex is disgusting.

Therapist: But if you didn't have flashbacks during sex, or freeze up, or switch to a scared child, what would happen?

Client: Then I'd have no reason to say, "No."

Therapist: Could you just tell your husband that you find him, his body, and his sexual drive disgusting?

Client: No way; he'd be devastated.

Therapist: So one function of the flashbacks during sex is to protect your husband's feelings?

Client: I guess so.

Therapist: That's a very kind and loving thing to do for him.

Client: I never thought of it that way.

Therapist: So you have a decision to make. Are you willing to say "No" to flashbacks, if that means learning how to have healthy, intimate sex with your husband? Or would you rather have PTSD the rest of your life?

Client: You make it sound like I'm choosing to have PTSD.

Therapist: Not at all. Getting PTSD was not your fault, it happened against your will, and you had no choice in the matter. You were just a child. I'm not talking about a choice to get PTSD in childhood; I'm talking about choosing to recover.

Client: But what if I don't want to have sex with my husband?

Therapist: If that's the bottom line, then you have to decide whether you want to stay in a sexless marriage. It seems to me you have three options: get out of the marriage and be celibate; stay in the marriage and be celibate; or, stay in the marriage, work in therapy, and have a normal sex life.

Client: Is that really possible, realistically?

Therapist: Only if that's what you really want, if that's the choice you make, and if you work really hard on it. If nothing changes, then you'll continue to try to have sex when you really don't want to, which will cause flashbacks, which will ruin the sex.

Client: But I really would like to be normal. My husband is a good guy. He deserves to have sex with his wife. It's normal.

Therapist: OK, your call then.

Client: What do you mean?

Therapist: Why don't we have your husband come into a session; we'll put all of this on the table, then talk about where to go from there?

Client: He'll die if he finds out how I feel.

Therapist: Can I tell you a secret?

Client: What?

Therapist: He already knows.

Client: Oh. Damn.

A final example of the "what if" cascade is:

Therapist: What if the voices just stopped one day, for good?

Client: That would be fantastic!

Therapist: And who would you have to talk to?

Client: No one.

Therapist: And how would that feel?

Client: Empty, lonely, bored.

Therapist: So one function of the voices is to keep you company.

Client: Sort of.

Therapist: What would happen if you were empty, lonely, and bored?

Client: I'd get wasted.

Therapist: What if you didn't hear voices, get stoned, or act out in any way?

Client: I couldn't stand it.

Therapist: And if you couldn't stand it, what would happen?

Client: I'd kill myself?

Therapist: And if you were dead, what would that be like?

Client: Peaceful.

Therapist: With no voices?

Client: I'd be asleep. I'd be dead.

Therapist: So when your voices tell you to kill yourself, they're telling you to try to find some peace?

Client: That's a weird way to look at it.

Therapist: Maybe, but it follows from what you said. Is it OK to kill yourself?

Client: It's my life.

Therapist: True. Would it be OK for your sister to kill herself?

Client: No. No way.

Therapist: Why?

Client: Because she's got a life.

Therapist: She does?

Client: Yeah, she's married and has kids.

Therapist: How old are you? Ninety-four?

Client: Very funny. You know I'm twenty-four.

Therapist: But you're talking like you're ninety-four and your life is over.

Client: It feels that way.

Therapist: I know, but remember what I said about the difference between facts and feelings? If you agree with your bad feelings, and see them as facts, they get worse and you feel more hopeless. This feeds the cycle of suicide and addiction.

Client: Right.

Therapist: OK, so you feel like your life is over, but in fact it isn't. If you state that your life is over, it's not surprising your voices recommend suicide. What do you think might happen if you chose life instead?

Client: You mean my voices might stop trying to kill me?

Therapist: Your voices are just your feelings talking to you.

Client: Doesn't seem like it.

Therapist: So your voices are the furniture talking to you?

Client: OK, it's me, but it doesn't feel like me.

Therapist: How do you think your voices would feel if you stopped wanting to get rid of them by killing them and yourself?

Client: I never thought of that.

Therapist: Well, now that you're thinking of it, what would happen if you stopped asking your voices to kill you?

Client: I thought you said I was trying to kill them?

Therapist: Chicken and egg.

Client: Which one am I?

Therapist: Both.

Client: Maybe they'd feel like living. Maybe they wouldn't be so scared.

Therapist: That might help the flashbacks to settle down.
Client: But then I'd have to have sex with my husband.
Therapist: See how it all fits together?
Client: Kind of.
Therapist: Kind of is better than zero understanding.
Client: So I used to be a zero?
Therapist: Zero point five.
Client: Oh, I feel better now.
Therapist: Glad I could help.

These three vignettes illustrate how therapy has the same structure, tasks, and goals no matter what the symptom, diagnosis, or addiction. The "what if" cascade can be pursued with a variety of wordings, and the therapist can divert to other matters before picking up the thread later in the same session, or in a subsequent session.

30
The Healing Power of Feeling: Working with Anger and Grief

One of the most difficult and challenging aspects of trauma therapy is safely connecting with, processing, and expressing feelings. Safety is an alien or abstract concept to many clients. They may never have experienced a sense of safety, either within themselves or with others. Some people simply do not believe it is possible to be or feel safe.

Clients say in various ways, "I want to feel better without having to feel." Feeling emotional pain, grief, terror, despair, and anger seems counterintuitive—after all, isn't that the point of dissociation—to not feel all that horrible *stuff*?

Tolerance levels to feeling vary from person to person and, at different times, vary within the same person. The person with DID or DDNOS will have differing levels of tolerance to feeling within different parts of the personality system. Different parts will also hold different feelings, allowing conflicting feelings to remain separate. However, this results in conflict between different parts, each having little tolerance or acceptance of the others' feelings and function.

Developing tolerance to intense feelings is a skill and capacity requiring time, patience, and courage. Courage is not an absence of fear. Courage is stepping toward and facing the things we fear the most.

This chapter will cover

- Normalizing Intense Feelings

- Learning the Difference Between Anger, Violence, Assertion, and Aggression

- Understanding the Link Between Anger and Grief

- Preparing, Planning, and Pacing Feeling Work

- Strategies to Assist Feeling Work

- The Healing Power of Anger: Transforming Shame and Guilt

- Role Play for an Anger-Phobic Person

Normalizing Intense Feelings

Reactions to trauma and abuse generally fall into two main categories of emotional defense. One reaction is experiencing an overwhelming flooding of feelings, intrusive images, memories, and sensations. The person who is flooded with feelings has difficulty containing, regulating, and self-soothing. This person is swept up in a tidal wave of feeling that frequently leaves a trail of devastation. Dreams of tidal waves, drowning, volcanoes, earthquakes, wars, and other disasters are common. Such dreams appear to be a metaphor for both the intensity and the fear of feelings.

The client who has difficulty containing feeling tends to be highly volatile, and emotionally, verbally, and/or physically aggressive toward self and/or others. This person very quickly becomes overcome with rage, despair, fear, and grief. These feelings can be externalized, internalized, or both. This client may constantly test and challenge the therapist's and others' boundaries. She tries to manage her distress by projecting her feelings onto others or blames herself for everything. She looks outside of herself to be rescued.

This client is not expressing or processing her feelings. Her behaviour reflects remaining stuck and re-enacting trauma. Clients may experience comments or feedback by the therapist as being judged, blamed, rejected, and shamed. Responses to such feedback might be, "What do you mean I'm not dealing with my feelings; I'm expressing them all the time. My problem is I feel too much."

This is in part true. This person needs assistance in learning containment and self-soothing skills, and in developing tolerance of her intense feelings. While this client experiences temporary relief from her outbursts of rage or tears, nothing is actually changing or shifting in her internal world or her external relationships. This suggests that she is not embracing or owning her feelings but (quite understandably) trying to get rid of them.

When she is not in crisis mode, she may possess deep insight and understanding about her experiences and behaviour. However, when triggered into feelings, she quickly escalates and spirals out of control; her insight is difficult to access or utilize. The therapist walks a delicate path, explaining these concepts with compassion, carefully avoiding words or behaviour that might intensify the client's feelings of shame or rejection, while rigorously maintaining clear and consistent boundaries.

The other common reaction to trauma and abuse is emotional numbing. Clients report a range of numbness, from an emotional flat-line to deep depression. While both flooded and numbed clients report depersonalization and derealization, the numbed client may report such distancing phenomena as a virtual way of life.

The numb client may present in a more obviously dissociative and disconnected manner. However, some clients reporting detachment and disconnection from self and others can possess effective social and communication skills. This person's inner experience of numbness and disconnection may not be obvious to others.

The person who is numb has shut down or dissociated his feelings. Disconnected from feelings, he lives in an empty no-man's-land where, seemingly, nothing or no one can reach him. However, as with all aspects of human experience, there are ironic paradoxes. The numbed client may report feeling nothing, but may express feeling distressed and upset about feeling nothing. While the flooded client might self-injure to distract and distance herself from overwhelming feelings, the numbed client may self-injure in an attempt to feel real and connected to himself.

A client with DID, who predominantly presents as numb, may report hearing crying, screaming, or raging inside but deny or dismiss that those voices or feelings have anything to do with him. He is likely to have little interest or compassion for these inner expressions of distress. Where the flooding client spills her feelings out all over the place in an attempt to *get rid of them*, the numb client is expert in ignoring, dismissing, and denying his feelings.

Some clients may bounce between these two defensive reactions. While each presentation looks very different, they are two sides of the same coin. Both clients are avoiding their feelings. Both clients may self-injure and experience suicidal ideation.

The idea of approaching and exploring feelings is terrifying. Rage may be used as a defense against feelings of powerlessness. Helplessness may be used as a defense against feelings of rage. The therapist's role is to help the client safely navigate the pathway to feelings.

Survivors of abuse often say that they don't feel, or are not *normal*—whatever normal might mean! Human beings have a propensity to compare themselves to others. We usually find ourselves lacking and deficient in some way. This very human condition is intensified in people who have been abused.

People with a history of abuse view themselves as being inherently bad and therefore, deserving of being abused. This belief serves several purposes, as explored in Chapters 11 and 12.

If the client was abused because she is bad, then everything about her is bad, including her feelings. She doesn't deserve to have any feelings about what happened to her.

If a person holds on to one particular feeling, be it grief, rage, fear, shame, guilt, or depression, then that person needn't face or feel the complex, multi-level conflicts and paradoxes created by abuse and trauma.

When the phobic reaction to feeling is more problematic in the client's life than the actual feeling, the therapist may intervene with *normalizing* strategies. This is where conundrums like *the problem is not the problem but a solution to another problem* and the *"what if" cascade* can help. These explanations often make immediate sense at a cognitive level and can help begin to reduce fear and anxiety.

Reframing defensive behaviours and reactions as useful solutions to problems that were insolvable at the time, helps decreases the client's feelings of shame and self-recrimination. When a person understands trauma dynamics and reactions, she can view feelings of shame in a different light. Such reframing paves the way to normalizing intense, uncomfortable, and frightening feelings, thoughts, and images.

Clients need repeated reassurance and validation that their feelings are normal and healthy. Abused children are likely to have been punished for showing or expressing feelings. Feeling angry or scared or upset didn't make any difference anyway. It was much safer to bury those feelings.

Encourage each small step toward connecting with feeling, while gently confronting and challenging old beliefs. As children they were powerless. As adults they can empower themselves through learning to value, honor, and embrace feelings.

Learning the Difference Between Anger, Violence, Assertion, and Aggression

Anger is a terrifying emotion for most traumatized and abused clients. Trauma clients often have an anger phobia. They describe a ball of intense, black energy buried in the abdomen. There it churns and boils, erupting every once in a while in violent acting out or turning it toward themselves.

Other clients get stuck in chronic anger in order to avoid their grief. They may be hypercritical, or verbally or physically abusive. These clients feel safer hiding in their anger instead of their emotional pain. Such people identify more with the perpetrator role—although they are usually horrified if this is how their behaviour is described.

At the other end of the anger spectrum is the severely depressed client. He will likely deny any feelings of anger toward those who have hurt him or, at best, he will intellectualize his anger. His internalized anger manifests through depression, with physical and/or emotional distress, which may result in his being diagnosed with a *mental illness*. This client is passive-aggressive and passive-resistant, emotionally withholding, and stonewalling. He does not recognize this behaviour as aggression. This client accepts the role of helpless victim—in the past, in current relationships, and in life in general.

The first client avoids feelings of helplessness and powerlessness through rage and anti-social behaviour. The second client avoids feelings of rage through depression and taking a victim stance. Both are avoiding deep feelings of grief.

Survivors of abuse perceive the violence of the perpetrator as evidence of his/her greater power and control. When a client has violent thoughts or feelings, they are experienced as proof of being like the perpetrator. This proof invokes feelings of shame, disgust, badness, and fear, which in turn serve to escalate the chosen defense.

A vital part of trauma therapy is tapping into the healing and restorative power of anger. Anger is rocket fuel for life. Anger is energy. Mobilized and channeled in a healthy fashion, anger fosters assertiveness. It improves posture and muscle tone and it has a powerful antidepressant effect. Getting in touch with, learning to tolerate, and then learning to use one's anger is a major component of healing and recovery.

This involves working with anger at cognitive, physical, emotional, and spiritual or philosophical levels. Normalizing and de-pathologizing anger is central to supporting clients' eagerness to explore and work with this powerful emotion. Understanding the differences between anger, violence, assertion, and aggression is key to effective anger work.

It is often helpful to use examples unrelated to the client's experience of abuse or her own behaviour. Sufficient distance and objectivity allows the client to apply understanding to her own experiences and behaviours. Feelings of shame and embarrassment are relieved by acknowledging that others have experienced and behaved in similar ways.

Identifying overt abusive and violent behaviour, such as name calling, putting another down, threats, or actual physical violence or destruction of property, is relatively easy. More covert behaviours and passive aggression, such as emotional withdrawal, stonewalling, forgetting to do things, breaking promises and agreements, consistently ignoring requests to do or not do something, or threatening to leave or commit suicide, can be harder for people to acknowledge as acts of aggression.

The simple gauge is that positive expression of anger and being assertive respects the rights of others. This does not mean liking the person; the client may in fact feel hate toward another person. Clients frequently need permission to feel hate. Feeling hate and acting hatefully are different. Violence and being aggressive do not respect the rights of others but are an emotional, mental, spiritual, and at times, physical assault.

Many clients have heightened integrity and ethical behaviour. However, there may be times when it is crucial to be direct and intervene if a client is currently behaving abusively and violently.

The Link Between Anger and Grief

Trauma, dissociation, conflicted attachment, and depression all go together in a package. The core dissociation is the disconnection between the positive feelings for the parents and the negative feelings. This leads to the two split behavioural states at the heart of borderline personality disorder—the *I hate you; don't leave me* dance.

The plus-minus, love-hate, approach-avoid, black-white, love-hate dichotomy is resolved by splitting the psyche into a good self and a bad self. The adult survivor of abuse then bounces back and forth from one half of reality to the other, but never has to look at the whole picture.

There are two split ways of thinking, feeling, speaking, perceiving, and behaving: all good and all bad. In the DSM criteria for borderline personality disorder, this is called *devaluation-idealization*. In cognitive therapy it is called *all-or-nothing thinking* or *dichotomization*, while in ego psychology language it is called *split object relations*. These are all different terms for the same thing—*unresolved conflict*.

The task of the client who dumps and projects emotional, verbal, or violent outbursts is to feel and express the grief beneath the rage, to learn constructive ways to express her anger, and to learn to be assertive.

The task for the depressed and helpless client is to learn to feel safe with his intense feelings of rage and deep grief, to let go of being in the victim role. The two clients take different routes to the same destination.

The therapist needs to guide the client to recognize when attachment to the perpetrator and locus of control dynamics are operating, and connecting this dynamic to the client's favored emotional style.

The client needs to perceive the therapist as able to tolerate intense expressions of anger and grief, thus providing a safe container for her feelings. The therapist's tolerance of these feelings creates a space to feel *safe enough* to do this vulnerable work, and to experience acceptance for expression of disavowed feelings and emotions.

Preparing, planning, and pacing all feeling work is important. The setting will determine when and how the feeling work will be approached.

Preparing, Planning, and Pacing Feeling Work

At some point, most trauma therapists explain the need for and benefits of working with feelings to their clients. These earnest discussions generally yield client-responses featuring variations of, "That sounds like a fun idea . . . Not." Understanding the need for working with feelings does not immediately diminish anxiety or resistance. Anxiety and resistance, like all reactions and responses in therapy, are a communication and need to be heeded. Just as many clients have not experienced safety, so they may not have experienced gentleness. They may become confused and suspicious when they first experience this in therapy.

There are two common approaches clients have to working with feelings. There is the *bull in a china shop* approach. This client wants to push through everything. The concepts of gentleness and pacing are not in his vocabulary.

The other common, but opposite, approach to feelings results in a therapy that is like trying to shuck an oyster. The oyster shell is clamped so tight it is almost impossible to open—unless you have the right tools and skills. This client doesn't have a concept of gentleness or pacing either.

Where the former client needs skills to shut down and contain, the latter needs skills to open up. Both clients are stuck in their respective *comfort zone*.

The metaphor for each style is that both the china and the pearl are precious and easily damaged. When an oyster is opened with skill and care it will present the pearl within—the wisdom that is contained within feelings.

Western society tends to revere Mind (cognition) and the Body (action). Soul (feeling) and Spirit (meaning) tend to be undervalued. Humans are a composite of mind, body, soul, and spirit; therefore, all aspects of the psyche need attention for health and well- being. The body remembers trauma, and feelings have a central role in the healing of trauma.

Feeling work and working with trauma memories are connected. Memories will surface when feelings are approached and feelings will surface when memories are approached. Before commencing working with feelings (and memories) the core foundations of therapy need to be in place: client safety and daily functioning; a solid understanding by the client of trauma and abuse dynamics; the client's capacity to ground and self-soothe; strong internal communication (when working with DID); and a strong therapeutic alliance.

Additional factors include being cognizant of the client's current circumstances. If an unexpected crisis or major life event occurs in the client's life, then proceeding with any planned feeling work related to past issues may be contraindicated. Working with feelings about the current event or situation, however, may be quite appropriate; a current crisis may also tap into old feelings. The client's capacity at any point in time must be the determining factor in when and how to work with feelings.

Regardless of whether the client is a flooder or a numb-er—a bull or an oyster—sessions for feelings require planning together and being given a clear structure. The structure might involve focus on a particular feeling in a broad sense or feelings connected to a specific event. Some clients will require assistance to begin identifying and naming feelings. It can take many months and, with highly traumatized clients, often years, and very small steps, to process and work through feelings safely.

Having a clear session format is important:

Beginning—Here the therapist and client cooperate in planning the approaching session. Clarifications include all special agreements between the client and therapist, such as signals to stop, grounding, and containing techniques that will be put in place, as well as the client's plans for supporting herself post-session.

Middle—This is where the work is undertaken, using any of the suggested strategies below, in addition to any the client and therapist may devise themselves.

End—This is where the client employs techniques she has discovered work for her to ground, contain, and bring closure to the session. This does not mean the issues are all dealt with, but that the client is able to leave the session and return to her daily life and commitments. An important part of this process (for all sessions, not only working with feelings) is for the client and therapist to make notes together about the content of the session. These notes record the feelings, associations, and meaning of the session, as well as any home support tasks to follow up on through the week.

Strategies to Assist with Feeling Work

These strategies are not limited to working with feelings. They can be utilized in any aspect of therapy; working with the locus of control shift, attachment to the perpetrator, developing internal communication and safe places, working with different parts of the DID system, understanding and exploring Victim–Rescuer–Perpetrator dynamics, etc. Trauma therapy requires being grounded in trauma theory and creative in therapeutic approaches.

- Talking

- Visualization/exploring Metaphors

- Art Work

- Body Work and Emotional Release

- Creative Writing/Music/Dance

- Dialoguing: Verbalized/Written

- Other Creative Mediums

Talking

Some clients use words to intellectualize their experience, stay in their heads, and distance from feelings. Simply talking does not assist these clients to connect with or express feelings.

Talking for other clients can be a direct pathway to connecting with feelings. Telling their story can be a powerful way to evoke feelings and to give their feelings a context and framework. The experience of having another person bear witness to their stories, and feeling the presence of another human being really listening and caring about what they have to say, can unlock the emotion that has been kept hidden before the words were said out loud.

The therapist can monitor and keep track of the client through observing the tone of her voice, how she is holding her body, and the look on her face as she talks. These cues can assist the therapist to guide the client deeper into her feelings, or to pull her back if she is moving beyond what she can safely process.

Visualization and Exploring Metaphors

Earlier in the chapter we acknowledged the content of dreams as a rich source of information about internal processes, feelings, and conflicts. Exploring dream content and imagery can open up the exploration of feelings in a variety of ways. Dreams may identify an emotion that is preparing to surface or the conflicts a person is experiencing about what they feel. Dreams may contain literal events or present information in more symbolic ways. The client may wish to explore her dreams through talking, making associations, visualization where she can talk to dream characters, painting, or story-telling. It is always important not to take the content of dreams too literally, and to remember that it may be symbolic rather than historical.

Dreams and nightmares evoke powerful feelings. They can be frightening, reassuring, confusing, and illuminating. Working with dreams offers a powerful and direct access to the inner workings of the psyche. The client is free to delve as far and wide as she feels ready to do.

Daily life experiences, whether they are our own experiences or world events, also provide an opportunity to explore aspects of feeling and emotion. A story that a client might tell, about something that happened to a friend, or that she saw on the news, can present a pathway into a feeling or experience.

Guided visualization or more structured symbol exercises about dreams and life events can yield rich insight and awareness. However, such exploration can open things up quickly and may result in the client being flooded and overwhelmed. It is important to monitor the client's tolerance level. Some trauma clients with PTSD or a dissociative disorder are afraid to do visualization for this reason. This wish should be respected and use of visualization approached cautiously.

Artwork

Artwork allows the client to tell a story or express a feeling without using words. Sometimes there are no words to adequately express a feeling or experience. Artwork can be done in session or at home. The client may want to talk about her painting or say nothing. Asking open questions or making observations may assist the client in talking about her picture or in connecting with a feeling that is being visually depicted but hasn't yet been voiced. As with visualization and guided imagery, artwork can also evoke powerful feeling responses.

Body Work and Emotional Release

The body holds the emotions of the trauma. Teaching body awareness can assist the client in becoming more connected to the physical body and less dissociated. It can also be a pathway into the emotions that are held in the body. Body work can take many forms; it may simply be reflecting to your client something about her posture. Is she slumped and hunched over? Is she clenching her jaw or fists? Is she sitting on the edge of the chair as if ready to take flight? Is her breathing deep or shallow? This gentle focus may bring attention and awareness that leads to accessing feelings being held in the body.

Sometimes, suggesting that a client shift or move position can help follow a feeling pathway. Focus on sensations in the body. Invite your client to let parts of the body speak. For example, "If you heart could speak what would it like to say?"

Encourage the client, when he is ready, to seek relaxation massage from a professional masseuse, osteopathy, or other forms of body work. These physical therapies can greatly assist in the process of connecting and releasing emotions.

Depending on the environment you work in, you may help clients work with deep feelings of anger, grief, and emotional pain, where they are free to yell, scream, and weep as loud as they wish. This is possible in some private practice environments and hospital settings. However, it may not be possible in other settings, where loud weeping or yelling would impact other clients and practitioners in the building. This work is an important part of the healing process. If it's not viable in your setting, teaching your client the skills to do this safely at home is another option. Encourage small sounds or changes in posture which the client can expand and build upon over time.

Sports, such as kick boxing, martial arts, gym work, swimming, yoga, and meditation and breath work can be great allies in assisting the expression of feelings and healing the body.

Dialoguing—Written or Verbalized

When knowledge, behaviour, feelings, memory, and skills are dissociated, the individual remains stuck in the cycle of trauma, the Victim–Rescuer–Perpetrator triangle, locus of control shift, and attachment to the perpetrator.

Dialoguing between parts of the DDNOS or DID system is one of the cornerstones of trauma therapy. Communication and support among parts is central to integrating traumas and therefore, dissociated parts of the psyche. Integration is a by-product of healing.

If dialoguing in written format is used, encourage writing with the non-dominant hand or using different coloured pens. This can facilitate access to different parts of the system and different feeling states.

Developing cooperation and co-consciousness between parts, so that information and feelings remain conscious, leads to integrating the trauma. There is no gain in working with different parts if the feelings remain dissociated from the rest of the system. This is counterproductive and reinforces internal splitting.

Sharing knowledge, experiences, feelings, and skills among parts of the internal system strengthens the whole person; this develops resilience and the capacity to manage and express the broad spectrum of human emotions.

Other Creative Mediums

The ways of exploring, connecting, and working with feelings are only limited by the imagination. Client and therapist can explore avenues together to discover what works best for each individual. Creative writing, poetry, playing and listening to music, and dance are valuable mediums to assist in accessing, exploring, and expressing feelings and integrating experiences.

The Healing Power of Anger: Transforming Shame and Guilt

Anger and depression are psycho-physiologically incompatible states. Anger is energy, arousal, adrenalin, good posture, aggression, and the fight response. Depression is withdrawal, learned helplessness, fatigue, hopelessness, and surrender.

The child in an abusive family learns that anger is bad and dangerous because she is punished if she ever gets angry, rebels, or resists in any way. She buries her anger inside in order to protect herself. She shifts the locus of control and blames herself for the abuse. This in turn reinforces her self-hatred, and increases the need to bury her anger even deeper. It is an endless vicious cycle.

Assisting clients to step into their anger leads to stepping out of depression. This is partly because of the state switch to an energized, activated state, and partly because it takes considerable energy to repress all that anger.

The client who learns to express anger effectively can begin to reverse the locus of control shift, acquire affect management skills, and increase inter-personality communication, cooperation, and cognitive restructuring. She is empowered to reconfigure the Victim-Rescuer-Perpetrator triangle, and many other components of therapy that go on at the same time.

Shame, guilt, and self-loathing are a crippling legacy of abuse and trauma. These feelings are intrinsically linked to the locus of control shift and attachment to the perpetrator. Explaining the difference between *good shame* and *bad shame* can be helpful.

Good shame is a feeling which alerts us that we are doing or have done something that goes against our sense of ethics and integrity. It propels us to take action to change. *Bad shame* is a feeling that keeps us stuck in self-defeating and unhealthy beliefs and behaviours. This explanation can assist clients to see the function of holding onto feelings of shame and guilt as a defense against their anger and grief.

Healthy expression of anger can transform the shame and guilt that undermines and debilitates so many trauma survivors. This transformation will lead to greater self worth, confidence, and personal agency.

Forgiveness is an issue related both to healing through feeling (Soul) work and through meaning (Spiritual) work. As with many aspects of healing from trauma, including working with anger and grief, forgiveness deserves a book of its own. In this manual it is discussed in the spirituality chapter, Chapter 33.

Role Play with an Anger-Phobic Person

Therapist: So you never get angry. Why?
Client: It's bad.
Therapist: What's bad about it?
Client: People get out of control. Bad things happen.
Therapist: That's a lesson you learned many times over as a child, right?
Client: Right.
Therapist: I'd like you to consider the differences between anger and rage, and between feelings and behaviour. Rage is anger ramped up to the max and turned into behaviour. Anger, on the other hand, is just a feeling.
Client: I don't see the difference.
Therapist: I think that's because in your family, there wasn't much difference. Anger exploded into rage and rage exploded into behaviour very quickly. They were all lumped together. But it's possible to separate them out. It's possible to be angry without being violent.
Client: Not in my family.
Therapist: I understand that, but you have decided not to copy your family and not to live by their rules. You've decided to change.
Client: I don't want to be like them.

Therapist: Then don't use their theory of anger. Get a better one.

Client: Like what?

Therapist: Well, first, let me ask you some questions.

Client: What else is new?

Therapist: That's what you pay me for. First, you go to church and you believe in God, you said.

Client: Right.

Therapist: So who designed your body, you or God?

Client: God.

Therapist: Why did God design two legs?

Client: For walking.

Therapist: Lungs?

Client: Breathing.

Therapist: The amygdala?

Client: The what?

Therapist: The amygdala. That's the part of the brain that gets angry. Also, why did God put adrenalin in your body?

Client: I don't know.

Therapist: What would happen if a mother bear had no adrenalin and no amygdala and another animal attacked her cub? She wouldn't have any fight response, and she would be unable to defend her cub.

Client: So anger can be good?

Therapist: Absolutely—channeled the right way in the right situation. All mammals have the ability to get angry. It's built into their DNA. When a mammal is cornered or attacked, the flight or fight response kicks in. It's survival. So when you were threatened or attacked as a child, your fight response kicked in, only you learned that it was dangerous to show any anger, so you stuffed the anger in your abdomen.

Client: So it was normal for me to be angry?

Therapist: 100% normal. In fact, it would have been abnormal for you not to get angry. So there's nothing evil, wrong, or bad about being angry. Anger is just a feeling. The question is what you do with it. If you get angry and start a rape crisis centre, that is a healthy thing to do. If you get angry and abuse your kids, that's unhealthy and wrong. But the problem isn't the anger—it's what you do with it. Does that make sense?

Client: Yes, but I don't know how to handle my anger.

Therapist: That's not surprising since you were never shown or taught healthy anger skills. But these are skills that can be learned.

Client: How?

Therapist: We're doing the first step right now. You can't learn to handle your anger in a healthy way if you define it as evil and a disgrace. With that definition, you can't even get started.

Client: OK, I see that anger isn't necessarily bad, but I'm still scared of it.

Therapist: Why does your anger scare you?

Client: It just does.

Therapist: What are you afraid might happen if you let your anger come up?

Client: I might lose control.

Therapist: Then what might happen?

Client: I might hurt someone.

Therapist: Like who?

Client: My boyfriend.

Therapist: Your boyfriend is six inches taller than you and about 80 pounds heavier.

Client: That's true—he can handle me with one arm. It pisses me off.

Therapist: No doubt. So if you got angry but didn't act out—didn't attack anyone or anything, including yourself—what's the worst that could happen?

From here the conversation will follow a *"what if"* cascade. The outcome of the conversation will be desensitization to the anger through de-catastrophization. This is the cognitive element of the work. The *in vivo exposure* component involves actually feeling the feeling of anger. The conversation might proceed as follows:

Therapist: Where is your anger?
Client: What do you mean?
Therapist: Well, it's not in the chair or the floor. If you had to locate it somewhere in your body, where would it be? Your left elbow?
Client: No, it's not in my left elbow.
Therapist: Where is it, then?
Client: Here, in my stomach.
Therapist: What size and shape is it? Does it have a color?
Client: It's about this big [eight inches] and it's a black ball.
Therapist: OK, so you know where your anger is and you know something about it. But you can't make angry statements, right?
Client: No way.
Therapist: Could you let the black ball of anger start moving up toward your throat?
Client: How do I do that?
Therapist: Just give it permission. Imagine that the angry energy is moving up into your chest. Take a minute . . . is it there yet?
Client: Yes.
Therapist: How do you feel?
Client: Scared.
Therapist: Scared of what?
Client: It might come up into my throat.
Therapist: Then what might happen?
Client: I might say something I don't mean.
Therapist: If you were to say something you don't mean, what is it you might say?
Client: I don't know.
Therapist: Take a guess.
Client: I hate my parents.
Therapist: Why do you hate your parents?
Client: They treated me like crap.
Therapist: Do you love your parents too?
Client: Yes. How sick is that?
Therapist: Remember, we talked about that. It's the problem of attachment to the perpetrator. By the way, congratulations.
Client: For what?
Therapist: You just got angry at your parents.
Client: I did?
Therapist: Yeah, you said that they treated you like crap.
Client: That's not anger. I was just talking.
Therapist: But that's the thing. You made an angry statement without exploding or getting violent. That's the whole idea. And you didn't forget that you also love your parents. Nice job.
Client: Oh. Thanks.

The client who is chronically angry requires a different approach. If she was working in an inpatient anger management group throwing balls of clay at a board, the therapist might say, "Now I want you to say, 'I couldn't make you love me.' Throw a ball and say that."

The idea is to bump the person out of her anger into her sadness. She is comfortable with her anger, and hides in it to avoid her grief. Also, she uses it to push people away so they don't come too close, then hurt or reject her. The reason they might reject her is because if they get too close, they will see the *real* her and be disgusted. This is the locus of control shift projected onto the other person.

The overtly angry person needs to desensitize herself to her sadness. Again, the first step is setting up the desensitization hierarchy and getting the client to agree to the plan and the rationale for it. The hierarchy can't be specified in concrete steps like it can with a spider phobia, but the client needs to agree to the general plan of approaching the sadness in tolerable small steps. She needs to agree that she has an anger addiction and say "no" to the drug of anger. Then the therapist can approach the sadness with a "what if" cascade and can help the client de-catastrophize just as would be done if the phobia was for anger rather than for sadness.

Once the sadness or the anger can be felt a little, then the therapy involves talking about it in a more generic processing format. The client needs to talk about the sad story. This involves some catharsis, some reversing of the locus of control shift, some commitment to sobriety from the anger addiction, some cognitive restructuring, some nurturing of the sad children within, and giving oneself permission to feel sad. This right was taken away by the parents. Giving it back to oneself is a healing gift in and of itself.

Briere, J., & Scott, C. (2006). *Principles of trauma therapy: A guide to symptoms, evaluation, and treatment*. Newbury Park, CA: Sage Publications.

Caldwell, M. (2004). The spectrum of emotions. International Society for the Study of Dissociation 21st International Conference, New Orleans, Louisiana, November 18-20.

Greenspan, M. (2003). *Healing through the dark emotions: The wisdom of grief, fear, and despair*. Boston: Shambala.

Lewis, M. (1992). *Shame: The exposed self*. New York: Free Press.

Ogden, P., Minton, K., & Pain, C. (2006). *Trauma and the body: A sensorimotor approach to psychotherapy*. New York: W.W. Norton.

Potter-Efron, R., & Potter-Efron, P. (1989). *Letting go of shame: Understanding how shame affects your life*. Center City, MN: Hazelden Press.

Rothschild, B. (2000). *The body remembers: the psychophysiology of trauma and trauma treatment*. New York: John Wiley & Sons.

31
Experiential Therapies

Therapy, from our perspective, involves a composite of didactic, cognitive-behavioural, systems, emotional processing and experiential work. Psychodynamic principles come into play as well, although we use the vocabulary of classical psychoanalysis sparingly. Some experiential therapies cannot be done in the private office setting during individual sessions because they are too noisy, require too much space, or require other people—for instance, psychodrama requires other clients, and anger work can be too disruptive in a poorly sound-insulated office building. The principles are the same in all settings, however.

Experiential therapies are essential to the work of desensitization. They can include art, music, movement, psychodrama, ROPES courses, and a wide range of different activities. As always, the content varies while the logic and structure remain the same.

In this chapter we cover

- Principles of Experiential Therapy

- Types of Experiential Therapy

- Experiential Treatment Strategies

Principles of Experiential Therapy

Experiential therapies and emotional processing are at the core of Trauma Model Therapy. They are integrated with the cognitive, behavioural, systems and didactic aspects of the work, and are not an add-on—they are not *adjunctive*. People learn most deeply by experience, by practicing and doing. Recovery can't be done solely at a cognitive, didactic, or intellectual level. This is true for recovery, learning a sport, learning how to paint or play an instrument, and countless other skills in life.

Basically, we can't just talk about feelings, we need to feel them. Experiential therapies are a set of structured procedures and tasks designed to desensitize a person to phobically avoided feelings and conflicts. Exposure therapy for single-event adult-onset trauma is usually regarded as a pure behavioural intervention, but it could just as easily be termed *experiential*. Once one is desensitized to the avoided feelings, they can be felt, tolerated, and lived without any need for addictions, acting out, and other unhealthy defenses. It isn't so much that therapy removes the defenses—it is more that it removes the *need* for the defenses.

Experiential therapies are not intrinsically different from standard exposure therapy. Although art, music, movement, psychodrama, or other creative techniques are used in experiential therapies, they are just the tools: the therapeutic power comes from the exposure, habituation, and desensitization. Within Trauma Model Therapy, experiential therapies are just as behavioural as behavioural interventions but are more than just behavioural interventions. While talking remains an integral part of the therapeutic experience, experiential therapies involve activities and processes that ultimately lead to behavioural changes.

In his *Four Quartets*, T.S. Eliot writes, "We had the experience, but missed the meaning."

This error can be made in experiential therapies—simply feeling a feeling or drawing a drawing doesn't lead to recovery. The exposure needs to be combined with cognitive processing and restructuring. The cerebral cortex and the limbic system have to be on the dance floor at the same time. Multiple parts of the brain have to talk to each other—the amygdala talks to the prefrontal cortex, the hippocampus talks to the temporal-parietal cortex, the visual cortex talks to the anterior cingulate, and the reticular activating system needs to be on for therapy to work. Parts of the mind and parts of the brain need to learn new patterns of communication, information sharing, and problem-solving. The problems to be solved are simultaneously emotional, intellectual, social, cultural, and biological in nature. The work of integration involves parts of the brain learning how to talk to each other. This is achieved through work with the mind.

Types of Experiential Therapy

A wide range of activities can be included in the general category of *experiential therapy*. There is no good reason to limit the number of different activities that can be used as experiential interventions. The type of exercise will need to be adapted to the setting. On an inpatient unit, for instance, one can use psychodrama easily because there are many people present in group therapy. In an individual therapy session in an outpatient office, the exercise could be modified to look more like the gestalt chair technique. In both instances, the purpose is for the client to experience a new viewpoint, to get a new perspective. This can help develop empathy for the parent, child, perpetrator, or other figure in the role play. When the client role-plays another person, the self sits in the other chair, so to speak.

On an inpatient unit that has a trained art therapist, a two-hour group can be called Art Therapy. When the therapist providing individual outpatient therapy is not an art therapist, it is still possible to use drawing exercises as therapy tasks, and integrated as part of the therapy.

Basic rules of ethics, boundaries, and professional conduct need to be adhered to in experiential therapies. Calling something an *experiential therapy* does not provide the therapist a justification for changing ethical boundaries, sexual misconduct, regressive interventions, or counter-therapeutic behaviour. Nor does it provide the client a license for acting out, self-indulgence, or lack of responsibility for her feelings, thoughts, and actions.

Experiential Treatment Strategies

A full description of experiential therapies will require a separate treatment manual. In this chapter the goal is to outline the general principles and provide brief examples of one experiential therapy technique—art therapy. Within Trauma Model Therapy, art therapy does not involve interpretation of drawings. The therapist does not look for symbols, evidence of child abuse, or other hidden information. Art therapy is not used to recover or uncover previously hidden information.

In hospital settings, art therapy requires the same rules, structure, and containment as any other group. Art therapy can dissolve into an escalating contest to produce the most graphic, triggering, and extreme drawings, with resulting behavioural chaos and regression. The rules of therapy need to be stated clearly, no matter which group is involved, be it cognitive therapy, psychodrama, trauma education, grief work, or art therapy.

Generally, on an inpatient or day hospital unit, the therapist will begin the art therapy group with an explanation of the task or assignment for the day. Alternatively, there can be group discussion in order to select a focus. If the topic is *your relationship with your mother*, the therapist might ask everyone to draw two people: mother on one side of the page, and self on the other side. Once this has been done, the therapist then asks everyone to write down a list of attributes for mother and a list of attributes for self, beside each figure.

The next step is then to discuss how the person is like her mother, and how she is different. Almost always, especially with women, there is a lot of difficulty maintaining a clear, bounded sense of *self* as separate from and differentiated from *mother*. The members of the group are then asked to write down a list of all the ways in which mother and self are different. This list is then discussed.

Another exercise would be to draw a primary perpetrator and the self. Often, the perpetrator is a big, powerful, angry male and the self is a small, defenseless child. The relationship between self and perpetrator in the present, emotionally, is indistinguishable from the relationship in childhood. After this portrait of the self is discussed, the person is then asked to draw a picture of the self that more closely resembles the present-day adult self. This can be followed with a list of all the ways in which the present-day self differs from the self of thirty years ago.

The list can be both concrete and abstract. It can include differences in height, weight, strength, size and age; where the person lives; having a driver's license; marital status; level of education completed; the adult took martial arts; no longer being abused; stood up to a boss at work; has a therapist; has told the secret to others; a network of supportive adults; more developed cognitive processes; a wider array of coping strategies; parents are divorced; more awareness of child abuse in her society; has a job and her own insurance; and so on.

The next exercise can be to redraw the perpetrator and the two selves, child and adult, so that the differences between the two selves are clear. Following this, the paper can be ripped down the middle so that the child and adult selves are on one piece and the perpetrator is on the other. Although the exercise is carried out by the host, a traumatized child part can participate or watch from close by, and can then learn lessons of safety. The exercise can increase internal communication, self-soothing, and orientation to the body and the present.

Such interventions may seem childish or make-believe to a skeptic, but most people with DID or DDNOS have very vivid internal worlds, imaginations, and absorptive capacity. Such exercises can be powerful and real for them, and can provoke intense feelings and significant changes in core beliefs. The skeptic might dismiss the power of art therapy for DID or DDNOS as based on *suggestibility*, but that is to miss the point. The suggestibility of the person with DID or DDNOS is her power for recovery. She can take a therapy technique that might seem foolish or ineffectual to someone else—drawing stick figures, talking about them, and ripping the page in half—and turn them into real and powerful recovery exercises. This is a talent and a gift, not a character flaw.

The suggestibility of people with DID and DDNOS is a two-edged sword: properly directed, it can lead to amazing recoveries; misdirected, it can lead to regression, chaos, dependency, and entrenchment in the patient role.

Music therapy can be used for relaxation, internal soothing of parts, de-escalation from more intense groups or therapy work, and as a gift to self that helps to reverse self-hatred, self-abuse, and low self-esteem. Inspirational recovery songs can help with motivation, and can help instill a belief that recovery is realistically possible. Other songs movingly explore various trauma themes: they mobilize intense feelings that are then worked on, processed, and desensitized. In this regard, music therapy is another experiential device for activating feelings.

In the person with DID or DDNOS, music can be played for specific parts. The host could do something kind for the inner children by choosing one of their favorite songs. Alternatively, traumatized children can be moved to a safe, well-lit, comfortable room in the inner world that has a suitable collection of books and CDs, plus a CD player. Music therapy can be prescribed as a homework assignment in both the internal and external worlds. Also, internal caretakers can read and sing to the children.

ROPES courses can be very useful in the treatment of DID and DDNOS. For example, the high elements require a great deal of communication, cooperation, internal negotiation, and problem-solving among the parts. This is illustrated vividly and with great wit in Cameron West's book, *First Person Plural*, when he has to walk across a narrow platform high above the ground during a ROPES group at the Trauma Program in Dallas.

These examples give a flavor of the range of experiential therapies that can be used in Trauma Model Therapy. Catharsis is a minor component of such work, which needs to be integrated into an overall plan of therapy, and then carried out in the context of specific, particular tasks and goals for the current session, in the current context, at the person's current life stage. Experiential therapies require solid moorings in order to be effective and healing.

32
Sexual Abuse and Dissociation: The Impact on Sexuality and Sex

The long-term consequences of sexual abuse are far reaching. This chapter will focus particularly on the impact on sexuality and sex.

Sexual contact is frequently a trigger for flashbacks of past abuse. This is frightening and distressing for the person who has been abused. Some people may not have flashbacks but instead experience a range of problems with arousal, orgasm, or other difficulties with sex and intimacy. For others, the legacy of abuse may manifest itself in behaviours, or situations, in which they do not want to participate. The person may not know how to say, "No," and later may experience regret.

Sexual abuse impacts an individual's sexuality, his or her sense of femininity or masculinity, and being comfortable in and with his or her body. It can impact how a person dresses and grooms, as well as his or her sexual behaviour. Some people experience confusion regarding sexual orientation.

There is often fear of sexual arousal and the content of sexual fantasies. People often have questions about whether their fantasies are *normal*. Similarly, there is often confusion around sexual behaviour.

It is also distressing for the partner who is the unwilling, and often times unknowing, catalyst for flashbacks and who may be cast into the role of perpetrator. This puts a painful strain on the relationship, for both parties.

The freedom to enjoy sexuality and sex has been sullied by abusive experiences. Not only has the person suffered during the abuse, they also suffer in sexual relationships in the present.

Confusion around sexuality, sex and relationships is not exclusive to the survivor of abuse. These fundamental human drives and needs are a source of anxiety and confusion, to varying degrees, for many people, from all walks of life, cultures and traditions. The survivor of sexual abuse is dealt a more complex hand to play in what is already a complex aspect of the human condition.

This chapter will cover

- The Impact of Sexual Abuse on Sexuality and Sex

- Flashbacks During Sex: Meaning and Managing

- Negotiating Sex in a Current Relationship or a New Relationship

- Working With Conflicts Around Sex and Sexuality

The Impact of Sexual Abuse on Sexuality and Sex

Self-blame, self-loathing, and self-harm, often of the genitals, are common reactions to sexual abuse.

These reactions may be understood in the context of the locus of control shift (*I am to blame*) and attachment to the perpetrator (*hating the sexual organs and having a sexual response*).

A child victim of incest or sexual abuse, or an adult victim of sexual assault or rape may make sense of the experience by blaming her looks (*it happened because I am pretty, or wore sexy clothes*), behaviour (*I was flirting, or out late at night*) or body (*I had a sexual response*).

No matter how much the therapist may say, "It was not your fault," or how much the client's adult self may understand that it wasn't her fault, entrenched emotional self-blame is likely to persist.

The outcome is often confusion about sexuality, sexual orientation, and difficulties with sex. Clients frequently express varying degrees of discomfort around their sexuality. This can range from guilt and shame about sex and their body, to an avoidance of acknowledging themselves as sexual beings, to questions about sexual orientation.

People who have been sexually abused often have a distorted image of, and attitude towards, their body and sexuality. The continuum ranges from the person who dresses and presents in an asexual demeanor, to the person who dresses in an overtly sexual way or exhibits behaviour that is inappropriately sexualized.

These above observations are generalizations and not intended to be judgmental. The authors are not attempting to outline what sexuality and sexual practices should or should not be, other than their view that rape and adult sexual contact with children are always abusive.

In our clinical experience, clients who engage in extreme sado-masochistic sexual relationships have been re-enacting unresolved ambivalent attachment to the perpetrator, the locus of control shift, and the Victim-Rescuer-Perpetrator triangle. Our clinical experience also suggests that clients with a sexual, physical and/or emotional abuse history who do not ever want to have sexual relationships tend to have unresolved trauma.

Clients may express not wanting sex and being disgusted by sex, at one extreme, or being consumed with thoughts and feelings of wanting sex all the time, at the other extreme. They may feel disgusted with themselves for wanting sex. There may also be indiscriminate sexual behaviour and / or placing themselves in risky situations, which can be understood in the context of attachment to the perpetrator dynamics.

Somewhere in the middle is the person who wants to have a healthy sexual relationship with herself and a partner but who experiences overwhelming flashbacks, sexual dysfunction, and self-hatred both for wanting sex and for having sexual difficulties.

The gender of the victim and the gender of the perpetrator are often key when there are conflicts regarding sexual orientation. If the perpetrator is the same gender as the client, the client may be confused as to whether his attraction to, or feelings of revulsion towards, the same gender are abuse related.

If the perpetrator is the opposite gender of the client, the client may be confused as to whether her orientation towards the opposite gender or towards particular physical attributes or ages is abuse related. If the client has been abused by both a male and a female perpetrator, this can create conflict as to what is her *true* sexual orientation.

The authors do not prescribe a specific code of sexual orientation or behaviour. Healthy, intimate, adult relationships are a therapy goal for most people.

Flashbacks During Sex: Meaning and Managing

Flashbacks are distressing and overwhelming. It is not difficult to understand how sexual contact in the present is a catalyst to flashbacks of past sexual abuse. However, the meaning and purposes of flashbacks are somewhat more complex and multi-layered.

At one level, flashbacks can be understood as the mind's best attempts to reassociate and resolve previously dissociated behaviour, affect, sensation, and knowledge. However, if unaddressed, flashbacks do not mitigate the trauma. In fact, flashbacks keep the client stuck and paralyzed, in much the same way that she was during the abuse. In this context, flashbacks during sex can be viewed as a reenactment of the trauma.

If flashbacks are worked with in therapy they provide invaluable information as to what issues require processing. However, what often happens is that the material is so overwhelming and distressing that the client is highly motivated to keep away from it. This sets up a pattern of avoidance of sex, which can be seen as another purpose of flashbacks.

Sex is understandably a huge trigger. Feelings of fear, terror, shame, humiliation, sexual arousal, feeling powerful and powerless, disgust, and betrayal rise up in a cacophony. There is a survival need to avoid these intense and conflicting emotions. While flashbacks present an opportunity to learn how to contain and address the trauma safely, they also provide a good reason to stay away from sex and sexual feelings, which are strong reminders of past abuse. It becomes a Catch-22 situation.

Raising the possibility that flashbacks may be helping the client avoid working with her abuse experiences requires sensitivity on the part of the therapist. The client may consciously want to work with the trauma and have a healthy relationship in the present, but not be connected to the fear this brings up. It is important that the client be well versed in the three core dynamics of abuse: the locus of control shift, attachment to the perpetrator and the Victim–Rescuer–Perpetrator triangle. This will help to give a framework for understanding her conflicts around sex.

Taking responsibility for the abuse (locus of control shift) is a defense against betrayal trauma, feelings of powerlessness, helplessness, rage, and grief. It is better to believe that if you had done something differently, or if you were not so pretty, or if you did not have normal bodily functions, there may have been a different outcome.

It is safer to hate and rage against your genitals than dare to feel hate and rage towards the perpetrator you were dependent on as a child. Some clients remain emotionally enmeshed with the perpetrator as an adult.

Challenging cognitive errors is the first step in addressing self-blame and self-harm. The second step is to process various aspects of the abuse. This requires the sharing of information between different parts of the system so that everyone understands the full picture of what happened, as opposed to dissociated and fragmented behaviour, affect, sensation, and knowledge.

Once the flashbacks are controlled and there is progress in working with the trauma, there is space for the client to begin to develop healthy sexual functioning.

The first step is to begin to address self-blame or blaming the genitals for the abuse.
A therapeutic exchange might go as follows:

Therapist: Why do you self-mutilate in your vaginal area?
Client: Because I hate my parts down there.
Therapist: It's understandable that you would, given your childhood sexual abuse, but specifically, why are you angry at your genitals?
Client: If I didn't have those parts, the abuse wouldn't have happened.
Therapist: That's true, but that doesn't mean it's your body's fault. If someone gets mugged and robbed, is it her wallet's fault?
Client: No.
Therapist: Same thing with your body. Robbery is a crime and it's the robber's fault, not the wallet's. Same thing with sexual abuse.
Client: That makes sense. But I still hate my vagina.
Therapist: Do you believe in God?
Client: No, not really.
Therapist: Oh, that's right. We talked about that before. Well, in that case, the human body developed over millions of years of evolution, right?
Client: Right.
Therapist: Why do all mammals have sex? To reproduce. Otherwise their species would die out. So sex is a natural part of life. Would you agree?
Client: What happened to me wasn't natural.
Therapist: True. Very true. OK, let me change tack a little. If I hit you on the head with a board, your body would react with bleeding and bruising, right? If I put your body in a tanning booth for too long, your body would react with sunburn. Neither of these reactions would be good or desirable, but they would be natural reactions of the body to what was going on. If you touch a hot stove, your body reacts with a blister because that is how it is designed. Would you agree with all that?
Client: Yes.
Therapist: Your body is also designed to experience sexual arousal when certain parts of it are stimulated. This is a completely normal bodily reaction. Without it, without sexual arousal and desire, the human race would die out. So when your body reacted with arousal, it was just reacting normally the way it was designed to do. Your body didn't know that it was your father touching you. It just did its job.
Client: OK.
Therapist: Therefore you're blaming your body when it wasn't your body's fault. This is a variation on the locus of control shift. The actual truth is that you, your elbows, your toes, and your genitals, were not in control of the situation. You couldn't stop the abuse or escape it, so you coped as best as you could. Your mind dissociated, because that's its job, and your genitals got aroused because that's their job.
Client: I see what you're saying. But I still hate my vagina.
Therapist: No doubt. But are you willing to consider forgiving your vagina for a crime it never committed—the crime of causing the abuse?
Client: I guess so.
Therapist: Good. "I guess so" is a lot further down the road of healing than "no." So, good work.
Client: Thanks.

Negotiating Sex in a Current Relationship or a New Relationship

The first step of negotiation in a current sexual relationship takes place not with the current or potential sexual partner but within the client. Internal communication and cooperation is fundamental to healing.

The client with DID or DDNOS is likely to have parts with different attitudes towards sex and sexual behaviours, ranging from aversion and avoidance, to having many sexual partners and for some, unsafe sexual practices. While these behaviours appear opposites, they are different sides of the same coin. Both extremes reflect unresolved trauma. In addition, there may be parts who are the opposite gender of the host, or who have a different sexual orientation than the host.

The parts of the system that tend to hold the most memories of the abuse are frequently young children and adolescents. It is often these parts who are among the ones activated during sexual contact in the present.

Parts who express their trauma through indiscriminate and dangerous sexual behaviours and situations, are often labeled as promiscuous by the host and other parts of the system. Unfortunately, this attitude may also be held and communicated overtly or subtly, by the therapist. This is unfair. The behaviour needs to be understood in the context that it developed: those parts taking on a role that other parts didn't want or couldn't do.

However, the parts who act out in this way also need to learn that their behaviour is part of a bigger picture that involves all three corners of the Victim–Rescuer-Perpetrator triangle. Continuing re-enacting trauma in this way exposes other parts to ongoing victimization, and therefore is part of the current problem.

People with a history of sexual abuse are more vulnerable to sexually abusive relationships and rape as adults, so the cycle of abuse is repeated and trauma is reactivated in the present. Working with safety in relationships is of primary importance. If the client is in abusive relationships, healing will be greatly impeded.

Usually, before improving sexual relations in the present can be addressed, a significant amount of processing of the sexual trauma needs to occur. Sometimes, the client may benefit from giving herself permission not to engage in sexual activity or limited activity while this processing takes place. This can assist the client in learning new patterns of sexuality that do not involve exchanging sex for favours and goods, and do not involve forcing herself to just *do it* through fear of losing her relationship, or in order to keep the peace. This is a combined Victim-Rescuer strategy that casts the partner in the role of Perpetrator. Choosing to refrain from or limit sexual activity can create additional anxiety for the client and stress on her relationship.

Clients are often fearful of discussing sex with their partners. The concept of boundaries, of being able to say no, or of asking for their needs be met, is completely foreign. Frequently the partners of abuse survivors do not know the extent of the abuse their partner has experienced, or the difficulties she experiences with sex. The client can have a great deal of fear of being rejected and abandoned.

Clients may need a lot of support, coaching, and role-playing to assist them to raise what may seem to be basic issues with their partner. Joint sessions with the partner may help to address and negotiate the concerns of both parties.

Working With Conflicts Around Sex and Sexuality

Exploring issues related to sex and sexuality is a slow and distressing process. Body image, identifying normal healthy sexual arousal as opposed to conditioned abuse stimuli, and being able to live within the body are among the many challenges of healing. Some of these conflicts will become clearer through processing memories.

Providing clients with books and DVD's can be very helpful. These can be read and watched in her own time and at her own pace, then the client can bring her feelings, reactions and questions in to therapy. It is important that the client feels that she can ask any questions, and that the therapist is non-judgmental and is comfortable with speaking about sex.

Learning to feel comfortable with her body is one of the first goals. This includes awareness of her body (living *in* the body, not outside it). Other aspects may involve learning to take better care of the body through attending to health needs, diet, exercise, hygiene, and personal grooming.

Visualization and relaxation techniques can help focus on healing the trauma to her body, reducing her fear and anxiety, and learning to be present. These exercises are intrinsically linked to working with grief, anger, betrayal, and body memory.

Exploring sexuality through masturbation, fantasies, and visualizations can assist the client to feel more comfortable with her body and more self-confident. When appropriate, the client can invite a partner to be involved in visualization and fantasy exercises. The client can learn to pace herself, becoming progressively more physical and intimate.

Developing communication skills and assertiveness not only assists in improving respectful non-sexual relationships, but will also lead to greater confidence when negotiating and exploring her sexuality and sex with a partner.

Often the person with a sexual abuse history will place great emphasis on the need to be able to trust her partner. While this is reasonable to a degree, primarily the need is to be able to trust in her own capacity to negotiate and handle all aspects of her life.

Sexual healing requires that the client learn to respect herself, her body, and her needs. It is a process requiring patience, courage, and tenacity. It is also a difficult road for partners; this is important for both the client and the therapist to acknowledge. However, it is possible for people who have been sexually abused to reclaim their bodies and to enjoy healthy adult sexual intimacy.

Courtois, C.A. (1988). *Healing the incest wound: Adult survivors in therapy*. New York: W.W. Norton.

Courtois, C.A. (1999). *Recollections of sexual abuse: Treatment principles and guidelines*. New York: W.W. Norton.

Gil, E. (1984). *Outgrowing the pain: A book for and about adults abused as children*. New York: Dell.

Gil, E. (1992). *Outgrowing the pain: A book for partners & spouses of adult survivors*. New York: Dell.

Jehu, D. (1988). *Beyond sexual abuse: Therapy with women who were childhood victims*. New

York: John Wiley & Sons.

Lewis, M.(1992). *Shame: The exposed self*. New York: Free Press.

Potter-Efron, R., & Potter-Efron, P. (1989). *Letting go of shame: Understanding how shame affects your your life*. Center City, MN: Hazelden Press.

van der Hart, O., Nijenhuis, E.R.S., & Steele, K. (2006). *The haunted self: Structural dissociation and the treatment of chronic traumatization*. New York: W.W. Norton.

33
The Impact of Trauma on Spirituality and the Role of Spirituality in Healing

Human beings are a composite of mind (cognitive functions), body (physical capacities), soul (feelings and emotions), and spirit (connection to God or something greater and *other* than Self, which gives a sense of meaning and purpose).

All aspects of the psyche are impacted by trauma and abuse. Clients with dissociative disorders from varied religious, spiritual, and cultural backgrounds frequently report profound spiritual experiences during and after traumatic events.

Conflict around the concepts of *Good* and *Evil*, the role of God or the universe and search for meaning, are inherent in healing from trauma. Yet, many therapists express feeling unsure as to how to approach spiritual issues and concerns about being intrusive, inadvertently imposing their own belief systems or causing offense.

Clients often raise spiritual experiences and beliefs tentatively. They can feel unsure as to whether their therapist is willing to explore these dimensions or if it's a legitimate issue to bring to therapy. Some fear their experiences or beliefs will be pathologized.

There is an increasing recognition and body of literature about the importance of incorporating spirituality in therapy. The authors' approach to spirituality includes, but is not limited to, formalized religion.

This chapter will explore spirituality in the context of cultural issues, socio-economic factors, gender, sexuality and the core dynamics of trauma. We will focus on assisting clients to reconcile spiritual conflicts and philosophical constructs and to draw on their spirituality as a profound resource in healing and well-being.

Practical guidance applicable to both religious and secular ideologies will be presented to assist therapists to enter into a spiritual dialogue with their clients, to explore how trauma impacts spirituality, and the role of spirituality in healing.

This chapter covers

- Definition of Spirituality

- Important Considerations in Relation to Spirituality and Trauma

- Spiritual Conflicts: Locus of Control Shift and Attachment to the Perpetrator

- The Victim–Rescue–Perpetrator Triangle

- Commonly Reported Spiritual Experiences

- Surrender to a Higher Power Versus Personal Responsibility

- Search for Meaning

- Forgiveness

- Entering a Spiritual Dialogue

- Spiritual Exercises

Definition of Spirituality

Therapists may have different beliefs and practices from their clients, even when they ostensibly belong to the same faith or spiritual philosophy. The authors don't believe this need be an impediment to assisting clients with spiritual conflicts or facilitating the spiritual aspect of healing from trauma. Respect for and embracing the beliefs and experiences of clients is paramount. The only caveat is where beliefs and practices infringe on the freedom, rights, safety and well-being of others.

The approach to working with spirituality presented is compatible for all religions, faiths, spiritual beliefs or philosophical constructs. The focus is providing a framework for the client to explore his or her beliefs, perceptions and experiences.

The definition of spirituality presented is

- A search for meaning and connection with something greater or *other than* Self and interpersonal relationships

- May or may not involve an organized religion

- May or may not be associated with belief in God/Gods

- An approach that embraces the essence of all religions and belief systems, and does not condone harm toward self and others

Important Considerations in Relation to Spirituality

In addition to acknowledgment and respect for clients' beliefs and faith systems there are other important considerations:

- Socio-political-cultural Context

- Race and Ethnicity

- Gender and Sexuality

- Age: Current and at Onset of Trauma

- Type of Trauma:

    Impersonal: natural disaster/car accident

Interpersonal: Child abuse, domestic violence, rape,
violent crime, chronic illness/hospitalizations, war, terrorist attack

The interaction of the above factors will have a bearing and influence on a person's experience; on the meaning she makes from the experience, as well as the individual's personality traits, resilience, and defense mechanisms.

People from the same faith or beliefs can have vastly differing social, cultural, and political contexts. A young girl raised as Roman Catholic in Australia, who becomes pregnant as a result of a rape, is unlikely to be shunned by her family and community, or pressured to marry her rapist. However, this was the experience of women in East Timor, whose rape by Indonesian troops resulted in pregnancy. In East Timor, pregnancy outside marriage brings shame upon the girl's family, regardless of the circumstances of the pregnancy.

Gender and sexuality are often significant factors. The roles of men and women are significantly different in many organized religions. This factor alone can have a major impact on some people. Trauma can add another dimension to this complex issue.

Lesbians and homosexuals face additional issues. Same sex relationships are seen to be against God's Will in the major religions. Once again, this is often experienced as a trauma, in and of itself. Oftentimes, lesbian and homosexual clients are not only grappling with issues of sexual abuse but also rejection by their faith due to their sexual orientation.

Just as emotional and psychological development occurs along an age continuum, so does spiritual development. Therefore, the current age of the client is a factor in his or her spiritual quest. The age of the onset of trauma also plays a significant part, not only in how a person makes sense of his experience at a personal level but also how it is integrated, or not integrated, with spiritual beliefs.

A belief and understanding in God or an intelligent universe or non-belief in God is different at age five than at age forty-five, for example. Oftentimes, in DDNOS and DID, parts of the system have arrested development, not only cognitively and emotionally, but also spiritually. The concrete and magical thinking of the child that manifests in attachment to the perpetrator and locus of control shift dynamics, frequently applies to spiritual and religious beliefs. However, trauma can challenge a person's belief system at any age.

Finally, the nature of the trauma can be significant to the perception, understanding, and meaning an individual makes of his experiences. An impersonal trauma may be experienced differently at a spiritual level than an interpersonal trauma. Abuse committed by spiritual leaders and abuse perpetrated ostensibly in the name of God inevitably adds an additional layer to the trauma experience.

Spiritual Conflicts

As discussed above, there are some spiritual conflicts that may be more specific to the nature of the trauma, the particular environment or circumstances of the individual. Some conflicts appear to be universal, centered around the themes of abandonment and betrayal. In clients with DDNOS and DID, different parts of the internal system may hold different explanations and meaning for the same experience. Some conflicts appear to be spiritual in nature but on exploration are revealed to be an extension of the core trauma conflicts of attachment to the perpetrator and the locus of control shift. Once these issues have been addressed, deeper spiritual questions, the search for meaning and spiritual expression may emerge.

Locus of Control Shift and Attachment to the Perpetrator

In some instances, God or the universe is a safe *object* onto whom feelings of rage, abandonment, pain, and grief about mum or dad can be displaced or projected. In this way the child can maintain her attachment to the people who are responsible for protecting her, but who are in fact the people responsible for her suffering.

Alternatively, a child can maintain her attachment to both her abuser and God or the universe by shifting the locus of control for the abuse to herself. This child's magical thinking is that God or the universe didn't stop dad from hurting her, because she is bad and deserved to be abused. This is God's or the universe's way of punishing her for being such a bad girl. However, if she tries harder to be a good girl, then she still has hope that she can win God's, the universe's and her daddy's love. By shifting the locus of control to herself she protects herself from feeling powerless, and feeling the overwhelming emotions associated with the betrayal by her father.

Victim–Rescuer–Perpetrator Triangle

Chapter 18 explained how the Victim-Rescuer-Perpetrator triangle operates within the client's internal and external worlds. Here, we explore how the triangle interacts with conflicts about God and the universe.

As stated in earlier chapters, the Victim-Rescuer-Perpetrator triangle is an expression of the dynamics inherent in the locus of control shift and attachment to the perpetrator. The triangle is often activated in relation to the trauma survivor's spiritual conflicts.

- Belief in a compassionate God or benign universe challenged

- God is loving or punishing depending on the client's innate goodness or badness

- Displacement of anger and betrayal onto God or the universe

- God or the universe as Rescuer or Perpetrator

- Judgmental and punishing beliefs about karma and destiny

- Abuse is proof that God doesn't exist

The Victim-Rescuer-Perpetrator triangle is an activation of cognitions, beliefs, and dissociated or suppressed emotions at the time of and subsequent to trauma. The cognitions and beliefs formed around the meaning of an experience are age-specific.

The locus of control shift, attachment to the perpetrator, and magical thinking result in fixed, concrete, and distorted cognitions. The child will come to the following conclusions about his or her experiences:

God made this happen because I am bad.

God doesn't love me or else He would have rescued me.

I hate God because He let bad things happen to me.

God loves me; He is trying to help me become a better boy by making uncle Jack do these bad things to me.

God loves me because He made daddy have an accident so he couldn't hurt me anymore.

God is punishing me for having bad thoughts about mummy.

Abuse means God doesn't exist because if He did, He wouldn't let it happen.

This is happening because I have bad karma.

I was cruel to my daddy in a past life and so that is why he left me.

I chose to come in to this family to work out past karma so I knew this would happen.

These are examples of common cognitive distortions in children. These beliefs may be shaped by things that the perpetrator told them, which were implied or which were gleaned from their cultural or religious context.

These explanations make sense to a child. However, in the DDNOS and DID client these distortions remain fixed and very difficult to shift. The adult client clings to these distortions to defend against feelings of powerlessness, rage, and grief.

Clients who do not have a belief in God will often feel betrayed and angry at the universe. Some clients feel their abuse proves there is no point or meaning to existence. There is often a profound sense of alienation and hopelessness that is more than social isolation. A universe that may be believed to be benign by some is often perceived to be indifferent at best, and hostile at worst, by survivors of trauma or abuse.

The Influence of Type of Abuse on Spiritual Conflicts

The type of abuse impacts the spiritual conflicts an individual may experience. Any kind of trauma, be it impersonal, interpersonal, or a combination, can lead to spiritual crisis. Whether the trauma is familial sexual abuse, a natural disaster, or terminal illness, a person may rage at or find solace and a deepening of his or her faith in God or the universe.

Abuse by spiritual or religious leaders, abuse perpetrated in the name of God (such as distorting scripture to justify the sexual abuse of a child or acts of terrorism), the performance of a deliverance ritual or exorcism, add another dimension to the experience of betrayal. Questions around God's Will and/or karma, complex issues in themselves, are complicated further by trauma and abuse.

Cognitive interventions can assist in exploring the layers of such conflicts. As with other aspects of healing from trauma, feelings and emotions need to be re-associated and given safe avenues of expression. Once some of the cognitive distortions and feelings have been processed the way is cleared for deeper spiritual exploration, meaning finding and healing.

Issues related to possession states, deliverance rituals or exorcisms will be explored below.

Commonly Reported Spiritual Experiences

Clients report a variety of spiritual experiences during and after traumatic experiences. Reports of feeling the presence of God, an angel, a saint, an ancestor, spirit guide, or *something* from another realm and dimension are common.

Some people report that this benevolent being spoke to them, offering comforting words and reassurance. They were told they would be OK, that they were being looked after, protected, and loved. Others report that there were no words but that the sense of a presence brought comfort, peace, and hope.

Some report a visual experience and others sensory, or a knowing that there was someone or something there.

Reports of spiritual attack, or being bombarded and terrorized by malevolent entities or forces are also common. Again, these experiences may be visual or a sense of a presence.

Clients with DDNOS or DID frequently express the belief of being possessed by Satan or one of his demons. This is common in clients who report ritual or organized sadistic abuse but is not limited to this group. As described above, some clients have had exorcisms or deliverance rituals to free them of evil spirits. The authors have clients or have consulted on cases where these experiences have been experienced as traumatic.

In the authors' experience, internal demons are an expression of a disavowed part of the internal DDNOS or DID system. These parts tend to hold a great deal of the pain and rage associated with the abuse. We have found that they are best approached in the same way as other persecutor parts of the internal system, as outlined in chapter 26.

Many of the world's major religions believe in demon and spirit possession. Yet, individuals within these faith systems may not believe in possession. Many people regard such beliefs as superstitions and psychologically based phenomenon.

The secular western world tends to be suspicious of phenomena and experiences that are normal and valid in other cultures. Indigenous Australian's and American Indian's daily life revolves around communion with the spirit world of ancestors and nature. Altered states of consciousness are actively pursued through initiation rites and rituals. In many cultures, possession by spirits is part of the cultural norm and viewed as a meaningful, real experience.

As therapists, we need to be mindful to not make assumptions about what a person might believe or how he interprets or practices his faith. Listening to clients we need to be aware of our own cultural and spiritual lenses.

Having stated the above, the authors also note that reports of external spiritual support or attack are often described as qualitatively different from experiences of internal support (such as inner self helper) or possession.

Whether the experience of spiritual support or attack is literal, symbolic, or another facet of dissociative experience, is not up to the therapist to know or determine. Our role is to assist the client to find his or her own meaning in these experiences.

The exception to this is when a client is clearly presenting as psychotic or delusional. Hallucinations, delusions, and psychosis are common reactions to and defenses against abuse and trauma. Yet it is equally important not to dismiss a client's experience because it occurred during a psychotic episode. Once the client has stabilized, working with the content of their experience will yield rich insight both into the client's trauma history as well as his or her spiritual beliefs and conflicts.

Clients reporting ritual abuse or who have been abused within a religious context, will often present with a combination of indoctrinated beliefs, having been terrorized and tricked into believing certain "magical" or "mystical" events have occurred, and having been subjected to various forms of mind manipulation resulting in distorted perceptions. The same clients may also have had genuine spiritual experiences that have not involved such manipulations. For these clients it can take a very long time to sift through the layers and levels of their experience before coming to a place of understanding.

Surrender to a Higher Power Versus Personal Responsibility

Confusion and conflict about surrender to a higher power and personal responsibility is not exclusive to trauma survivors. Implicit in faith in God or a conscious and intelligent universe, is the concept of surrender. This requires putting one's faith, trust, and life in the hands of God or the universe.

Inherent in this concept is the notion that as limited human beings we may not understand why or how things happen, but we believe that there is a divine plan that we are part of and that within this plan we each have a part to play. Whatever happens is either God's Will or happens for a reason.

Fundamental to psychotherapy is the concept of personal responsibility. This does not imply that we are responsible for everything that happens to us. Clearly, there are many events in our lives over which we have little or no control. Personal responsibility means that we are responsible for making our best efforts to deal with issues which life presents. Personal responsibility requires taking ownership of the things over which we can assert some influence and control.

It follows, that while we are not responsible for the bad things that others may do to us, we are responsible for our own healing and living the best life we can. This includes owning our projections, addressing the defenses that arose out of trauma, and self-empowerment.

Are faith in God or a higher order in the universe and the concept of personal responsibility, mutually exclusive? The authors' approach is that faith and personal responsibility are compatible.

Rather than entering into a theological or philosophical debate with clients, which is potentially fraught with moral judgments and assumptions, it is more helpful to explore with the client how he or she is living. Does the person have compassion and humility for self and others? Is he or she actively engaged in a healing process both in and outside therapy? Is he or she stuck in the locus of control shift, attachment to the perpetrator, or Victim–Rescuer–Perpetrator dynamics?

Search for Meaning

When something traumatic happens, whatever type of trauma it may be, at some point most people ask, "Why did this happen to me?" The search for meaning is not limited to people who have experienced trauma but appears to be inherent in the human condition. Sometimes, it is not until a major life-changing event occurs that a person embarks on a spiritual quest or experiences a spiritual awakening.

When an individual feels there is no meaning or purpose in life, this can precipitate profound despair and an existential crisis. The spiritual path and the search for meaning is a challenging, complex, confusing, and oftentimes, painful process. Clients who have experienced trauma will return to the same questions time and again.

As therapists, it is not our role to interpret events according to our personal beliefs, or to suggest meaning, but rather to walk alongside our clients as they search for their own truth. Among the common questions clients and therapists will ask is, "How do I know whether I am rationalizing why something happened as an avoidance of the feeling?," or "Am I being superstitious?," or "Have I truly discerned the meaning, or that there was no meaning?"

It is not our job to know, or to answer these questions for clients. We can assist them to explore the meaning behind delusions, the locus of control shift, attachment to the perpetrator, or triangle dynamics. We can gently reflect on their experiences and questions. We can help them hold their map, but we are not the map-makers.

Forgiveness

Forgiveness is a huge and emotionally charged word. It is a major issue that arises in trauma therapy, regardless of the nature of the trauma. However, the nature of the trauma will often have a bearing on an individual's desire, need, struggle or ease in forgiving.

What does forgiveness mean? As therapists it is important to clarify what forgiveness means to yourself and to clarify what it means for your client. These meanings may not match.

To say forgiveness is a complicated issue is an understatement. The authors' perspective about forgiveness is that it is not about condoning, saying something was OK, or that it doesn't matter. Forgiveness is not about forgetting and it doesn't mean being forced to have someone in your life and loving them.

Our perspective is that forgiveness means to not remain stuck in hate and revenge fantasies or behaviours. It means not treating oneself or others badly or reliving the trauma in myriad ways. From this perspective, forgiveness may be seen as a *letting go*. Some clients feel at peace with the idea of 'letting go' but can remain endlessly stuck in their associations with the word forgiveness.

Many clients believe that if they forgive the person who hurt them, then that person is getting away with it. Sometimes, not getting better is a way to punish the perpetrator. Not getting better makes the statement, "*See, look what you did. I hope you feel bad and guilty.*" While some perpetrators may feel guilt for causing their victim's suffering, ultimately it is the client who continues to suffer.

In most ways, forgiveness is less about setting the other person free and more about the clients setting themselves free. If the perpetrator finds some peace from either the client being able to move on, or directly being forgiven, that is a byproduct and not the purpose of forgiveness.

The authors' belief is that we never get away with wrong doing, whether it's discovered or not, whether a person is brought to account or not. We believe this to be true even when it appears on the outside that the wrongdoer got what he or she wanted and is living happily.

The issue of forgiveness is inherent in the spiritual conflict and quest of the client. Some people believe forgiveness comes exclusively through the Grace of God. This belief is not incompatible with the views reflected here. The client will still battle with the notion of what forgiveness means to him or her, whether she or he can forgive or not, whether he or she is bad if they don't, whether she or he is good if they do, and how to go about forgiving.

Forgiveness would seem to be less of a *doing* than a way of *being*. The authors believe that forgiveness is a natural result of healing and is not something that can be forced or intellectualized. Certainly individuals can decide that they want to reach a point of forgiveness. This may precipitate acting with more compassion to self and others. This decision may signal an important first step along the road to forgiveness. However, as discussed in chapter 30, clients will still need to feel the pain, rage, hate, grief, and loss. There are no shortcuts.

Spirituality has a large role to play in forgiveness. However, as therapists we need to be mindful of becoming the perpetrator on the triangle if we push forgiveness as a goal or make judgments about a client's readiness, willingness, or ability to forgive. Everyone will travel their own unique road to healing.

Entering a Spiritual Dialogue

Therapy has a beginning stage—developing a therapeutic alliance, work on stabilizing and daily functioning; a middle stage—working with trauma material and conflicts; and an end stage—working with the grief about what was, what wasn't, and what can never be. End stage therapy focuses on developing life beyond trauma. The reality of therapy is that it is not a linear process. These stages intersect, crossover, and go back and forth continually. A useful image for the therapy process is a spiral. Therapy progresses through the levels of the spiral, seemingly returning to the same point but at the next level.

Spiritual issues fit well with the concept of a spiral. Just as at different stages in the life cycle our spirituality develops, twisting and turning, being redefined, further understood, and integrated as we mature; oftentimes the role of spirituality in healing will twist and turn.

Spirituality can be, but is not necessarily, a stand-alone issue. It weaves in and out of the therapeutic journey. At times it may appear to be a backdrop and at others to take centre stage. At times it is appropriate to wait for the client to raise spiritual concerns and at other times it may be pertinent to initiate questions that may lead to spiritual exploration:

How do you make sense of this?

How does this fit in with your beliefs?

Questions about spirituality can be subtle or direct. Some clients are very clear that they need to explore and understand how their experiences have impacted and influenced their beliefs and spiritual practices. Others may feel they can't bring spirituality into therapy, that it's not relevant, allowed, or something you can or are willing to address. Others may not know how to begin to articulate it. Others may be very disconnected or dissociated from their spirituality.

Opening the door to spirituality as part of therapy can begin in the assessment process, through the case history questionnaire or direct questioning. It may take the form of a direct question such as, *"Do you have a spiritual and/or religious belief and practice?"*

Spirituality may be approached through an open question, such as, *"What in your life nourishes you or gives you a sense of meaning and purpose?"* This offers the possibility of discussing many aspects of the person's life, relationships, work, hobbies, and interests, as well as spirituality.

By asking questions about a person's beliefs and practices at the beginning of therapy, we immediately inform the client that spiritual conflicts and beliefs are something he or she can bring into therapy, and give the message that spirituality is seen as a relevant and important aspect of life and experiences.

When people have been raised in a belief system or practice that they experienced to be restrictive, dogmatic or alienating, once they have left home they may have made a decision not to adhere to these beliefs and practices. Similarly, if someone has been abused in the context of particular beliefs or by a spiritual leader, faith and abuse become entangled. For some, the solution to this conflict may be to abandon and discredit the religion in its entirety.

This may be an appropriate choice for many. They may find different beliefs that feel more compatible with their understanding of spirituality. Others may at some point wish to return to the beliefs and faiths in which they were raised, or reclaim some aspect of the belief, rituals or practices.

Healing, reclaiming, developing, and strengthening the spiritual aspect of Self for survivors of trauma requires soul searching, resolution of the locus of control shift, attachment to the perpetrator, and victim-rescuer-perpetrator triangle dynamic, and emotional work.

So, how can we help clients explore spiritual questions and conflicts? The strategies outlined in chapter 30 are also applicable to exploring spiritual issues. They are not grounded in any belief system and so can be utilized for all people, whatever beliefs they have and whatever aspect of spirituality they are exploring; positive experiences, conflicts, the search for meaning, or integrating experiences with spiritual beliefs.

Giving clients permission to bring their spiritual beliefs, practices, experiences and conflicts in to the room opens another pathway toward healing. Engaging a client in an ongoing dialogue about spiritual experiences and concerns simultaneously offers many opportunities. It bears witness and can be experienced as validating and respectful. It offers an opportunity to explore and challenge cognitive distortions, e.g. the locus of control shift, attachment to the perpetrator, and triangle dynamics. It also recognizes spirituality as a legitimate and important aspect of the human experience.

Spirituality Exercises

In addition to the strategies in chapter 30, these exercises are designed to facilitate the exploration of spirituality, the impact trauma has had on an individual's spirituality and the role spirituality plays in the healing process. The exercises can be done in therapy sessions, as homework assignments, or in groups.

Introduction to exercise 1: Bring something to the therapy session or group that symbolizes or represents something about your spirituality and what spirituality means to you. Write or draw something about what this object reflects or expresses about your spirituality

The exercise is followed by an invitation to share with the therapist or group. (If the exercise is done as a group exercise, allow 15 minutes for the exercise and 10 minutes for feedback to the group).

Introduction to exercise 2: Some people say that trauma or abuse has challenged their beliefs and perceptions about God or what spirituality means. They felt abandoned, angry, and betrayed. They view life as pointless and meaningless.

Some people became attuned to and connected with their spirituality through their abuse and traumatic experiences. They describe feeling the presence of God, angels, a spirit guide, ancestor or connection with something greater than and beyond the physical, which sustained and nurtured them through difficult times.

How have your experiences of abuse or trauma influenced your spirituality?

What are some of the challenges you have faced regarding spirituality?

The exercise is followed by an invitation to share with the therapist or group. (If the exercise is done in a group exercise, allow 15 minutes for the exercise and 10 minutes for feedback to the group).

Introduction to exercise 3: Dissociation, auditory, visual, olfactory, sensory hallucinations, delusions, and psychosis are common reactions to and defenses against abuse and trauma. Spiritual experiences that are accepted and seen as the norm in other cultures are often treated with suspicion in western society. Some people may be confused as to the validity or realness of some spiritual experiences.

How do you work out what is real and what may be delusional or a projection of inner experiences and conflicts? Can you ever know for sure? If you work with the meaning of an experience, does it matter, or when might it matter?

The exercise is followed by an invitation to share with the therapist or group. (If the exercise is done in a group exercise, allow 15 minutes for the exercise and 10 minutes for feedback to the group).

Introduction to exercise 4: Healing from trauma and abuse is a journey of the mind (cognitions), body (connection with the body), soul (expression of feelings and emotions) and spirit (beliefs, meaning, philosophies).

In what ways has spirituality been a part of your healing?

The exercise is followed by an invitation to share with the therapist or group. (If the exercise is done in a group exercise, allow 15 minutes for the exercise and 10 minutes for feedback to the group).

Introduction to exercise 5: Spirituality is a way of being with oneself and being in the world. Some of the ways it may be expressed are through prayer; attending a place of worship; practicing meditation or yoga; through creative expression; being in nature; working with dreams, and the symbolism reflected in daily life experiences. The place of, and connection with spirituality impacts how we treat ourselves and others. It may be a private and personal expression, or through varied forms of contribution to the community, environment, or global issues.

In what ways do you express your spirituality in daily life?

Are there things you want to do or think you might like to try to deepen, express, or practice your spirituality more fully?

The exercise is followed by an invitation to share with the therapist or group. (If the exercise is done in a group exercise, allow 15 minutes for the exercise and 10 minutes for feedback to the group).

Frazier, R.E., Hansen, N.D. (2009). Religious/spiritual psychotherapy behaviors: Do we do what we believe to be important? *Professional Psychology: Research and Practice*, 40, 81-87.

Griffith, J.L., & Griffith, M.E. (2003). *Encountering the sacred in psychotherapy: How to talk with people about their spiritual lives*. New York: Guilford Press.

Moore, T. (1992). *Care of the soul: A guide for cultivating depth and sacredness in everyday life*. New York: Harper Perrenial.

Moore, T. (2005). *Dark nights of the soul: A guide to finding your way through life's ordeals*. New York: Gotham Books.

Pargament, K.I. (2007). *Spiritually integrated psychotherapy: Understanding & addressing the sacred*. New York: Guilford Press.

Passmore, N.L. (2003). Religious issues in counseling: Are Australian psychologists "dragging the chain"? *Australian Psychologist*, 38, 183-192.

Richo, D. (2005). *The 5 things we cannot change: and the happiness we find by embracing them*. Boston: Shambala.

Smith, A.F. (2007). Do clients want their spiritual and religious beliefs to be discussed in therapy? *Psychotherapy in Australia*, 14, 55-59.

Somer, E. (2004). Trance possession disorder in Judaism: sixteenth-century dybbuks in the Near-East. *Journal of Trauma and Dissociation*, 5, 131-146.

Tacey, D. (2003). *The spirituality revolution: The emergence of contemporary spirituality*. New York: Harper Collins.

Young-Eisendrath, P. (1996). *The gifts of suffering: Finding insight, compassion, and renewal*. Boston: Addison-Wesley.

34
The Role of Hypnosis

In North America in the 1990s, therapists were intimidated into under-utilization of hypnosis in trauma therapy because of false memory lawsuits. These lawsuits occurred, in part, because of excessive use of hypnosis, too much memory work, and failure to maintain therapeutic neutrality. In terms of medico-legal survival in North America, it is a fact of life that hypnosis carries risk, and this risk should not be ignored. One must balance purely clinical considerations against the therapist's professional survival. The net outcome is caution about the role of hypnosis in trauma therapy.

This chapter does not contain instruction on hypnotic techniques. The reader is advised to take courses from the American Society of Clinical Hypnosis or a similar organization, to seek supervision in any use of formal hypnotic inductions, and to use consent forms provided by professional organizations. In the Appendix, statements by professional organizations concerning hypnosis and trauma memories are referenced.

This chapter briefly covers

- Overview of Liability Risks of Hypnosis

- Recommendations for Risk Management

- Non-hypnotic Techniques for Managing the Client's Trance Logic and Auto-hypnotic Skills

Liability Risks of Hypnosis

In the United States, rules about hypnosis vary from state to state. In many courts, no testimony from a witness is allowed if the person has previously been hypnotized. Therefore all clients offered hypnosis must be informed of this risk. There are many misconceptions and myths about hypnosis, and there are diametrically opposed schools of thought about the reality of hypnotic trance. Indeed, some schools of thought adopt the position that hypnosis is just an elaborate form of role play. This viewpoint is often referred to as the *sociocognitive model* of hypnosis. The sociocognitive model is best explained by Nicholas Spanos (1996).

In any lawsuit concerning treatment of a dissociative disorder, the expert witnesses for the plaintiff are likely to be proponents of the sociocognitive model. Such experts generally believe that most or all cases of DID are created unwittingly by misinformed therapists. They believe that, like hypnotic trance, DID is a form of role enactment. According to this viewpoint, the client adopts the social role of DID sufferer in response to subtle cues and suggestions, leading questions, and sources of information about DID in books, in movies, and on the internet.

From the sociocognitive perspective, DID is not a legitimate psychiatric disorder. If you ignore it, stop talking about it, don't feed into it, and don't reinforce it, DID will just melt away, according to the sociocognitive model. Therapists using hypnosis for treatment of DID, DDNOS, complex PTSD, borderline personality disorder, or related conditions, are advised to educate themselves about the sociocognitive model of hypnosis, and the arguments for and against that model in the literature.

Recommendations for Risk Management

Fortunately, lawsuits for implantation of false memories and creation of iatrogenic DID peaked in 1994–1995 and are now quite rare. Therapists can treat dissociative disorders with a low and tolerable degree of medico-legal risk. Therapists can protect themselves by practicing within the Treatment Guidelines of the International Society for the Study of Trauma and Dissociation, by maintaining good boundaries, by seeking sub-specialty training and supervision, and by adhering to the practice guidelines of their licensing boards and national associations.

In our experience providing clinical supervision and expert witness testimony in malpractice lawsuits, lawsuits are rarely filed if the therapy has involved good boundaries, and has followed standard ethical guidelines. In the lawsuits we have seen, there have always been violations of many different boundaries, violations of therapeutic neutrality, counter-transference acting out on the Victim-Rescuer-Perpetrator triangle, and other serious problems in the therapy process. When no such problems occur in a therapy, a lawsuit is highly unlikely. The only exception to this is litigation filed by individuals with factitious DID, but such lawsuits can be successfully defended based on current literature, research, and practice guidelines.

Non-Hypnotic Techniques for Managing the Client's Trance Logic and Auto-Hypnosis

In our experience, formal hypnotic inductions are not necessary in treatment of DID because treatment goals can be met without them. In fact, it is the opposite procedure that is more important: grounding the client and bringing her out of trance states. Techniques for doing so are described in previous chapters. Here we are simply emphasizing the conceptual principle: the goal of treatment is to learn a more healthy, fluid, balanced use of self-hypnosis and dissociation. Overall, treatment is more about helping the client come out of trance than it is about induction of trance states.

35
The Role of Medication

Most people in treatment for DID or DDNOS are on some type of psychiatric medication. Anyone who has been an inpatient is almost certain to be on meds. In this chapter we will briefly review medications from the perspective of psychotherapy. This chapter covers

- The History and Effectiveness of Psychiatric Medications

- How Medications are Prescribed to People with Complex Dissociative Disorders

The History and Effectiveness of Psychiatric Medications

Before 1950, a few different medications were used for sleep and sedation but not much was available. The modern era of psychopharmacology began in the early 1950s with chlorpromazine (Thorazine). The antipsychotic effect of chlorpromazine was discovered by accident. Subsequent to this, and after it had been in use for a number of years in psychiatry, lab scientists discovered by studying slices of rat brains that chlorpromazine works on the neurotransmitter *dopamine*.

One nerve cell communicates with the next nerve cell in the brain by sending a chemical across the gap between the two nerve cells. The gap is called a *synapse* and the chemical messenger is called a *neurotransmitter*. After the neurotransmitter crosses the synapse, it locks onto a receptor called a *post-synaptic receptor*. When enough receptors have been occupied by neurotransmitter molecules, the cell on the far side of the synapse reacts by sending an electrical signal down its long thin body—through the nerve cell *axon*.

The electrical signal travels down the axon and then stimulates that nerve cell to release a neurotransmitter, which diffuses across a second synapse and stimulates a third nerve cell or neuron. This is how the brain talks to itself in endless, complex, feedback loops. When a drug interacts with a receptor, it can do one of two things: stimulate the receptor, or simply occupy it without stimulating it. A medication that stimulates a receptor is called an *agonist*. A medication that occupies a receptor but does not stimulate it is called an *antagonist*, or a *blocker*. Chlorpromazine and the other antipsychotic medications are *postsynaptic dopamine receptor blockers*. There is also a third option: some medications partly stimulate a receptor and are called *partial agonists*. Partial agonists don't play much role in psychiatry, however.

Antipsychotic medications block postsynaptic dopamine receptors. They thereby prevent the brain's own dopamine from locking onto the receptors, which prevents the postsynaptic neuron from being stimulated and firing electrically. The net effect is to calm down the dopamine system.

When lab scientists showed that chlorpromazine is a postsynaptic dopamine receptor blocker, psychiatrists theorized that psychosis must be caused by too much dopamine. This is how the dopamine theory of schizophrenia came into being. It was worked out after the fact. The same is true for the serotonin theory of depression—it was worked out by discovering that the antidepressants can improve depression, then discovering that they interact with the serotonin system, then deciding that serotonin must be involved in depression.

Antidepressants like fluoxetine (Prozac) are called *selective serotonin reuptake inhibitors* or SSRIs. Instead of blocking the postsynaptic receptor, they block the presynaptic receptor. A neuron releases serotonin into a synapse in order to stimulate another neuron. The serotonin diffuses across the synapse, locks onto the postsynaptic receptors for a while, then unlocks itself and falls off the receptor. After the serotonin molecule falls off the postsynaptic receptor, it diffuses back across the synapse and interacts with a receptor on the original neuron.

This receptor is called a *presynaptic receptor*. Once the serotonin locks onto the presynaptic receptor it is taken back into the original neuron for storage where it is either broken down or used again. An SSRI antidepressant blocks the reuptake process. This results in serotonin molecules staying in the synapse longer. They therefore can diffuse back across the synapse and lock onto a postsynaptic receptor again instead of undergoing reuptake into the presynaptic neuron. The net effect is to boost the serotonin system.

This is why psychiatrists theorize that depression is caused by low levels of serotonin. Although that is a reasonable theory, it isn't supported by the facts. Despite lots of effort and many investigations, there is no evidence that serotonin levels are low in depression. The *chemical imbalance* theory of mental disorders is just a theory. It is not based on facts. Actually, there are numerous studies that show there is no consistent chemical imbalance of any kind in mental illness. This is true for all the common psychiatric diagnoses.

That is why psychiatrists never actually order serotonin, noradrenalin, or dopamine levels in order to make a diagnosis or choose a medication. Neurologists and internists study levels of many different things in blood, urine, and cerebrospinal fluid on a routine basis. Psychiatrists never order neurotransmitter levels because there is no evidence they are abnormal in mental disorders.

The idea that people with mania, schizophrenia, depression, or other psychiatric disorders have a biological disease or a chemical imbalance is an unproven theory. It is not a scientific fact. If a specific biological abnormality had been demonstrated in any psychiatric disorder, then psychiatrists would order a test for it as part of regular clinical practice.

Do internists ever diagnose anemia without taking a hemoglobin level? Do they diagnose diabetes without taking a blood sugar level? Never. Psychiatrists often compare depression to diabetes, explaining that both are medical diseases based on abnormally low levels of natural body chemicals. In depression, serotonin is low, while in diabetes insulin is low, they say.

Treatment of diabetes, the psychiatrist will explain, involves replacing the missing insulin to restore a chemical balance in the body. Treating depression involves replacing the missing serotonin. The problem is, there is no consistent evidence that serotonin levels are low in depression. The analogy is based on belief and theory, not scientific fact. Therapists need to be wary of the idea that some symptoms or diagnoses are inherently *biological* and therefore will respond to medication, but not to psychotherapy. Overall, psychotherapy is just as effective as antidepressants.

Pooling large numbers of drug studies, 30% of clinically depressed people respond to placebo and 50% respond to antidepressants. Psychiatric medications are not powerful or highly effective. They help a bit, but only a minority of people given antidepressants—at most one-third—go into full remission. The 50% classified as *responders* includes people who improve but are still significantly depressed.

Medications and psychotherapy are not either/or options. In actual practice, almost everyone in treatment for DID or DDNOS gets both. The most medications do, for most people, is to provide a buffer and help a person get through the process of therapy. After a person reaches stable integration, few if any psychiatric medications are required. Many people early in the recovery process are on four to eight different psychiatric medications. Post-integration, most people are on zero to two. Usually this is one SSRI antidepressant and maybe a small dose of one sleeping pill or anti-anxiety medication.

Don't misunderstand: psychiatric medications are definitely more effective than placebo. The difference is statistically significant. But they aren't *powerful,* they aren't miracle cures, and they don't prove that the person has a biological disease.

How Medications Are Prescribed to People with Complex Dissociative Disorders

Throughout psychiatry, medications tend to be prescribed in a 'hit or miss' fashion, with four, five, or six prescribed at a time. This is true regardless of the diagnosis, be it schizoaffective disorder, rapid-cycling bipolar mood disorder, borderline personality disorder, or schizophrenia. The same prescribing pattern applies when the person has DID or DDNOS.

The pattern is called *irrational polypharmacy*, but it is the norm in psychiatry, except for simple, straightforward clients, who are mostly private practice outpatients. There are many problems with irrational polypharmacy. Psychiatrists not uncommonly make the following prescribing errors

- Too many medications prescribed at one time

- Dosages too high or too low

- Different medications stopped, started, increased, and deceased within a short time period

- Medications not matched to diagnoses

- Medications prescribed for reasons not supported by scientific data (so-called *off-label* uses)

- Medications prescribed for too long or too short a time period

- Symptoms not documented or tracked systematically

- Medications with opposite actions prescribed simultaneously, i.e., a stimulant and a sedative

- Addictive medications prescribed to known abusers of them

- Patients discharged on high doses of numerous medications without adequate follow-up

- Side effects and drug-drug interactions not recognized and/or not explained to patients

- Patient non-compliance attributed to a bad attitude by the patient when, actually, the medications make no sense, aren't helping, or are toxic

- Telling the patient that improvement is definitely due to medications when it could be due to numerous other factors

- Telling patients that medications are required because they have a *biological illness* when this has not been demonstrated scientifically

- Overstating the effectiveness of medications while understating the effectiveness of psychotherapy

In the inpatient setting, with average lengths of stay less than two weeks in the United States, it is not possible to do anything about polypharmacy. It simply has to be tolerated and then resolved over the long term. Most people in treatment for complex trauma disorders receive irrational polypharmacy. At a practical level, this situation is unlikely to change in the near future.

Many psychiatrists claim that they have had "good experience" with this or that medication. The problem is, these opinions are not scientific. There are so many of the above prescribing errors that it is impossible to tell which medication, or which medication change, is causing what. This is especially true when numerous medication changes are made at the same time as a major psychosocial intervention like hospitalization.

We are not trying to discourage therapists from sending their clients to psychiatrists for an assessment for medication. Nor are we against medications in any rigid, simplistic manner. It simply is a fact that the state of the art in psychopharmacology is chaotic—at the level of actual practice with complex patients. This is true irrespective of diagnosis.

Therapists are encouraged to find a prescribing psychiatrist who is careful with medications, and receptive to trauma. Medications are slightly more effective than placebo in simple, pure, straightforward cases, but there are no large studies of polypharmacy in complex, real-world patients. (By *real world* patients we mean individuals with complex histories, presentations and chronic symptomatology, as seen in the daily routine of clinical practice.) In the end, the therapist's role is to concentrate on the therapy and leave the prescribing of medications to the psychiatrists. This manual is a guide to psychotherapy, not to medication, and this chapter has been included only to help therapists understand the complexities and limitations of psychiatric medication.

36
Inpatient Treatment

Inpatient treatment could be the subject of an entire book. One of the authors, (Ross) has been treating dissociative disorders on an inpatient basis since 1979, and in a dedicated specialty program since 1991. Inpatient treatment is based on the same principles as therapy in general, but with the addition of milieu management strategies that are not required in individual therapy.

Because of the structure, containment, support, and nursing staff available in a hospital, treatment can proceed at a much faster pace, and with greater intensity than on an outpatient basis. Also, patients are withdrawn from current life stresses and responsibilities, and so can focus all their energy on their therapy.

This chapter is based on the programs at the trauma units at Timberlawn Mental Health System, Dallas, Texas, Forest View Hospital, Grand Rapids, Michigan and Del Amo Hospital, Torrance, California.

This chapter covers

- Purposes of Inpatient Treatment

- Behavioural Management Strategies

- Group Therapy Schedule

Purposes of Inpatient Treatment

The purposes of inpatient treatment for dissociative disorders are generic and the same as for inpatient treatment in general. In the United States, inpatients must meet *acuity criteria* in order for the hospital to be reimbursed by the insurance company. If the hospital is not reimbursed, the specialty program closes and no one gets specialty treatment. This illustrates a core principle of inpatient treatment that is not required in outpatient therapy: *balancing the needs of the milieu against the needs of the individual.*

Admission criteria for Ross Institute Trauma Programs are: acutely suicidal, acutely homicidal, or unable to maintain basic stability, safety, and function at a lower level of care.

Individuals are *not* admitted for social respite, to do *memory work*, or other aspects of therapy, in order to adjust medications, or for any vague, undefined, or non-emergency reasons. Certainly, medications get adjusted during an admission, and certainly there is respite, but these are not the reasons for admission.

The inpatient acuity criteria have been imposed by the insurance industry and managed care, but they are not something to chafe against. In fact, lengths of stay on both general and specialty units were too long thirty years ago. No outcome data existed to justify such expensive interventions and, clinically, they often caused deterioration, hospital dependency, regression, and institutionalization. It is healthier for people with DID and DDNOS to not stay in the hospital for months or years.

The purpose of inpatient treatment is acute stabilization and return to day hospital or outpatient treatment. On a Ross Institute Trauma Program, inpatient stabilization is achieved in an average of about twelve days, with an upper limit of twenty-one days. This is achieved through intense therapy work. The insurer-imposed upper limit is also a good limit clinically. After three weeks, the incremental return from attending more groups declines to minimal, while regression and dependency are either imminent or already setting in.

For some people, unfortunately, it is more comfortable in a psychiatric hospital than in the real world. The food, socialization, furniture, décor, and safety are better. The outside world can be overtly abusive and traumatic, lonely and isolated, monotonous, devoid of social support, and triggering. Living in a psychiatric hospital for prolonged periods does not solve any of these problems; it only increases the phobic avoidance of them, and the desperation of the self-destructive measures required to block discharge.

Behavioural Management Strategies

On a Trauma Program, close to 100% of patients meet lifetime criteria for major depressive episode; most often it is currently active. Average scores on measures of depression are well above cutoffs to qualify for a drug company-funded antidepressant study. Levels of suicidal ideation are high. About 65% of patients meet criteria for borderline personality disorder (BPD). The average number of DSM personality disorders per patient is four, a fact that illustrates a core problem with Axis II: It is not conceptually possible to have four different personality disorders at the same time, but many people in the mental health system meet criteria for two, three, four, or more Axis II disorders.

Of the 35% of patients who do not meet diagnostic criteria for BPD, many satisfy three or four criteria, and fall just short of the required five; therefore principles of borderline management apply to the population as a whole. It is not kind, helpful, therapeutic, or humane to accept the role of a passive enabler with respect to borderline behaviour. Without necessary rules, boundaries, containment, and behavioural strategies, the milieu can deteriorate into chaos: chronic abreactions, self-mutilation, crises, regression, intensified PTSD symptoms, disorganized switching, and prolonged executive control by child alters. A chaotic environment fosters staff burnout and counter-acting out, such as excessive use of restraints, seclusion, involuntary intramuscular medication, take-downs, codes, and one-on-one nursing care.

With such chaos, less work gets done; finite and precious insurance money is wasted; patients get worse, and eventually the unit closes. This outcome is not theoretical: it has occurred repeatedly in North America. Behavioural rules and guidelines are required for both patients and staff. All too often, for instance, the attending psychiatrist and individual therapist *advocate* for more inpatient days, more lenient rules and consequences, and special exceptions for their individual patients. This is a natural byproduct of the individual treatment alliance, but it can be toxic to both the individual and the milieu.

Inconsistent application of rules and consequences retraumatizes those who do not get the special exceptions, reduces their self-esteem, damages their treatment alliance, and increases their justifiable anger and resentment. This is one way in which the needs of the individual and the milieu need to be balanced; it is a balancing act that never ends.

Some professionals see limits and consequences as further punishment of a victim-patient who has already experienced excessive abuse and trauma. This is a counter-transference distortion, not a good management strategy. It is helpful, healthy, and therapeutic to be treated as a rational adult of whom others have normal expectations, and for whom the normal rules of life apply. To be treated as an incompetent victim who cannot manage her thoughts, feelings, or behaviour, places the patient in the role of helpless child and the professional in the role of grandiose good parent. This is a formula for childish acting out, not for healing.

Inpatients in a Trauma Program rise to expectations. If they are expected to act out, regress, and abreact, and if this behaviour is reinforced by more attention, staff time, privileged status, and interventions, it will happen more frequently rather than less. If patients are expected to work hard, and if there are clear consequences for acting out and avoidance, then they will act out less and make more progress. In our clinical experience these facts about inpatient treatment have been shown to be consistent outcomes over two decades.

The primary behavioural strategy, then, is to expect more work and better behaviour—the expectation itself is the primary intervention. When the expectation is not met, then rules and consequences are required. One of our primary techniques is called Connect and Refocus.

A patient receives a Connect and Refocus exercise for behaviour the treatment team decides requires it. There are clear guidelines for types of behaviour that warrant receiving a Connect and refocus. Receiving a Connect and Refocus is not negotiable. The second Connect and Refocus in a given admission results in immediate transfer off the Trauma Program for the remainder of that admission. Depending on the severity of the behaviour, a person may be barred from the Trauma Program for weeks, months, or forever, after discharge. In eighteen years, permanent expulsion has occurred only a few times.

Behaviours that result in a Connect and Refocus include: self-mutilation; head-banging; smuggling in contraband including sharps and drugs; throwing furniture; threatening or assaulting other patients or staff; sleeping all the time; not attending groups; excessive abreactions; sexual contact with other patients, which can include sexualized hugging and touching and need not include sex; inadequate work ethic or treatment progress; blocking discharge; too much demanding behaviour; dominating groups; and too much rescuing behaviour.

Connect and Refocus (C&R) is described in detail in the written patient packet and is reviewed in groups and individual therapy. Initially the rule was that three C&R's were required for transfer off the Trauma Program. We dropped the limit to two when a patient explained that she and others were deliberately getting two and stopping there, because they knew they were allowed three. Now patients get only one "free" C&R.

The Connect and Refocus is a structured homework exercise in which the person has to identify her acting out and avoidance strategies, and how they are interfering with her work. She then states defined, operationalized treatment goals, specific tasks and steps for meeting them, and makes a plausible commitment to her work. If the treatment team assesses that the C&R has been done adequately in all its elements, the person is allowed back in the Program. The C&R is done during a compulsory 24-hour time out from the Program during which the person is on another unit. If the first C&R is not satisfactory, the person is not allowed back into the Program until it is completed.

The treatment team has the option of giving a Therapeutic Assignment, which is exactly the same structured homework task, without the 24-hour time out, and which does not count as a C&R. It is clearly stated, and the patients know, that a Therapeutic Assignment means the person is inching toward a C&R.

The power of the C&R is two-fold. The impending consequence of a C&R prevents the behaviour from occurring; and the C&R prevents it from recurring. The C&R works because patients value the Trauma Program and want to stay in it. Many have come from other states at considerable personal expense to attend the program. If the program was not valued, then transfer off the program would have no effect as a behavioural management strategy.

There are many micro-strategies used in the inpatient setting. For instance, when I (Ross) am doing cognitive therapy group, I never stop the work to attend to another person's abreaction, trance state, pseudoseizure, faint, departure from the group, or other behaviour, because doing so would reward and reinforce the behaviour. There are technicians and nursing staff to handle such situations. Likewise, I never participate in or respond to codes, take-downs, patient crises or other behaviour occurring while I am in the building because such special attention from Dr. Ross would be too reinforcing. Over the course of a quarter-century career, these rules also prevent burnout for me, which is a benefit to all the patients.

One day in the early nineties, I was standing by the nursing station talking with staff. We were all ignoring an "unconscious" patient lying nearby on the floor who had had numerous factitious faints and pseudoseizures.

When I asked a nurse what time the next group started, the unconscious patient said, without opening her eyes, "Two-fifteen." We continued to ignore her.

Although this response by the staff might seem like doing nothing, it is actually a planned, considered, active treatment intervention based on the behavioural principle of extinction. Extinction only works for some behaviours, and is only one strategy in the tool box. Like all tools, it should not be overused or applied thoughtlessly. It can become a rationalization for indifference, apathy, and staff burnout. Nevertheless, doing nothing is often the best plan of action.

Clear rules and consequences are combined with Rogerian principles: accurate empathy, genuine positive regard, and congruent behaviour by the staff. Otherwise, rules become heartless, mean, tyrannical, and traumatic. The rules and consequences on Ross Institute Trauma Programs are tougher than on the average general adult inpatient unit. Calling a spade a spade is a standard approach, as is empathic confrontation. Confrontation does not mean "getting in your face"—it means accurate feedback and clear communication. If a person is holding tight to flagrant cognitive errors in order to justify suicide, pointing this out is kind, not confrontational in the aggressive or adversarial sense. One confronts the *defenses*, not the person.

The rules, limits, and consequences are designed to protect the patient from him or her self. Patients frequently say that they want to feel *safe*, and often they are currently in abusive relationships, but usually the person who poses the greatest danger to the patient is the patient him or her self. The attack on self can be through words, beliefs, passive acceptance of abuse by others, substance abuse, eating-disordered behaviour, overdoses, self-mutilation, self-neglect, or countless other channels. To reiterate, it is not kind or helpful to adopt the position of the passive bystander or the absent rescuer while this attack on a human being continues.

Confrontation can be delivered in a quiet voice, through a Socratic dialogue, through hypotheticals, and in styles that are not blatantly confrontational. Ultimately, on an inpatient unit, the needs of the majority can override the needs of an individual. A person can get a first or second C&R for being too disruptive to the milieu. The disruptive behaviour robs the other patients of their opportunity to make progress, and wastes their insurance money.

Most often, the needs of the individual and the milieu are aligned. Simultaneously, the milieu needs the person removed, and the person is making it clear that she needs to be removed. For behavioural management, we listen to the patient's behaviour, not her words. Her words will often contradict her behaviour, as she pleads to remain in the program and makes an implausible claim that she will *be good*. This, often, is a reenacted childhood strategy for management of past perpetrators of rejection and abuse, not a real adult commitment to recovery. The patient is trying to manage her perpetrators in a reenactment of her family of origin dynamics.

The patient's behaviour says, *The milieu is too triggering, demanding, and overwhelming for me. I'm not ready to do the work. I'm too phobic of the feelings. I don't really believe that I deserve a better life, and I'll do whatever it takes to get kicked out.*

The patient's words say, "I can't believe you won't give me another chance. Why are you punishing me? Am I that bad? Do you hate me that much? I thought you were supposed to help people here, not throw them out when you get tired of them. Your rules suck. You call yourselves professionals?"

In this scenario, the ghost of the plaintiff's lawyer lurks nearby, and tries to intimidate the treatment team into being *nice*. Being intimidated or controlled by this much-feared Grim Reaper results in paralysis, loss of leverage, therapeutic impotence, and reinforcement of the patient's unhealthy defenses and sick role. The solution is to treat all the patients like competent, responsible adults—which they are—and simultaneously, like behaviourally disturbed, traumatized children—which they are, emotionally. The goal is to get the inner adult and the inner child working together in a more integrated, healthy fashion, rather than as a dissociated kamikaze attack team. Analysis of the Victim-Rescuer-Perpetrator triangle is a major component of behavioural management on an inpatient unit.

About once a year, there is a unit shut-down. During a shut-down, all individual therapy, group therapy, phone calls, doctor's rounds, visitors, smoke breaks, and other activities are stopped except for meals and bathroom breaks. Cessation of smoke breaks is probably the most powerful component of this package. Every single patient must be in the shut-down, must be awake, and must attend without acting out. Everyone sits in the shut-down group and it continues until the cause of the milieu disruption, acting out, or stabilization is explained and solved.

Unit shut-downs are ordered when the amount of acting out, conflict, sleeping, avoidance, non-attendance at groups, or other behaviours escalates too high for too long. The underlying cause is often a patient hiding sharps or medication, keeping some other secret, or entangling the other patients in a reenactment of family dynamics. There are usually cliques, coalitions, and clearly defined victims and perpetrators. Usually, some patients know what is going on but are keeping "the family secret" out of fear, misplaced loyalty, or in order to avoid their work.

Physical restraint with straps has not been used for over a decade. Take-downs with intramuscular injections are rare. Sustained seclusion (days or a week) of individual patients has not occurred for over a decade. A second C&R with transfer off the unit occurs about once a month, or less. The degree of destabilization on the unit waxes and wanes depending on the mix of people admitted. Since 90% of the patients are women, sexual issues that rise to the level of Therapeutic Assignment or C&R are more frequently lesbian than heterosexual. Overall, from a medico-legal liability point of view, the Trauma Program poses less risk than the general adult and adolescent units. The reverse would be true if it was mismanaged.

C&R and Therapeutic Assignments can be used in a day hospital or outpatient setting as well. The principles and counter-transference are the same across settings, but greater flexibility is possible in outpatient therapy because the level of acuity is lower.

Group Therapy Schedule

The group therapy schedule on a Ross Institute Trauma Program involves about 25 hours a week of structured groups that are integrated into the overall model, and delivered by professionals trained in the Trauma Model. Unavoidably, the level of training, experience, and expertise varies with budget, insurance reimbursement rates, recruitment and retention difficulties, and other factors. Inpatient groups are about 50% cognitive-behavioural-didactic and about 50% experiential. They are delivered almost entirely by full and part-time staff and interns of the hospital, not by outside consultants, other than two employees of the Ross Institute (Dr. Ross and Melissa Engle, MS, ATR, LPC).

Groups are scheduled so that the most difficult and arousing groups do not come at the end of the day, and are followed by process, didactic, discharge planning, or more task-oriented groups that allow for de-escalation and stabilization. Milieu and hospital issues and conflicts are restricted to community groups, and are not allowed to overtake or dominate other groups. Which specific groups are provided can vary depending on the skill and training of the available staff. For instance, a trained psychodrama expert is not always available.

A more complete account of an inpatient Trauma Program requires another manual. The program at Timberlawn hospital in Dallas has a visiting professional program.

37
Life After Trauma

A client once asked, poignantly, "Who am I if I am not the pain?" Another client spoke about the fear that surfaced when the flashbacks stopped and the arguing and crying inside her head subsided. Coping with the aftermath of trauma can be all consuming of time and energy. For many clients in the early and mid-stages of healing there is often little time, energy, or space for life. A client may be employed, have relationships, and friends. To the observer everything may appear fine. However, the client's inner world can be tormented and intensely painful. Other people have very limited functioning and are unable to work or sustain relationships early in therapy. These clients are often very isolated and alienated, living on the edge of society.

The child living in a chaotic and violent household lives minute by minute, her attention focused on how to avoid the next attack, or how to get it over and done with as quickly as possible. As an adult, the focus turns to managing the next flashback, or panic attack, or how get through another day struggling with urges to self-injure, or suicidal ideation. Some clients may still be experiencing abusive relationships. There may be financial struggles due to impaired functioning and limited ability to work.

The person who has resolved her major traumas and conflicts presents very differently at the end stages of therapy. There is no longer active major substance abuse, she does not require hospital-based treatment, and individual therapy sessions are less frequent. The client no longer self-harms; she is not suicidal, does not hear voices, or experience periods of missing time. The symptoms of other DSM disorders are either no longer present or are greatly reduced. There may be residual depression and anxiety at times, but it is manageable, not debilitating or constant. These are very positive and encouraging outcomes of trauma therapy.

However, difficulty conceptualizing a future is common in abuse survivors. Like the clients mentioned above, identity and meaning can be bound up in being a *survivor*. The prospect of relinquishing this identity can be frightening. Life beyond trauma is an unknown and unimaginable for many. What if life after trauma isn't all it's cracked up to be? Trauma and abuse survivors often live life with the adrenaline pumping. Life at a slower and less chaotic pace can feel unreal or boring.

As opportunities open up that the client didn't dare dream about, simultaneously there is grief in coming to terms with what was, as well as what wasn't—all the lost years and possibilities that may no longer be an option. It is important that these losses are not minimized by the therapist or counteracted with, "Yes, but look at how much better things are now." These are real and legitimate losses that require grieving.

Life after trauma presents new challenges and new responsibilities. These range from developing new and healthier friendships and relationships, to furthering or developing a career and creating financial security. There is the possibility of developing new skills and interests. These challenges occur much later in life than they do for their peers. This can give rise to feelings of anger, frustration, and insecurity. Clients often express feeling as if they lack experience and knowledge of how life works.

Being responsible for oneself and the realization that what happens now is in one's own hands can feel frightening and overwhelming. While it has always been true that her life is her responsibility—this is a fundamental principle of trauma therapy—once the client is no longer managing trauma symptoms, the reality of what this means comes more sharply into focus.

Life after trauma is simultaneously exciting and daunting. Once the trauma work of therapy is over the focus turns to developing and building skills, confidence, and competency in visioning and planning for the future, and finding meaning, enjoyment, and pleasure in the present. The main tasks of life after trauma and the end stages of therapy are to

- Let go of the *survivor* identity

- Face and find acceptance for losses: people, opportunities, finances

- Learn to live in the present

- Conceptualize and plan for the future

The strategies previously outlined in the manual will assist with these important tasks. It is a stage of therapy that cannot be rushed or viewed as not as important as the early and mid-stages. The work is different but can still be challenging. There will be steps forward and setbacks. In many ways clients are much stronger by this stage of therapy. In other ways there will still be some fragility. There is a parallel with the adolescent who is almost grown and wants independence and freedom, yet who at the same time needs to know he can still come home.

Life after trauma also heralds the end of therapy. Reducing the frequency of sessions evolves naturally. Grief for the end of therapy is an end stage therapy issue. The client will mourn the loss of her relationship with the therapist who has been her witness, mentor, champion, and role model. The therapist has been the consistent *other* in a long line of inconsistencies. The client may need permission to leave. It has been a long road that has been traveled together. Abandonment issues may resurface. Ending therapy is another loss that is often experienced as bittersweet. Reassure the client that he or she can come back for follow up sessions or in an emergency. Review the therapy, acknowledging the stages, the struggles, the triumphs, and the challenges still ahead.

At the beginning of therapy the client may have had no concept of there being life after trauma. At times, when therapy is tough, the therapist may doubt this as well. However, it is the role of the therapist to hold and contain the faith, hope, and possibilities for the client at times when the client cannot do this for him or herself. Life after trauma sees the client leaving the therapy room holding the container within herself.

38
Trauma and Self-Care of the Therapist

This chapter has been left until last, but it may have been more appropriately placed at the beginning of the section titled *General Principles of Treatment*. When therapists do not attend to self-care, the impact of working with this client group greatly increases the risk of boundary transgressions, counter-transference responses that engage the Victim–Rescuer–Perpetrator triangle and burnout.

Vicarious traumatization (VT) and working with trauma, go hand in glove. It is not something a "good" therapist will escape. However, paying attention to oneself and one's reactions to client's stories will assist in identifying VT. The sooner VT is recognized the earlier its impact can be mitigated.

Self-care when working with profoundly distressed people is crucial for remaining focused and for being able to effectively manage the complex symptomatology that clients present. Managing VT is essential to keeping therapy on track.

This chapter will cover

- Factors Contributing to Vicarious Trauma

- Identifying Signs and Symptoms of Vicarious Trauma

- Managing Vicarious Trauma

Factors Contributing to Vicarious Trauma

One of the roles of the therapist is to sit with clients as they tell their painful and intimate life stories. Navigating the healing process and accompanying clients on their journey is challenging and confronting. It is a long road. The therapist provides a container and *safe enough* space for the client to do the work of healing.

Our clients' stories defy basic assumptions about protecting the young and vulnerable in society. So what happens to the therapist when the client leaves the room? How can we remain present and connected with clients without becoming overwhelmed by their suffering?

Research by Laurie Anne Pearlman and others, has identified that therapists with a history of trauma not only experience vicarious traumatization (VT) as a consequence of exposure to their clients' material, but they may also experience a reactivation of their own stories. This additional risk factor increases the potential for counter-transference reactions going unchecked, and of the therapist stepping onto the Victim–Rescuer–Perpetrator triangle.

Clients with post traumatic stress disorder (PTSD) and dissociative disorders (DD) present with a complex array of distressing and debilitating symptomatology. Functioning at a day-to-day level is frequently severely compromised. Often there is on-going trauma in clients' current circumstances.

For therapists in private practice, competing demands of 'making a living,' while providing a professional ethical service can be a difficult balancing act. Many therapists in private practice work from home offices or consulting suites without regular contact with colleagues.

Increasingly, therapists working within an agency are in situations where their organization does not provide the option of long-term therapy. This creates stress for the client, for the therapist and between the therapist and his supervisor and/or agency. There may be little understanding of trauma, and a lack of support from managers, supervisors, and colleagues. Clients with high needs may be viewed by the agency as 'too difficult' and time consuming, and be labeled with the negative interpretation of 'borderline.'

Professional development forums in trauma and abuse are more plentiful now than twenty years ago. However, therapists may have limited access to, or funding for, ongoing training, supervision, or case consultation. This can result in therapists spending precious training budgets on consultations or workshops that are client focused rather than therapist and self-care focused.

All of the above factors contribute to VT, and increase the risk of VT going unrecognized and unaddressed.

Identifying Signs and Symptoms of Vicarious Trauma

The warning signs of VT are clear when you are attuned to them. However, they may be easily attributed to other life issues and stressors. Therapists can at times be more attuned at identifying signs of stress and trauma in their clients than they are in themselves!

As acknowledged above, VT is a normal reaction to hearing clients' traumatic stories. Signs that may indicate VT include: less time, energy, and interest in family and friends. Routines and daily functioning may fall by the wayside. There can be a loss of enjoyment in activities that had previously provided pleasure and relaxation. There may be a decrease in libido. Problems in relationships with partner, children, family, colleagues and friends may develop or escalate. Health problems may develop. Misusing alcohol, prescription medications, and illicit drugs to numb, escape, or relax are all warnings that VT is going unchecked.

Some therapists report experiencing sadness or anger for which they cannot identify the source. Becoming more serious, cynical or disinterested in life are also potential indicators of VT. In case consultations, some therapists have acknowledged avoiding the evening news and violent movies or TV shows. During the recent bushfires in Victoria, Australia, therapists, as well as clients, reported that the endless news footage of raging fires, burnt out townships and traumatized and displaced families became overwhelming. This normal response to such a devastating situation exacerbated trauma symptoms in clients and VT symptoms in therapists.

VT can precipitate a spiritual or existential crisis. Meaning and purpose can be profoundly shaken. Some therapists report preoccupation with seemingly irrational fears for their own or loved ones' safety.

The therapist may collude with clients to avoid distressing material. Boundary transgressions, feeling de-skilled and inadequate professionally, can reflect unchecked VT. Intrusive thoughts and feelings about clients' material or behaviour may alternate with feeling numb, detached, disconnected and/or hopeless.

Unrecognized and unaddressed VT may result in some therapists deciding they don't want to work with trauma, PTSD, and DD's. This can be a perfectly valid personal and professional choice. If it is driven by unrecognized and unaddressed VT, however, it may serve to undermine personal and professional confidence and self-esteem.

Increased and mismanaged counter-transference responses and burn-out are often linked to unrecognized VT. Transference and counter-transference, all grist for the therapy mill, are more complex with severely traumatized, abused, and dissociative clients. The different parts of clients with DID and DDNOS have their own unique thoughts and feelings about the therapist and therapy. Further, each part of the system is likely to have its own particular and separate transference issues. This can be taxing for the therapist, and increase counter-transference, which in turn increases the risk of engaging in Victim–Rescuer–Perpetrator dynamics.

The handling of transference and counter-transference plays a significant role in strengthening or weakening the therapeutic alliance. Therefore, unchecked VT can have a profound influence on the outcome of therapy.

Managing Vicarious Trauma

Experiencing VT doesn't equate with being a "bad" therapist. It means the therapist is a normal human being. VT goes with the territory. However, we not only have a duty of care to clients. We need to apply the duty of care rule to ourselves: *self-care.* There is no doubt that exposure to other people's trauma has a profound impact. Therapists need to take their own advice and create balance between work, rest, and play.

In your personal life, spend time with the people you like, pursuing the interests and activities that nurture and sustain you. Explore, develop, and maintain philosophies, belief systems, practices, and forms of self-expression that provide meaning, purpose, and direction in your life.

At a professional level, it is important to build a network of colleagues. Talking to colleagues about the impact of your work can be validating and supportive. Case consultation, supervision, peer supervision and study groups offer a forum to explore the impact of working with trauma, in an empathic and holding environment.

Therapists with a trauma history need to be alert to the possibility that their experiences may be activated by clients' material. In such cases, pursuing or returning to therapy is recommended where reactivation is interfering with your work and/or personal life.

Creating balance in your work can help to maintain perspective. You may wish to pursue other professional interests and activities that are not trauma-related or not directly client focused. For both of the authors, this was achieved through providing professional development training in the trauma field.

Be mindful of how you engage with clients emotionally. Develop self-protective strategies that enable you to remain present and connected with clients, but keep yourself at a *safe enough* distance. In the same way we teach clients mindfulness exercises, it is helpful for therapists to be mindful of their thoughts and feelings. Visualization, meditation and other types of relaxation techniques can be enormously helpful. These can be practiced for a few minutes between client sessions, as well as being part of self care outside of work hours.

The appropriate use of humour with clients and colleagues can also be healing and help to regain equilibrium. It is important to acknowledge and express your feelings about your client's experiences. While it can be healing for clients to experience another's genuine feelings about their stories, venting and other more expressive outpourings of feelings need to be done in a supportive professional or personal environment, not with clients.

Finally, know that you, like your clients, have choices; to do this work or not. If you perceive yourself as having no choice and feel trapped, you take the victim position on the triangle. This will affect your presence and effectiveness with clients, and will create further stress, which in turn will increase the likelihood of unmitigated counter-transference, boundary transgressions, enactment of triangle dynamics and VT.

Most importantly, remember that VT is not a failing as a therapist; it is a normal response to another's pain and suffering. To provide the best service to our clients, we need to take care of ourselves. This is also positive modeling for our clients. Ultimately, self-care is paramount to our effectiveness and longevity in what is both a challenging and rewarding profession.

Figley, C.R. (1995). *Compassion fatigue: Coping with secondary traumatic stress disorder in those who treat the traumatized.* New York: Brunner/Mazel.

Moore, T. (1992). *Care of the soul: A guide for cultivating depth and sacredness in everyday life.* New York: Harper Perrenial.

Moore, T. (2005). *Dark nights of the soul: A guide to finding your way through life's ordeals.* New York: Gotham Books.

Pearlman, L.A. , & Saakvitne, K.W. (1995). *Trauma and the therapist: Countertransference and vicarious traumatization in psychotherapy with incest survivors.* New York: W.W. Norton.

Rothschild, B. (2006). *Help for the helper: The psychophysiology of compassion fatigue and vicarious trauma.* New York: W.W. Norton.

Somer, E.,Buchbinder, E., Peled-Avram, M., & ben-Yizhack, Y. (2004). The stress and coping of Israeli emergency room social workers following terrorist attacks. *Qualitative Health Research*, 14, 1077-1093.

Stamm, B.H. (1995). *Secondary traumatic stess: Self-care issues for clinicians, researchers & educators.* Lutherville, MD: Sidran Press.

APPENDICES

THE DISSOCIATIVE EXPERIENCES SCALE (DES)

DES

Eve Bernstein Carlson, Ph.D.   Frank W. Putnam, M.D.

DIRECTIONS

This questionnaire consists of twenty-eight questions about experiences that you may have in your daily life. We are interested in how often you have these experiences. It is important, however, that your answers show how often these experiences happen to you when you are not under the influence of alcohol or drugs.

To answer the questions, please determine to what degree the experience described in the question applies to you and circle the number to show what percentage of the time you have the experience.

EXAMPLE

0%   **10**   **20**   **3.0**   **40**   **50**   **60**   **70**   **80**   **90**   **100%**
(never)   **(always)**

Date _____

1. Some people have the experience of driving or riding in a car or bus or subway and suddenly realizing that they don't remember what has happened during all or part of the trip. Circle a number to show what percentage of the time this happens to you.

   0%   10   20   30   40   50   60   70   80   90   100%

2. Some people find that sometimes they are listening to someone talk and they suddenly realize that they did not hear part or all of what was said. Circle a number to show what percentage of the time this happens to you.

   0%   10   20   30   40   50   60   70   80   90   100%

3. Some people have the experience of finding themselves in a place and having no idea how they got there. Circle a number to show what percentage of the time this happens to you.

   0%   10   20   30   40   50   60   70   80   90   100%

4. Some people have the experience of finding themselves dressed in clothes that they don't remember putting on. Circle a number to show what percentage of the time this happens to

you.

0%   10   20   30   40   50   60   70   80   90   100%

5.   Some people have the experience of finding new things among their belongings that they do not remember buying. Circle a number to show what percentage of the time this happens to you.

0%   10   20   30   40   50   60   70   80   90   100%

6.   Some people sometimes find that they are approached by people that they do not know who call them by another name or insist that they have met them before. Circle a number to show what percentage of the time this happens to you.

0%   10   20   30   40   50   60   70   80   90   100%

7.   Some people sometimes have the experience of feeling as though they are standing next to themselves or watching themselves do something and they actually see themselves as if they were looking at another person. Circle a number to show what percentage of the time this happens to you.

0%   10   20   30   40   50   60   70   80   90   100%

8.   Some people are told that they sometimes do not recognize friends or family members. Circle a number to show what percentage of the time this happens to you.

0%   10   20   30   40   50   60   70   80   90   100%

9.   Some people find that they have no memory for some important events in their lives (for example, a wedding or graduation). Circle a number to show what percentage of the time this happens to you.

0%   10   20   30   40   50   60   70   80   90   100%

10.   Some people have the experience of being accused of lying when they do not think that they have lied. Circle a number to show what percentage of the time this happens to you.

0%   10   20   30   40   50   60   70   80   90   100%

11.   Some people have the experience of looking into a mirror and not recognizing themselves. Circle a number to show what percentage of the time this happens to you.

0%   10   20   30   40   50   60   70   80   90   100%

12.   Some people have the experience of feeling that other people, objects, and the world around them are not real. Circle a number to show what percentage of the time this happens to you.

0%   10   20   30   40   50   60   70   80   90   100%

13. Some people have the experience of feeling that their body does not seem to belong to them. Circle a number to show what percentage of time this happens to you.

0%   10   20   30   40   50   60   70   80   90   100%

14. Some people have the experience of sometimes remembering a past event so vividly that they feel as if they were reliving that event. Circle a number to show what percentage of time this happens to you.

0%   10   20   30   40   50   60   70   80   90   100%

15. Some people have the experience of not being sure whether things that they remember happening really did happen or whether they just dreamed them. Circle a number to show the percentage of time this happens to you.

0%   10   20   30   40   50   60   70   80   90   100%

16. Some people have the experience of being in a familiar place but finding it strange and unfamiliar. Circle a number to show the percentage of time this happens to you.

0%   10   20   30   40   50   60   70   80   90   100%

17. Some people find that when they are watching television or a movie they become so absorbed in the story that they are unaware of other events happening around them. Circle a number to show the percentage of time this happens to you.

0%   10   20   30   40   50   60   70   80   90   100%

18. Some people find that they become so involved in a fantasy or daydream that it feels as though it were really happening to them. Circle a number to show what percentage of the time this happens to you.

0%   10   20   30   40   50   60   70   80   90   100%

19. Some people find that they sometimes are able to ignore pain. Circle a number to show what percentage of the time this happens to you.

0%   10   20   30   40   50   60   70   80   90   100%

20. Some people find that they sometimes sit staring off into space, thinking of nothing, and are not aware of the passage of time. Circle a number to show what percentage of time this happens to you.

0%   10   20   30   40   50   60   70   80   90   100%

21. Some people sometimes find that when they are alone they talk out loud to themselves. Circle a number to show what percentage of the time this happens to you.

0%   10   20   30   40   50   60   70   80   90   100%

22. Some people find that in one situation they may act so differently compared with another situation that they feel almost as if they were two different people. Circle a number to show what percentage of the time this happens to you.

     0%   10   20   30   40   50   60   70   80   90   100%

23. Some people sometimes find that in certain situations they are able to do things with amazing ease and spontaneity that would usually be difficult for them (for example, sports, work, social situations, etc.). Circle a number to show what percentage of the time this happens to you.

     0%   10   20   30   40   50   60   70   80   90   100%

24. Some people sometimes find that they cannot remember whether they have done something or have just thought about doing that thing (for example, not knowing whether they have just mailed a letter or have just thought about mailing it). Circle a number to show what percentage of the time this happens to you.

     0%   10   20   30   40   50   60   70   80   90   100%

25. Some people find evidence that they have done things that they do not remember doing. Circle a number to show what percentage of the time this happens to you.

     0%   10   20   30   40   50   60   70   80   90   100%

26. Some people sometimes find writings, drawings, or notes among their belongings that they must have done but cannot remember doing. Circle a number to show what percentage of the time this happens to you.

     0%   10   20   30   40   50   60   70   80   90   100%

27. Some people sometimes find that they hear voices inside their head that tell them to do things or comment on things that they are doing. Circle a number to show what percentage of time this happens to you.

     0%   10   20   30   40   50   60   70   80   90   100%

28. Some people sometimes feel as if they are looking at the world through a fog so that people and objects appear far away or unclear. Circle a number to show what percentage of the time this happens to you.

     0%   10   20   30   40   50   60   70   80   90   100%

THE SOMATOFORM DISSOCIATION
QUESTIONNAIRE (SDQ)

S.D.Q. – 20

This questionnaire asks about different physical symptoms or body experiences, which you may have had either briefly or for a longer time.

Please indicate to what extent these experiences apply to you *in the past year*.

For each statement, please circle the number in the first column that best applies to YOU.

The possibilities are:

1 = this applies to me NOT AT ALL
2 = this applies to me A LITTLE
3 = this applies to me MODERATELY
4 = this applies to me QUITE A BIT
5 = this applies to me EXTREMELY

If a symptom or experience applies to you, please indicate whether a *physician* has connected it with a *physical disease*.

Indicate this by circling the word YES or NO in the column "Is the physical cause known?"
If you wrote YES, please write the physical cause (if you know it) on the line.

Example:

	Extent to which the symptom or experience applies to you	Is the physical cause known:

Sometimes:

my teeth chatter	1 2 3 4 5	NO	YES, namely_____
I have cramps in my calves	1 2 3 4 5	NO	YES, namely _____

If you have circled a 1 in the first column (i.e., This applies to me NOT AT ALL), you do NOT have to respond to the question about whether the physical cause is known.

On the other hand, if you circle 2, 3, 4, or 5, you must circle NO or YES in the "Is the physical cause known?" column.

Please do not skip any of the 20 questions.
Thank you for your cooperation.

Here are the questions:

1 = this applies to me NOT AT ALL
2 = this applies to me A LITTLE
3 = this applies to me MODERATELY
4 = this applies to me QUITE A BIT
5 = this applies to me EXTREMELY

	Extent to which The symptom or experience applies to you	Is the physical cause known?	

Sometimes:

1. I have trouble urinating	1 2 3 4 5	NO	Yes, namely _____
2. I dislike tastes that I usually like (women: at times OTHER THAN pregnancy or monthly periods)	1 2 3 4 5	NO	Yes, namely _____
3. I hear sounds from nearby as if They were coming from far way	1 2 3 4 5	NO	Yes, namely _____
4. I have pain while urinating	1 2 3 4 5	NO	Yes, namely _____
5. My body or a part of it, feels numb	1 2 3 4 5	NO	Yes, namely _____
6. People and things look bigger than usual	1 2 3 4 5	NO	Yes, namely _____
7. I have an attack that resembles an epileptic seizure	1 2 3 4 5	NO	Yes, namely_____
8. My body, or a part of it, is insensitive to pain	1 2 3 4 5	NO	Yes, namely _____
9. I dislike smells that I usually like	1 2 3 4 5	NO	Yes, namely_____

1 = this applies to me NOT AT ALL
2 = this applies to me A LITTLE
3 = this applies to me MODERATELY
4 = this applies to me QUITE A BIT
5 = this applies to me EXTREMELY

	Extent to which The symptom or experience applies to you	Is the physical cause known?	

Sometimes:

10. I feel pain in my genitals (at times OTHER THAN sexual intercourse)

1 2 3 4 5   NO   Yes, namely _____

11. I cannot hear for a while (as if I am deaf)

1 2 3 4 5   NO   Yes, namely _____

12. I cannot see for a while (as if I am blind)

1 2 3 4 5   NO   Yes, namely _____

13. I see things around me differently than usual (for example as if looking through a tunnel, or seeing merely a part of an object

1 2 3 4 5   NO   Yes, namely _____

14. I am able to smell much BETTER or WORSE than I usually do (even though I do not have a cold)

1 2 3 4 5   NO   Yes, namely _____

15. It is as if my body, or part of it, has disappeared

1 2 3 4 5   NO   Yes, namely _____

16. I cannot swallow, or can swallow Only with great effort

1 2 3 4 5   NO   Yes, namely_____

17. I cannot sleep for nights on end but remain very active during daytime

1 2 3 4 5   NO   Yes, namely_____.

18. I cannot speak (or only with great effort) or I can only whisper

1 2 3 4 5   NO   Yes, namely_____.

1 = this applies to me NOT AT ALL
2 = this applies to me A LITTLE
3 = this applies to me MODERATELY
4 = this applies to me QUITE A BIT
5 = this applies to me EXTREMELY

	Extent to which The symptom or experience applies to you	Is the physical cause known?
19. I am paralyzed for a while _____	1 2 3 4 5	NO Yes, namely____
20. I grown stiff for a while _____	1 2 3 4 5	NO Yes, namely____

Before continuing, will you please check whether you have responded to all 20 statements?

You are asked to fill in and place an X beside what applies to you.

21. Age _____ years

22 Sex _____ female
_____ male

23. Marital status: ____ single
____ married
____ living together
____ divorced
____ widower/widow

24. Education: ____ Number of years

25: Date _____

6. Name: _____

S.D.Q. – 5

This questionnaire asks about different physical symptoms or body experiences, which you may have had either briefly or for a longer time.
Please indicate to what extent these experiences apply to you *in the past year*.

For each statement, please circle the number in the first column that best applies to YOU.

The possibilities are:

1 = this applies to me NOT AT ALL
2 = this applies to me A LITTLE
3 = this applies to me MODERATELY
4 = this applies to me   QUITE A BIT
5 = this applies to me EXTREMELY

If a symptom or experience applies to you, please indicate whether a *physician* has connected it with a *physical disease*.
Indicate this by circling the word YES or NO in the column "Is the physical cause known?"
If you wrote YES, please write the physical cause (if you know it) on the line.

Example:

	Extent to which the symptom or experience applies to you	cause	Is the physical known:

Sometimes:

my teeth chatter	1 2 3 4 5	NO	YES, namely ....
I have cramps in my calves	1 2 3 4 5	NO	YES, namely ....

If you have circled a 1 in the first column (i.e., This applies to me NOT AT ALL), you do NOT have to respond to the question about whether the physical cause is known.

On the other hand, if you circle 2, 3, 4, or 5, you must circle NO or YES in the "Is the physical cause known?" column.

Please do not skip any of the 5 questions.
Thank you for your cooperation.

Here are the questions:

1 = this applies to me NOT AT ALL
2 = this applies to me A LITTLE
3 = this applies to me MODERATELY
4 = this applies to me QUITE A BIT
5 = this applies to me EXTREMELY

	Extent to which The symptom or experience applies to you	Is the physical cause known?	

Sometimes:

1. I have pain while urinating	1 2 3 4 5	NO	Yes, namely _____
2. My body, or a part of it, is Insensitive to pain	1 2 3 4 5	NO	Yes, namely _____.
3. I see things around me differently than usual (for example as if looking through a tunnel, or seeing merely a part of an object)	1 2 3 4 5	NO	Yes, namely _____
4. It is as if my body, or a part of it, has disappeared	1 2 3 4 5	NO	Yes, namely _____
5. I cannot speak (or only with great effort) or I can only whisper	1 2 3 4 5	NO	Yes, namely _____

THE DISSOCIATIVE DISORDERS
INTERVIEW SCHEDULE (DDIS)

THE DISSOCIATIVE DISORDERS INTERVIEW SCHEDULE - DSM-IV VERSION

The Dissociative Disorders Interview Schedule (DDIS) is a highly structured interview which makes DSM-IV diagnoses of somatization disorder, borderline personality disorder and major depressive disorder, as well as all the dissociative disorders. It inquires about positive symptoms of schizophrenia, secondary features of DID, extrasensory experiences, substance abuse and other items relevant to the dissociative disorders.

The DDIS can usually be administered in 30-45 minutes.

Permission to copy and distribute is granted by Colin A. Ross, M.D.

CONSENT FORM FOR THE DISSOCIATIVE DISORDERS INTERVIEW SCHEDULE

I agree to be interviewed as part of a research project on dissociative disorders. Dissociative disorders involve problems with memory.

I understand that the interview contains some personal questions about my sexual and psychological history, however, all information that I give will be kept confidential. My name will not appear on the research questionnaire.

I understand that my answers will have no direct effect on how I am treated in the future.

I understand that the overall results of this research will be published and these results will be available to authorities or therapists involved with me.

I understand that the interviewer and other researchers cannot offer me treatment.

I understand that the purpose of this interview is for research and that I cannot expect any direct benefit to myself other than knowing that I have helped the researchers understand dissociative disorders better.

I agree to answer the interviewer's questions as well as I can but I know that I am free not to answer any particular questions I do not want to answer.

Although I have signed my name to this form, I know that it will be kept separate from my answers and that my answers cannot be connected to my name, except by the interviewer and his/her research colleagues.

I also understand that I may be asked to participate in further dissociative disorders interviews in the future, but that I will be free to say no. If I do say no this will have no consequences for me and any authorities or therapists involved with me will not be told of my decision not to be interviewed again.

Signed: _____   Witness: _____

Date: _____

DEMOGRAPHIC DATA FOR DISSOCIATIVE DISORDERS INTERVIEW
SCHEDULE

Age: [   ]

                                                                        [   ]

Sex: Male=1   Female=2   [   ]

Marital   Single=1   Married (including common-law)=2
Status: Separated/Divorced=3   Widowed=4   [   ]

Number of Children: (If no children, score 0)   [   ]

Occupational Status: Employed=1   Unemployed=2   [   ]

Have you been in jail in the past?
Yes=1   No=2   Unsure=3   [   ]

Physical diagnoses currently active: [   ]
                                                                  [   ]
                                                                  [   ]

Current and past diagnoses must consist of written diagnoses provided by
the referring physician or available in the patient's chart (give DSM-IV codes
if possible, if not write DSM-IV diagnoses to the right of the brackets).

Psychiatric diagnoses currently active: [   ]
                                                                  [   ]
                                                                  [   ]

Psychiatric diagnoses currently in remission: [   ]
                                                                  [   ]

DISSOCIATIVE DISORDERS INTERVIEW SCHEDULE

DSM-IV VERSION

Questions in the Dissociative Disorders Interview Schedule must be asked in the order they occur in the Schedule. All the items in the Schedule, including all the items in the DSM-IV diagnostic criteria for dissociative disorders, somatization disorder, and borderline personality disorder must be inquired about. The wording of the questions should be exactly as written in order to standardize the information gathered by different interviewers. The interviewer should not read the section headings aloud. The interviewer should open the interview by thanking the subject for his/her participation and then should say:

"Most of the questions I will ask can be answered Yes, Nor or Unsure. A few of the questions have different answers and I will explain those as we go along."

1. Somatic Complaints

      1. Do you suffer from headaches? Yes=1 No=2 Unsure=3   [   ]

If subject answered No to question 1, go to question 3:

      2.   Have you been told by a doctor that you have migraine headaches?
         Yes=1   No=2   Unsure=3   [   ]

Interviewer should read the following to the subject:

"I am going to ask you about a series of physical symptoms now. To count a symptom as present and to answer yes to these questions, the following must be met:

    a)   no physical disorder or medical condition has been found to account for the symptom.
    b)   if there is a related general medical condition, the problems the symptom causes in terms of occupational or social impairment are more than would be expected.
    c)   the symptom is not caused by a street drug or medication."

Interviewer should now ask the subject, "Have you ever had the following physical symptoms for which doctors could find no physical explanation?"

The interviewer should review criteria a-c for the subject immediately following the first positive response to ensure that the subject has understood.

      3.   Abdominal pain (other than when menstruating)
         Yes=1   No=2   Unsure=3   [   ]

4.   Nausea (other than motion sickness)
      Yes=1   No=2   Unsure=3   [   ]

5.   Vomiting (other than motion sickness)
      Yes=1   No=2   Unsure=3   [   ]

6.   Bloating (gassy)
      Yes=1   No=2   Unsure=3   [   ]

7.   Diarrhea
      Yes=1   No=2   Unsure=3   [   ]

8.   Intolerance of (gets sick on) several different foods
      Yes=1   No=2   Unsure=3   [   ]

9.   Back pain
      Yes=1   No=2   Unsure=3   [   ]

10.   Joint pain
      Yes=1   No=2   Unsure=3   [   ]

11.   Pain in extremities (the hands and feet)
      Yes=1   No=2   Unsure=3   [   ]

12.   Pain in genitals other than during intercourse
      Yes=1   No=2   Unsure=3   [   ]

13.   Pain during urination
      Yes=1   No=2   Unsure=3   [   ]

14.   Other pain (other than headaches)
      Yes=1   No=2   Unsure=3   [   ]

15.   Shortness of breath when not exerting oneself
      Yes=1   No=2   Unsure=3   [   ]

16.   Palpitations (a feeling that your heart is beating very strongly)
      Yes=1   No=2   Unsure=3   [   ]

17.   Chest pain
      Yes=1   No=2   Unsure=3   [   ]

18.   Dizziness
      Yes=1   No=2   Unsure=3   [   ]

19.   Difficulty swallowing
      Yes=1   No=2   Unsure=3   [   ]

20. Loss of voice
    Yes=1   No=2   Unsure=3   [   ]

21. Deafness
    Yes=1   No=2   Unsure=3   [   ]

22. Double vision
    Yes=1   No=2   Unsure=3   [   ]

23. Blurred vision
    Yes=1   No=2   Unsure=3   [   ]

24. Blindness
    Yes=1   No=2   Unsure=3   [   ]

25. Fainting or loss of consciousness
    Yes=1   No=2   Unsure=3   [   ]

26. Amnesia
    Yes=1   No=2   Unsure=3   [   ]

27. Seizure or convulsion
    Yes=1   No=2   Unsure=3   [   ]

28. Trouble walking
    Yes=1   No=2   Unsure=3   [   ]

29. Paralysis or muscle weakness
    Yes=1   No=2   Unsure=3   [   ]

30. Urinary retention or difficulty urinating
    Yes=1   No=2   Unsure=3   [   ]

31. Long periods with no sexual desire
    Yes=1   No=2   Unsure=3   [   ]

32. Pain during intercourse
    Yes=1   No=2   Unsure=3   [   ]

Note: If subject is male ask question 33 and then go to question 38. If female, go to question 34.

33. Impotence
    Yes=1   No=2   Unsure=3   [   ]

34. Irregular menstrual periods
    Yes=1   No=2   Unsure=3   [   ]

35.   Painful menstruation
       Yes=1   No=2   Unsure=3   [   ]

36.   Excessive menstrual bleeding
       Yes=1   No=2   Unsure=3   [   ]

37.   Vomiting throughout pregnancy
       Yes=1   No=2   Unsure=3   [   ]

38.   Have you had many physical symptoms over a period
       of several years beginning before the age of 30 that resulted
       in your seeking treatment or which caused occupational
       or social impairment?
       Yes=1   No=2   Unsure=3   [   ]

39.   Were the physical symptoms you described deliberately
       produced by you?
       Yes=1   No=2   Unsure=3   [   ]

II.   <u>Substance Abuse</u>

40.   Have you ever had a drinking problem?
       Yes=1   No=2   Unsure=3   [   ]

41.   Have you ever used street drugs extensively?
       Yes=1   No=2   Unsure=3   [   ]

42.   Have you ever injected drugs intravenously?
       Yes=1   No=2   Unsure=3   [   ]

43.   Have you ever had treatment for a drug or alcohol problem?
       Yes=1   No=2   Unsure=3   [   ]

III.   <u>Psychiatric History</u>

44.   Have you ever had treatment for an emotional problem
       or mental disorder?
       Yes=1   No=2   Unsure=3   [   ]

45.   Do you know what psychiatric diagnoses, if any, you
       have been given in the past?
       Yes=1   No=2   Unsure=3   [   ]

46.   Have you ever been diagnosed as having:
       a)   depression   [   ]
       b)   mania   [   ]
       c)   schizophrenia   [   ]

        d)   anxiety disorder   [   ]
        e)   other psychiatric disorder (specify)   [   ]
              _____

        Yes=1   No=2   Unsure=3

If subject did not volunteer a diagnosis for 46 (e) go to question 48.

47.   If the subject volunteered diagnoses for (e), did the subject volunteer   any   of
       the following:
       a)   dissociative amnesia   [   ]
       b)   dissociative fugue   [   ]
       c)   dissociative identity disorder (multiple personality
             disorder)   [   ]
       d)   depersonalization disorder   [   ]
       e)   dissociative disorder not otherwise specified   [   ]
       Yes=1   No=2   Unsure=3

48.   Have you ever been prescribed psychiatric medication?
       Yes=1   No=2   Unsure=3   [   ]

49.   Have you ever been prescribed one of the following medications?
       a)   antipsychotic   [   ]
       b)   antidepressant   [   ]
       c)   lithium   [   ]
       d)   anti-anxiety or sleeping medication   [   ]
       e)   other (specify) _____   [   ]
       Yes=1   No=2   Unsure=3

50.   Have you ever received ECT, also know as electroshock treatment?
       Yes=1   No=2   Unsure=3   [   ]

51.   Have you ever had therapy for emotional, family, or psychological
       problems, for more than 5 sessions in one course of treatment?
       Yes=1   No=2   Unsure=3   [   ]

52.   How many therapists, if any, have you seen for emotional problems
       or mental illness in your life.
       Unsure=89   [   ]

If subject answered No to both questions 51 and 52, go to question 54.

53.   Have you ever had a treatment for an emotional problem or mental
       illness which was ineffective?
       Yes=1   No=2   Unsure=3   [   ]

IV.   Major Depressive Episode

The purpose of this section is to determine whether the subject has ever had or currently has a major depressive episode.

54.   Have you ever had a period of depressed mood lasting at least two weeks in which you felt depressed, blue, hopeless, low, or down in the dumps?
Yes=1   No=2   Unsure=3   [   ]

If subject answered No to question 54, go to question 62.

If subject answered Yes or Unsure, interviewer should ask, "During this period did you experience the following symptoms nearly every day for at least two weeks?

55.   Poor appetite or significant weight loss (when not dieting) or increased appetite or significant weight gain.
Yes=1   No=2   Unsure=3   [   ]

56.   Sleeping too little or too much.
Yes=1   No=2   Unsure=3   [   ]

57.   Being physically and mentally slowed down, or agitated to the point where it was noticeable to other people.
Yes=1   No=2   Unsure=3   [   ]

58.   Loss of interest or pleasure in usual activities, or decrease in sexual drive.
Yes=1   No=2   Unsure=3   [   ]

59.   Loss of energy or fatigue nearly every day.
Yes=1   No=2   Unsure=3   [   ]

60.   Feelings of worthlessness, self-reproach, or excessive or inappropriate guilt nearly every day.
Yes=1   No=2   Unsure=3   [   ]

61.   Difficulty concentrating or difficulty making decisions.
Yes=1   No=2   Unsure=3   [   ]

62.   Recurrent thoughts of death, suicidal thoughts, wishes to be dead, or attempted suicide.
Yes=1   No=2   Unsure=3   [   ]

       If you have made a suicide attempt, did you:
       a)   take an overdose   [   ]
       b)   slash your wrists or other body areas   [   ]
       c)   inflict cigarette burns or other self injuries [   ]
       d)   use a gun, knife, or other weapons   [   ]

e)   attempt hanging   [   ]

f)   use another method   [   ]

Yes=1   No=2   Unsure=3

63.   If you have had an episode of depression as described above,
is it: [   ]

currently active, first occurrence   =1

currently in remission   =2

currently active, recurrence   =3

uncertain   =4

due to a specific organic cause   =5

V.   <u>Positive Symptoms of Schizophrenia (Schneiderian First Rank Symptoms)</u>

64.   Have you ever experienced the following:

Yes=1   No=2   Unsure=3

a)   voices arguing in your head   [   ]

b)   voices commenting on your actions   [   ]

c)   having your feelings made or controlled by someone
or something outside you   [   ]

d)   having your thoughts made or controlled by someone
or something outside you   [   ]

e)   having your actions made or controlled by someone
or something outside you   [   ]

f)   Influences from outside you playing on or affecting your
body such as some external force or power.   [   ]

g)   having thoughts taken out of your mind   [   ]

h)   thinking thoughts which seemed to be someone else's   [   ]

i)   hearing your thoughts out loud   [   ]

j)   other people being able to hear your thoughts as if they're
out loud   [   ]

k)   thoughts of a delusional nature that were very out of
touch with reality   [   ]

If subject answered No to all schizophrenia symptoms, go to question 67,

otherwise, interviewer should ask:

"If you have experienced any of the above symptoms are they clearly limited to one of the following:"

65. Occurred only under the influence of drugs, or alcohol.
Yes=1   No=2   Unsure= 3   [   ]

66. Occurred only during a major depressive episode.
Yes=1   No=2   Unsure= 3   [   ]

VI. <u>Trances, Sleepwalking, Childhood Companions</u>

67. Have you ever walked in your sleep?
Yes=1   No=2   Unsure= 3   [   ]

If subject answered No to question 67, go to question 69.

68. If you have walked in your sleep, how many times roughly?
1-10=1   11-50=2   >50= 3   Unsure=3   [   ]

69. Have you ever had a trance-like episode where you stare off into space, lose awareness of what is going on around you and lose track of time?
Yes=1   No=2   Unsure= 3   [   ]

If subject answered No to question 69, go to question 71.

70. If you have had this experience, how many times, roughly?
1-10=1   11-50=2   >50=3   Unsure=4   [   ]

71. Did you have imaginary playmates as a child?
Yes=1   No=2   Unsure= 3   [   ]

If subject answered No to question 71, go to question 73.

72. If you had imaginary playmates, how old were you when they stopped.   Unsure=0   [   ]

If subject still has imaginary companions score subject's current age.

VIII.   <u>Childhood Abuse</u>

73. Were you physically abused as a child or adolescent?
Yes=1   No=2   Unsure= 3   [   ]

If subject answered No to question 73, go to question 78.

74.   Was the physical abuse independent of episodes of sexual abuse?
        Yes=1   No=2   Unsure= 3   [   ]

75.   If you were physically abused, was it by:
        a)   father   [   ]
        b)   mother   [   ]
        c)   stepfather   [   ]
        d)   stepmother   [   ]
        e)   brother   [   ]
        f)   sister   [   ]
        g)   male relative   [   ]
        h)   female relative   [   ]
        i)   other male   [   ]
        j)   other female   [   ]
        Yes=1   No=2   Unsure= 3

76.   If you were physically abused, how old were you when it started?
        Unsure=89. **If less than 1 year, score 0.**   [   ]

77.   If you were physically abused how old were you when it stopped?
        Unsure=89   **If less than 1 year, score 0. If ongoing score subject's
        current age.**   [   ]

78.   Were you sexually abused as a child or adolescent? Sexual abuse
        includes rape, or any type of unwanted sexual touching or fondling
        that you may have experienced.
        Yes=1   No=2   Unsure= 3   [   ]

If the subject answered No to question 78, go to question 86. If the subject answered Yes or Unsure to question 78, the interviewer should state the following before asking further questions on sexual abuse:

"The following questions concern detailed examples of the types of sexual abuse you may or may not have experienced. Because of the explicit nature of these questions, you have the option not to answer any or all of them. The reason I am asking these questions is to try to determine the severity of the abuse that you experienced. You may answer Yes, No, Unsure or not give an answer to each question."

79.   If you were sexually abused was it by:

        a)   father   [   ]
        b)   mother   [   ]
        c)   stepfather   [   ]
        d)   stepmother   [   ]
        e)   brother   [   ]
        f)   sister   [   ]
        g)   male relative   [   ]

h)   female relative   [   ]
i)   other male   [   ]
j)   other female   [   ]
Yes=1   No=2   Unsure= 3   No Answer=4

If subject is female skip question 80. If male skip question 81.

80.   If you are male and were sexually abused, did the abuse involve:

a)   hand to genital touching   [   ]
b)   other types of fondling   [   ]
c)   intercourse with a female   [   ]
d)   anal intercourse with a male - you active   [   ]
e)   you performing oral sex on a male   [   ]
f)   you performing oral sex on a female   [   ]
g)   oral sex done to you by a male   [   ]
h)   oral sex done to you by a female   [   ]
i)   anal intercourse - you passive   [   ]
j)   enforced sex with animals   [   ]
k)   pornographic photography   [   ]
l.)   other (specify) _____   [   ]
Yes=1   No=2   Unsure=3   No Answer=4

81.   If you are female and were sexually abused, did the abuse involve:

a)   hand to genital touching   [   ]
b)   other types of fondling   [   ]
c)   intercourse with a male   [   ]
d)   simulated intercourse with a female   [   ]
e)   you performing oral sex on a male   [   ]
f)   you performing oral sex on a female   [   ]
g)   oral sex done to you by a male   [   ]
h)   oral sex done to you by a female   [   ]
i)   anal intercourse with a male   [   ]
j)   enforced sex with animals   [   ]
k)   pornographic photography   [   ]
l)   other (specify) _____   [   ]
Yes=1   No=2   Unsure=3   No Answer=4

82.   If you were sexually abused, how old were you when it started?
         Unsure=89. **If less than 1 year, score 0.**   [   ]

83.   If you were sexually abused, how old were you when it stopped?
         Unsure=89 **If less than 1 year, score 0. If ongoing score subject's
         current age.**   [   ]

84. How many separate incidents of sexual abuse were you subjected
to up until the age of 18?
0=1 1-5=2 6-10=3 11-50=4 >50=5 Unsure=6　　　　[　　　]

85. How many separate incidents of sexual abuse were you subjected to
after the age of 18?
0=1 1-5=2 6-10=3 11-50=4 >50=5 Unsure=6　　　　[　　　]

VIII.　　Features Associated with Dissociative Identity Disorder

For questions 86-95, if subject answers Yes, ask subject to specify whether it is occasionally, fairly often or frequently, excluding question 93.

86. Have you ever noticed that things are missing from your personal
possessions or where you live?
Never=1　　Occasionally=2　　Fairly Often=3　　Frequently=4
Unsure=5　　　　　　　　　　　　　　　　　　　　[　　　]

87. Have you ever noticed that there are things present where you live, and you
　　　　don't know where they came from or how they got there? e.g. clothes
jewelry, books, furniture.

Never=1　　Occasionally=2　　Fairly Often=3　　Frequently=4
Unsure=5　　　　　　　　　　　　　　　　　　　　[　　　]

88. Have you ever noticed that your handwriting changes drastically or that
there are things around in handwriting you don't recognize?
Never=1　　Occasionally=2　　Fairly Often=3　　Frequently=4
Unsure=5　　　　　　　　　　　　　　　　　　　　[　　　]

89. Do people ever come up and talk to you as if they know you but you don't
know them, or only know them faintly?
Never=1　　Occasionally=2　　Fairly Often=3　　Frequently=4
Unsure=5　　　　　　　　　　　　　　　　　　　　[　　　]

90. Do people ever tell you about things you've done or said, that you can't
remember, not counting times you have been using drugs or alcohol?
Never=1　　Occasionally=2　　Fairly Often=3　　Frequently=4
Unsure=5　　　　　　　　　　　　　　　　　　　　[　　　]

91. Do you ever have blank spells or periods of missing time that you can't
remember, not counting times you have been using drugs or alcohol?
Never=1　　Occasionally=2　　Fairly Often=3　　Frequently=4
Unsure=5　　　　　　　　　　　　　　　　　　　　[　　　]

92.   Do you ever find yourself coming to in an unfamiliar place, wide awake, not sure how you got there, and not sure what has been happening for the past while, not counting times when you have been using drugs or alcohol?

Never=1   Occasionally=2   Fairly Often=3   Frequently=4
Unsure=5   [   ]

93.   Are there large parts of your childhood after age 5 which you can't remember?
Yes=1   No=2   Unsure=3   [   ]

94.   Do you ever have memories come back to you all of a sudden, in a flood or like flashbacks?
Never=1   Occasionally=2   Fairly Often=3   Frequently=4
Unsure=5   [   ]

95.   Do you ever have long periods when you feel unreal, as if in a dream, or as if you're not really there, not counting when you are using drugs or alcohol?
Never=1   Occasionally=2   Fairly Often=3   Frequently=4
Unsure=5   [   ]

96.   Do you hear voices talking to you sometimes or talking inside your head?
Yes=1   No=2   Unsure=3   [   ]

If subject answered No to question 96, go to question 98.

97.   If you hear voices, do they seem to come from inside you?
Yes=1   No=2   Unsure=3   [   ]

98.   Do you ever speak about yourself as "we" or "us"?
Yes=1   No=2   Unsure=3   [   ]

99.   Do you ever feel that there is another person or persons inside you?
Yes=1   No=2   Unsure=3   [   ]

If subject answered No to question 99, go to question 102.

100.   Is there another person or person inside you that has a name?
Yes=1   No=2   Unsure=3   [   ]

101.   If there is another person inside you, does he or she ever come out and take control of you body?
Yes=1   No=2   Unsure=3   [   ]

IX. Supernatural/Possession/ESP Experiences/Cults

102. Have you ever had any kind of supernatural experience?
Yes=1   No=2   Unsure=3   [   ]

103. Have you ever had any extrasensory perception experiences such as:
a)   mental telepathy   [   ]
b)   seeing the future while awake   [   ]
c)   moving objects with your mind   [   ]
d)   seeing the future in dreams   [   ]
e)   deja vu (the feeling that what is happening to you has
       happened before)   [   ]
f)   other (specify) _____   [   ]
Yes=1   No=2   Unsure=3

104. Have you ever felt you were possessed by a:
a)   demon   [   ]
b)   dead person   [   ]
c)   living person   [   ]
d)   some other power or force   [   ]
Yes=1   No=2   Unsure=3

105. Have you ever had any contact with:
a)   ghosts   [   ]
b}   poltergeists (cause noises or objects to move around) [   ]
c)   spirits of any kind   [   ]
Yes=1   No=2   Unsure=3

106. Have you ever felt you know something about past lives or
      incarnations of yours?
Yes=1   No=2   Unsure=3   [   ]

107. Have you ever been involved in cult activities?
Yes=1   No=2   Unsure=3   [   ]

X.   Borderline Personality Disorder

Interviewer should state, "For the following nine questions, please answer
Yes only if you have been this way much of the time for much of your life.
Have you experienced:

108. Impulsive or unpredictable behavior in at least two areas that are potentially
      self-damaging, e.g., spending, sex, substance use, reckless driving, binge eating.
Yes=1   No=2   Unsure=3   [   ]

109. A pattern of intense, unstable personal relationships characterized by your

alternating between extremes of positive and negative feelings.
Yes=1   No=2   Unsure=3   [   ]

110.   Intense anger or lack of control of anger, e.g., frequent displays of temper,
            constant anger, recurrent physical fights.
            Yes=1   No=2   Unsure=3   [   ]

111.   Unstable identity, self-image, or sense of self.
            Yes=1   No=2   Unsure=3   [   ]

112.   Frequent mood swings: noticeable shifts from normal mood to
            depression, irritability or anxiety, usually lasting only a few hours
            and rarely more than a few days.
            Yes=1   No=2   Unsure=3   [   ]

113.   Frantic efforts to avoid real or imagined abandonment.
            Yes=1   No=2   Unsure=3   [   ]

114.   Recurrent suicidal behavior, e.g., suicidal attempts, self-mutilation,
        or threats of suicide.
            Yes=1   No=2   Unsure=3   [   ]

115.   Chronic feelings of emptiness.
            Yes=1   No=2   Unsure=3   [   ]

116.   Transient, stress-related paranoia or severe   [   ]
            Dissociative symptoms.

XI. Dissociative Amnesia

117.   Have you ever experienced inability to recall important personal
            information, particularly of a traumatic or stressful nature, that
            is too extensive to be explained by ordinary forgetfulness?
            Yes=1   No=2   Unsure=3   [   ]

If subject answered No or Unsure to question 117, go to 120.

118.   If you answered Yes to the previous question was the disturbance due
            to known physical disorder (e.g., blackouts during alcohol intoxication,
            or stroke), substance abuse, or another psychiatric disorder?
            Yes=1   No=2   Unsure=3   [   ]

119.   Did the symptoms cause you significant distress or impairment
            in social or occupational function?
            Yes=1 No=2   Unsure=3   [   ]

XII. Dissociative Fugue

120. Have you ever experienced sudden unexpected travel away from your home or customary place of work, with inability to recall your past?
Yes=1   No=2   Unsure=3   [   ]

121. During this period did you experience confusion about your identity or assume a partial or complete new identity?
Yes=1   No=2   Unsure=3   [   ]

If subject answered No to one or both of questions 120 and 121, go to 124.

122. If you answered Yes to both the previous two questions was the disturbance due to a known physical disorder? (e.g., blackouts during alcohol intoxication or stroke)?
Yes=1   No=2   Unsure=3   [   ]

123. Did the symptoms cause you significant distress or impairment in occupational or social function?
Yes=1 No=2   Unsure=3   [   ]

XIII.   Depersonalization Disorder

124.   **Interviewer should say,** "I am now going to ask you a series of questions about depersonalization. Depersonalization means feeling unreal, feeling as if you're in a dream, seeing yourself from outside your body or similar experiences."

   a)   Have you had one or more episodes of depersonalization sufficient to cause problems in your work or social life?
Yes=1   No=2   Unsure=3   [   ]

   b)   Have you ever had the feeling that your feet and hands or other parts of your body have changed in size?
Yes=1   No=2   Unsure=3   [   ]

   c)   Have you ever experienced seeing yourself from outside your body?
Yes=1   No=2   Unsure=3   [   ]

   d)   Have you ever had a strong feeling of unreality that lasted for a period of time, not counting when you are using drugs or alcohol?
Yes=1   No=2   Unsure=3   [   ]

If subject did not answer Yes to any of 124 a-d, go to question 127.

125.   If you answered Yes to any of the previous questions about
        depersonalization was the disturbance due to another disorder,
        such as Schizophrenia, Anxiety Disorder, or epilepsy, substance abuse,
        or a general medical condition?
        Yes=1   No=2   Unsure=3   [   ]

126.   During the periods of depersonalization, did you stay in touch
        with reality and maintain your ability to think rationally?
        Yes=1 No=2   Unsure=3   [   ]

XIV.   Dissociative Identity Disorder

127.   Have you ever felt like there are two or more distinct identities
        or personalities within yourself, each of which has its own
        pattern of perceiving, thinking, and relating to self and others?
        Yes=1   No=2   Unsure=3   [   ]

If subject answered No to question 127, go to question 131.

128.   Do at least two of the identities or personalities recurrently
        take control of your behavior?
        Yes=1   No=2   Unsure=3   [   ]

Interviewer should score question 129 based on the subject's response to Question 117, and should not read question 129 aloud.

129.   Have you experienced inability to recall important personal
        information that is too extensive to be explained by
        ordinary forgetfulness?
        Yes=1   No=2   Unsure=3   [   ]

130.   Is the problem with different identities or personalities
        due to substance abuse (e.g. alcohol blackouts)
        or a general medical condition?
        Yes=1 No=2   Unsure=3   [   ]

Interviewer should not read the following two questions aloud.

XV. Dissociative Disorder Not Otherwise Specified

131.Subject appears to have a dissociative disorder but does not satisfy the criteria for a specific dissociative disorder. Examples include trance-like states, derealization unaccompanied by depersonalization, and those more prolonged dissociated states that may occur in persons who have been subjected to   periods of prolonged and intense coercive persuasion (brainwashing, thought reform, and indoctrination while captive).
        Yes=1   No=2   Unsure=3   [   ]

XVI. <u>Concluding Item</u>

132. During the interview, did the subject display unusual, illogical, or idiosyncratic thought processes?

                Yes=1   No=2   Unsure=3   [   ]

Interviewer should make a brief concluding statement telling subject that there are no more questions, and thanking the subject for his/her participation.

SCORING THE DISSOCIATIVE DISORDERS INTERVIEW SCHEDULE

The Dissociative Disorders Interview Schedule (DDIS), is divided into 16 sections. Each section is scored independently. All DSM-IV diagnoses are made according to the rules in DSM-IV.

There is no total score for the entire interview. However, average scores for 166 dissociative identity disorder (DID) subjects on selected subsections are given below (Ross et al, Differentiating Multiple Personality Disorder and Dissociative Disorder Not Otherwise Specified, Dissociation, 5, 87-90, 1992).

Following presentation of scoring rules for each section, you will find a description of a typical profile for a DID patient. The DDIS has been administered to over 500 subjects with a confirmed false positive diagnosis of DID in 1% of cases. The sensitivity of the DDIS for the diagnosis of DID in 196 clinically diagnosed cases was 95.4%.

I. Somatic Complaints

This is scored according to DSM-IV rules. To receive a diagnosis of somatization disorder by DSM-IV rules one must be positive for a least four pain symptoms, two gastrointestinal symptoms and one sexual symptom and one pseudoneurological symptom:

  1. Pain - questions 9-14, 17, 32, 35
  2. Gastrointestinal - questions 3-8
  3. Sexual - questions 31, 33-37
  4. Pseudoneurological - questions 19-30

One must also answer "yes" to question 38 and "no" to question 39.

A history of somatization disorder distinguishes DID from schizophrenia, eating disorders, and controls, but not from panic disorder. The average number of symptoms positive from questions 3-37 for DID was 14.1. Out of 166 subjects, 39.8% met DSM-III-R criteria for somatization disorder: these data have not been reanalyzed by DSM-IV criteria.

II. Substance Abuse

We score the subject as positive for substance abuse if he or she answers "yes" to any question in this section. A history of substance abuse differentiates DID from schizophrenia, eating disorders, panic disorder, and controls: 51.2% of 166 DID subjects were positive.

III. Psychiatric History

This is a descriptive section that does not yield a score as such. In a questionnaire study (Ross, Norton, & Wozney, 1989) we found that in 236 cases of DID, the average patient had received 2.74 other psychiatric diagnoses besides DID.

IV. *Major Depressive Episode*

This is scored according to DSM-IV rules, which underwent only minor changes in wording from DSM-III-R. To be positive the subject must answer "yes" to question 54. He or she must answer "yes" to 4 questions from 55-62.

A history of depression does not discriminate DID from other diagnostic groups: out of 166 subjects, 89.8% had been clinically depressed at some time.

V. *Schneiderian First Rank Symptoms*

In this section we score the total number of "yes" responses. The total number of Schneiderian symptoms positive discriminates DID from all groups tested including schizophrenia. The average number of positive symptoms in 166 subjects was 6.5.

VI. *Trances, Sleepwalking, Childhood Companions*

Each of these items is scored independently. The subject is positive for sleepwalking if he or she answers "yes" to question 67, positive for trances if "yes" to 69, positive for imaginary playmates if "yes" to 71. Each of these items discriminates DID from schizophrenia, eating disorder, panic disorder, and controls.

VII. Childhood Abuse

The subject is scored positive for physical abuse if he or she answers "yes" to question 73. Other data are descriptive. A history of physical abuse discriminates DID from schizophrenia, eating disorders, and panic disorder.

The subject is positive for sexual abuse if he or she answers "yes" to question 78. Sexual abuse also discriminates DID from the other three groups. Out of 166 subjects 84.3% reported sexual abuse, 78.3% physical abuse, and 91.0% physical and/or sexual abuse.

VIII. *Features Associated with Dissociative Identity Disorder*

The responses in this section are added up to give a total score. A positive response in this section is either "yes" or else "fairly often" or "frequently," depending on the structure of the question. "Never" and "occasionally" are scored as negative. Secondary features discriminate DID from panic disorder, eating disorders and schizophrenia. The average number of features positive in 166 subjects with DID was 10.2.

IX. *Supernatural/Possession/ESP Experiences/Cults*

In this section the positive answers are added up to give a total score. These experiences discriminate DID from the other groups. The average number of positive responses for 166 subjects was 5.3.

X. Borderline Personality Disorder

This is scored by DSM-IV rules. The subject must be positive for 5 items to meet the criteria for borderline personality. Borderline personality does not discriminate DID from other groups tested to date, except for panic disorder and controls. However, the average number of borderline criteria positive does discriminate DID from schizophrenia, eating disorders, and panic disorder. The average for 166 DID subjects was 5.1.

XI.   Dissociative Amnesia

This is scored by DSM-IV rules. The subject must be positive for question 117, negative for question 118, and positive for question 119.

XII.   Dissociative Fugue

This is scored by DSM-IV rules. The subject must be positive for questions 120 and 121, negative for 122, and positive for 123.

XIII.   Depersonalization Disorder

This is scored by DSM-IV rules. The subject must be positive for question 124a, negative for 125, and positive for 126. Questions 124b-d are examples of depersonalization that are not required for the DSM-IV diagnosis. This diagnosis discriminates DID from other groups very poorly.

XIV.   Dissociative Identity Disorder

This is scored by DSM-IV rules. The subject must be positive for questions 127-129 and negative to 130 to receive a diagnosis of DID.

XV.   Dissociative Disorder Not Otherwise Specified

This is scored positive based on the interviewer's judgment. A patient can be positive for dissociative disorder not otherwise specified only if he or she does not have any other dissociative disorder.

XVI.   Concluding Item

This is a descriptive question and is not scored.

Most DID patients will exhibit the DDIS profile but some will score lower than usual in some or all sections.

Individuals with dissociative disorder not otherwise specified have the same profile, but to a lesser degree than those with full DID. It is not unusual for subjects to meet criteria for both dissociative amnesia and depersonalization disorder and to have elevated symptom profiles in the rest of the DDIS: these people usually have a chronic, complex dissociative disorder that is not well classified by the DSM-IV system. One might diagnose them as having a partial form of DID and classify them as dissociative disorder not otherwise specified, but this is not allowed by DSM-IV rules. One should bear in mind that subjects who are positive for dissociative amnesia and depersonalization disorder but negative for DID on the DDIS might actually have DID, in which case they have received a false negative diagnosis of DID from the DDIS.

THE MULTIDIMENSIONAL INVENTORY OF DISSOCIATION (MID)

MID6.0

Multidimensional Inventory of Dissociation v.6.0

© 2004, Paul F. Dell, PhD.   FAX: 757-626-3318

Instructions: How often do you have the following experiences when you are **not under the influence of alcohol or drugs?** Please circle the number that best describes you. Circle a "0" if the experience never happens to you; circle a "10" if it is always happening to you. If it happens sometimes, but not all the time, circle a number between 1 and 9 that best describes how often it happens to you.

Never										Always
0	1	2	3	4	5	6	7	8	9	10

1. While watching TV, you find that you are thinking about something else.	0 1 2 3 4 5 6 7 8 9 10
2. Forgetting what you did earlier in the day.	0 1 2 3 4 5 6 7 8 9 10
3. Feeling as if your body (or certain parts of it) are unreal.	0 1 2 3 4 5 6 7 8 9 10
4. Having an emotion (for example, fear, sadness, anger, happiness) that doesn't feel like it is 'yours.'	0 1 2 3 4 5 6 7 8 9 10
5. Things around you suddenly seeming strange.	0 1 2 3 4 5 6 7 8 9 10
6. Hearing the voice of a child in your head.	0 1 2 3 4 5 6 7 8 9 10
7. Having pain in your genitals (for no known medical reason).	0 1 2 3 4 5 6 7 8 9 10
8. Having another personality that sometimes 'takes over.'	0 1 2 3 4 5 6 7 8 9 10
9. Hearing yourself talk, but you don't feel that you are choosing the words that are coming out of your mouth.	0 1 2 3 4 5 6 7 8 9 10
10. Forgetting errands that you had planned to do.	0 1 2 3 4 5 6 7 8 9 10
11. Feeling that your mind or body has been taken over by a famous person (for example, Elvis Presley, Jesus Christ, Madonna, President Kennedy, etc.).	0 1 2 3 4 5 6 7 8 9 10
12. Trying to make someone jealous.	0 1 2 3 4 5 6 7 8 9 10
13. Feeling as if close friends, relatives, or your own home seems strange or foreign.	0 1 2 3 4 5 6 7 8 9 10
14. Reliving a traumatic event so vividly that you totally lose contact with where you actually are (that is, you think that you are 'back there and then').	0 1 2 3 4 5 6 7 8 9 10

15. Having difficulty swallowing (for no known medical reason).

0 1 2 3 4 5 6 7 8 9 10

16. Having trance-like episodes where you stare off into space and lose awareness of what is going on around you.

0 1 2 3 4 5 6 7 8 9 10

17. Being puzzled by what you do or say.

0 1 2 3 4 5 6 7 8 9 10

18. Seeing images of a child who seems to 'live' in your head.

0 1 2 3 4 5 6 7 8 9 10

19. Being told of things that you had recently done, but with absolutely no memory of having done those things.

0 1 2 3 4 5 6 7 8 9 10

20. Thoughts being imposed on you or imposed on your mind.

0 1 2 3 4 5 6 7 8 9 10

21. Pretending that something upsetting happened to you so that others would care about you (for example, being raped, military combat, physical or emotional abuse, sexual abuse, etc.).

0 1 2 3 4 5 6 7 8 9 10

22. Strong thoughts in your head that "come from out of nowhere."

0 1 2 3 4 5 6 7 8 9 10

23. Having blank spells or blackouts in your memory.

0 1 2 3 4 5 6 7 8 9 10

24. Not remembering what you ate at your last meal — or even whether you ate.

0 1 2 3 4 5 6 7 8 9 10

25. Feeling like you're only partially 'there' (or not really 'there' at all).

0 1 2 3 4 5 6 7 8 9 10

26. Your mind being controlled by an external force (for example, microwaves, the CIA, radiation from outer space, etc.).

0 1 2 3 4 5 6 7 8 9 10

27. Having no feeling at all in your body (for no known medical reason).

0 1 2 3 4 5 6 7 8 9 10

28. Feeling divided, as if you have several independent parts or sides.

0 1 2 3 4 5 6 7 8 9 10

29. Nobody cares about you.

0 1 2 3 4 5 6 7 8 9 10

30. Hearing voices in your head that argue or converse with one another.

0 1 2 3 4 5 6 7 8 9 10

31. 'Losing' a chunk of time and having a total blank for it.

0 1 2 3 4 5 6 7 8 9 10

32. Strong feelings of emotional pain and hurt that come from out of nowhere.

0 1 2 3 4 5 6 7 8 9 10

33. While reading, you find that you are thinking about something else.

0 1 2 3 4 5 6 7 8 9 10

34. Having strong impulses to do something — but the impulses don't feel like they belong to you.

0 1 2 3 4 5 6 7 8 9 10

35. Feeling empty and painfully alone.

0 1 2 3 4 5 6 7 8 9 10

36. Feeling mechanical or not really human.

0 1 2 3 4 5 6 7 8 9 10

37. Things around you feeling unreal.

0 1 2 3 4 5 6 7 8 9 10

38. Pretending that you have a physical illness in order to get sympathy (for example, flu, cancer, headache, having an operation, etc.).

0 1 2 3 4 5 6 7 8 9 10

39. Not being able to see for a while (as if you are blind) (for no known medical reason).

0 1 2 3 4 5 6 7 8 9 10

40. Feeling that the color of your body is changing.

0 1 2 3 4 5 6 7 8 9 10

41. Feeling split or divided inside.	0 1 2 3 4 5 6 7 8 9 10
42. Hearing a voice in your head that tries to tell you what to do.	0 1 2 3 4 5 6 7 8 9 10
43. Finding things at home (for example, shoes, clothes, toys, toilet articles, etc.), that you don't remember buying.	0 1 2 3 4 5 6 7 8 9 10
44. Feeling very detached from your behavior as you "go through the motions" of daily life.	0 1 2 3 4 5 6 7 8 9 10
45. Feeling mad.	0 1 2 3 4 5 6 7 8 9 10
46. Being unable to remember who you are.	0 1 2 3 4 5 6 7 8 9 10
47. Talking to others about how you have been hurt or mistreated.	0 1 2 3 4 5 6 7 8 9 10
48. Being in a familiar place, but finding it strange and unfamiliar.	0 1 2 3 4 5 6 7 8 9 10
49. Feeling uncertain about who you really are.	0 1 2 3 4 5 6 7 8 9 10
50. 'Coming to' in the middle of a conversation with someone and having no idea what you and that person have been talking about — you didn't even know that you were having a conversation.	0 1 2 3 4 5 6 7 8 9 10
51. Talking to others about very serious traumas that you have experienced.	0 1 2 3 4 5 6 7 8 9 10
52. Your thoughts being broadcast so that other people can actually hear them.	0 1 2 3 4 5 6 7 8 9 10
53. Being told that there were times when you did not recognize friends or family members (for example, asking your spouse or friend, "Who are you?").	0 1 2 3 4 5 6 7 8 9 10
54. Being rejected by others.	0 1 2 3 4 5 6 7 8 9 10
55. Feeling the presence of an old man inside you who wants to read his newspaper or go to the bathroom.	0 1 2 3 4 5 6 7 8 9 10
56. Being unable to remember your name, or age, or address.	0 1 2 3 4 5 6 7 8 9 10
57. Your moods changing so rapidly that you don't know what you are going to feel from one minute to the next.	0 1 2 3 4 5 6 7 8 9 10
58. Feeling that other people, objects, or the world around you are not real.	0 1 2 3 4 5 6 7 8 9 10
59. Being angry that your life is ruined.	0 1 2 3 4 5 6 7 8 9 10
60. Being paralyzed or unable to move (for no known medical reason).	0 1 2 3 4 5 6 7 8 9 10
61. Hearing a voice in your head and, at the same time, seeing an image of that 'person' or of that voice.	0 1 2 3 4 5 6 7 8 9 10
62. Nobody understands how much you hurt.	0 1 2 3 4 5 6 7 8 9 10
63. Exaggerating the symptoms of a physical illness (that you genuinely have) in order to get sympathy or attention (for example, flu, cold, headache, fever, pain, etc.).	0 1 2 3 4 5 6 7 8 9 10
64. Finding yourself lying in bed (on the sofa, etc.) with no memory of how you got there.	0 1 2 3 4 5 6 7 8 9 10
65. Being impulsive.	0 1 2 3 4 5 6 7 8 9 10
66. Being so bothered by flashbacks that it was hard to get out of bed and face the day.	0 1 2 3 4 5 6 7 8 9 10

67. Not remembering large parts of your childhood after age 5.	0 1 2 3 4 5 6 7 8 9 10
68. Not being able to keep friends.	0 1 2 3 4 5 6 7 8 9 10
69. Feeling disconnected from everything around you.	0 1 2 3 4 5 6 7 8 9 10
70. Having to 'stretch the truth' to get your doctor's (or therapist's) concern or attention.	0 1 2 3 4 5 6 7 8 9 10
71. Not being able to hear for a while (as if you are deaf) (for no known medical reason).	0 1 2 3 4 5 6 7 8 9 10
72. Feeling like you are often different from yourself.	0 1 2 3 4 5 6 7 8 9 10
73. Feeling the pain of never being really special to anyone.	0 1 2 3 4 5 6 7 8 9 10
74. Suddenly 'waking up' in the middle of doing something (that you were completely unaware you were doing) (for example, vacuuming the carpet, cooking dinner, spanking the children, driving the car, etc.).	0 1 2 3 4 5 6 7 8 9 10
75. Hurting yourself so that someone would care or pay attention.	0 1 2 3 4 5 6 7 8 9 10
76. Finding things in your shopping bags, which you don't remember buying.	0 1 2 3 4 5 6 7 8 9 10
77. People think that you live "in a world of your own."	0 1 2 3 4 5 6 7 8 9 10
78. Feeling that pieces of your past are missing.	0 1 2 3 4 5 6 7 8 9 10
79. Immediately forgetting what other people tell you.	0 1 2 3 4 5 6 7 8 9 10
80. Not being sure about what is real (and what is unreal) in your surroundings.	0 1 2 3 4 5 6 7 8 9 10
81. Being so bothered by flashbacks that it is hard to function at work (or it is hard to carry out your daily responsibilities).	0 1 2 3 4 5 6 7 8 9 10
82. Having difficulty walking (for no known medical reason).	0 1 2 3 4 5 6 7 8 9 10
83. Switching back and forth between feeling like an adult and feeling like a child.	0 1 2 3 4 5 6 7 8 9 10
84. Hearing a voice in your head that wants you to hurt yourself.	0 1 2 3 4 5 6 7 8 9 10
85. When something upsetting happens, you go blank and lose a chunk of time.	0 1 2 3 4 5 6 7 8 9 10
86. After a nightmare, you wake up and find yourself not in bed (for example, on the floor, in the closet, etc.).	0 1 2 3 4 5 6 7 8 9 10
87. Not being able to remember something, but feeling that it is "right on the tip of your tongue."	0 1 2 3 4 5 6 7 8 9 10
88. Making decisions too quickly.	0 1 2 3 4 5 6 7 8 9 10
89. Feeling very confused about who you really are.	0 1 2 3 4 5 6 7 8 9 10
90. Feeling that important things happened to you earlier in your life, but you cannot remember them.	0 1 2 3 4 5 6 7 8 9 10
91. Standing outside of your body, watching yourself as if you were another person.	0 1 2 3 4 5 6 7 8 9 10
92. Feeling as if you were looking at the world through a fog so that people and objects felt far away or unclear.	0 1 2 3 4 5 6 7 8 9 10

93. Seeing or talking with others who have the same disorder that you have.	0 1 2 3 4 5 6 7 8 9 10
94. Having seizures for which your doctor can find no reason.	0 1 2 3 4 5 6 7 8 9 10
95. Going into trance so much (or for so long) that it interferes with your daily activities and responsibilities.	0 1 2 3 4 5 6 7 8 9 10
96. Thinking about how little attention you received from your parents.	0 1 2 3 4 5 6 7 8 9 10
97. Hearing a lot of noise or yelling in your head.	0 1 2 3 4 5 6 7 8 9 10
98. Hearing voices, which come from unusual places (for example, the air conditioner, the computer, the walls, etc.), that try to tell you what to do.	0 1 2 3 4 5 6 7 8 9 10
99. Words just flowing from your mouth as if they were not in your control.	0 1 2 3 4 5 6 7 8 9 10
100. Listening to someone and realizing that you did not hear part of what he/ she said.	0 1 2 3 4 5 6 7 8 9 10
101. Sudden strong feelings of anger that seem to come from out of nowhere.	0 1 2 3 4 5 6 7 8 9 10
102. Feeling that there are large gaps in your memory.	0 1 2 3 4 5 6 7 8 9 10
103. Feeling as if you are two different people — one who is going through the motions of daily life and the other who is just watching.	0 1 2 3 4 5 6 7 8 9 10
104. Feeling that your surroundings (or other people) were fading away or disappearing.	0 1 2 3 4 5 6 7 8 9 10
105. Having traumatic flashbacks that make you want to inflict pain on yourself.	0 1 2 3 4 5 6 7 8 9 10
106. Going into trance for hours.	0 1 2 3 4 5 6 7 8 9 10
107. Feeling like some of your behavior isn't really 'yours.'	0 1 2 3 4 5 6 7 8 9 10
108. Finding something that has been done (for example, the lawn mowed, the kitchen painted, a task at work completed, etc.), that you don't remember doing — but knowing that you must be the one who did it.	0 1 2 3 4 5 6 7 8 9 10
109. Forgetting where you put something.	0 1 2 3 4 5 6 7 8 9 10
110. Having dreams that you don't remember the next day.	0 1 2 3 4 5 6 7 8 9 10
111. Desperately wanting to talk to someone about your pain or distress.	0 1 2 3 4 5 6 7 8 9 10
112. Feeling the presence of an angry part in your head that tries to control what you do or say.	0 1 2 3 4 5 6 7 8 9 10
113. Your mind blocking or going totally empty.	0 1 2 3 4 5 6 7 8 9 10
114. Feeling like time slows down or stops.	0 1 2 3 4 5 6 7 8 9 10
115. Bad memories coming into your mind and you can't get rid of them.	0 1 2 3 4 5 6 7 8 9 10
116. Drifting into trance without even realizing that it is happening.	0 1 2 3 4 5 6 7 8 9 10
117. Words come out of your mouth, but you didn't say them — you don't know where those words came from.	0 1 2 3 4 5 6 7 8 9 10
118. Hearing voices crying in your head.	0 1 2 3 4 5 6 7 8 9 10

119. Suddenly finding yourself standing someplace and you can't remember what you have been doing before that.	0 1 2 3 4 5 6 7 8 9 10
120. Something in your mind interferes when you think about things that you 'shouldn't' think about.	0 1 2 3 4 5 6 7 8 9 10
121. Daydreaming.	0 1 2 3 4 5 6 7 8 9 10
122. Being able to remember very little of your past.	0 1 2 3 4 5 6 7 8 9 10
123. Not recognizing yourself in the mirror.	0 1 2 3 4 5 6 7 8 9 10
124. Feeling hurt.	0 1 2 3 4 5 6 7 8 9 10
125. Re-experiencing body sensations from a past traumatic event.	0 1 2 3 4 5 6 7 8 9 10
126. Part of your body (for example, arm, leg, head, etc.) seems to disappear and doesn't re-appear for several days.	0 1 2 3 4 5 6 7 8 9 10
127. When something upsetting starts to happen, you 'go away' in your mind.	0 1 2 3 4 5 6 7 8 9 10
128. Telling others about your psychological disorder(s).	0 1 2 3 4 5 6 7 8 9 10
129. When you are angry, doing or saying things that you don't remember (after you calm down).	0 1 2 3 4 5 6 7 8 9 10
130. Exaggerating the symptoms of a psychological illness (that you genuinely have) in order to get sympathy or attention (for example, depression, bulimia, posttraumatic stress disorder, memory blackouts, being suicidal, etc.).	0 1 2 3 4 5 6 7 8 9 10
131. Being able to do something really well one time — and then not being able to do it at all at another time.	0 1 2 3 4 5 6 7 8 9 10
132. Being unable to recall something — then, something "jogs" your memory and you remember it.	0 1 2 3 4 5 6 7 8 9 10
133. Feeling like you are 'inside' yourself, watching what you are doing.	0 1 2 3 4 5 6 7 8 9 10
134. Not being able to remember important events in your life (for example, your wedding day, the birth of your child, your grandmother's funeral, taking your final exams, etc.).	0 1 2 3 4 5 6 7 8 9 10
135. Feeling distant or removed from your thoughts and actions.	0 1 2 3 4 5 6 7 8 9 10
136. Things around you seeming to change size or shape.	0 1 2 3 4 5 6 7 8 9 10
137. Having traumatic flashbacks that make you want to die.	0 1 2 3 4 5 6 7 8 9 10
138. Feeling that you have multiple personalities.	0 1 2 3 4 5 6 7 8 9 10
139. Being bothered by how much you 'trance out.'	0 1 2 3 4 5 6 7 8 9 10
140. Hearing a voice in your head that calls you names (for example, wimp, stupid, whore, slut, bitch, etc.).	0 1 2 3 4 5 6 7 8 9 10
141. Suddenly realizing that hours have gone by and not knowing what you were doing during that time.	0 1 2 3 4 5 6 7 8 9 10
142. Having to go back and correct mistakes that you made.	0 1 2 3 4 5 6 7 8 9 10
143. Poor memory causing serious difficulty for you.	0 1 2 3 4 5 6 7 8 9 10

144. Feeling that your vision was suddenly sharper or that colors suddenly seemed more vivid or more intense.	0 1 2 3 4 5 6 7 8 9 10
145. Reliving a past trauma so vividly that you see it, hear it, feel it, smell it, etc.	0 1 2 3 4 5 6 7 8 9 10
146. Your thoughts and feelings are so changeable that you don't understand yourself.	0 1 2 3 4 5 6 7 8 9 10
147. Going into trance several days in a row.	0 1 2 3 4 5 6 7 8 9 10
148. Not feeling together, not feeling whole.	0 1 2 3 4 5 6 7 8 9 10
149. Having other people (or parts) inside you who have their own names.	0 1 2 3 4 5 6 7 8 9 10
150. Discovering that you have changed your appearance (for example, cut your hair, or changed your hairstyle, or changed what you are wearing, or put on cosmetics, etc.) with no memory of having done so.	0 1 2 3 4 5 6 7 8 9 10
151. Thoughts coming into your mind that you cannot stop.	0 1 2 3 4 5 6 7 8 9 10
152. Being told about things that you did — that you don't remember doing and would never do (for example, swearing like a sailor, being very mad, acting like a young child, or being very sexual).	0 1 2 3 4 5 6 7 8 9 10
153. Having trance-like episodes during which you see yourself being taken into a spaceship and experimented on by aliens.	0 1 2 3 4 5 6 7 8 9 10
154. Being bothered or upset by how much you forget.	0 1 2 3 4 5 6 7 8 9 10
155. Exaggerating something bad that once happened to you (for example, rape, military combat, physical or emotional abuse, sexual abuse, mistreatment by our spouse, etc.) in order to get attention or sympathy.	0 1 2 3 4 5 6 7 8 9 10
156. Reliving a traumatic event so totally that you think that a present-day person is actually a person from the trauma (for example, being home with your partner, suddenly reliving being raped by your alcoholic uncle, and actually thinking that your partner is your uncle — that is, you see your uncle in front of you instead of seeing your partner).	0 1 2 3 4 5 6 7 8 9 10
157. Thinking about nothing.	0 1 2 3 4 5 6 7 8 9 10
158. Feeling like you are not the same kind of person all the time.	0 1 2 3 4 5 6 7 8 9 10
159. Hearing a voice in your head that wants you to die.	0 1 2 3 4 5 6 7 8 9 10
160. Suddenly finding yourself somewhere odd at home (for example, inside the closet, under a bed, curled up on the floor, etc.) with no knowledge of how you got there.	0 1 2 3 4 5 6 7 8 9 10
161. Feeling as if there is something inside you that takes control of your behavior or speech.	0 1 2 3 4 5 6 7 8 9 10
162. Totally forgetting how to do something that you know very well how to do (for example, how to drive, how to read, how to use the computer, how to play the piano, etc.).	0 1 2 3 4 5 6 7 8 9 10
163. Hearing a voice in your head that keeps talking about AIDS and homosexuals.	0 1 2 3 4 5 6 7 8 9 10
164. Feeling that part of your body is disconnected (detached) from the rest of your body.	0 1 2 3 4 5 6 7 8 9 10
165. Wishing you knew why you feel and behave the way you do.	0 1 2 3 4 5 6 7 8 9 10
166. Hearing sounds from nearby as if they were coming from far away (for no known medical reason).	0 1 2 3 4 5 6 7 8 9 10
167. Going into trance and being possessed by a spirit or demon.	0 1 2 3 4 5 6 7 8 9 10

168. Having snapshots of past trauma that suddenly flash in your mind.	0 1 2 3 4 5 6 7 8 9 10
169. Feeling no pain (when you should have felt pain) (for no known medical reason).	0 1 2 3 4 5 6 7 8 9 10
170. Discovering that you have a significant injury (for example, a cut, or a burn, or many bruises), and having no memory of how it happened.	0 1 2 3 4 5 6 7 8 9 10
171. Hearing a voice in your head that calls you a liar or tells you that certain events never happened.	0 1 2 3 4 5 6 7 8 9 10
172. Feeling as if part of your body (or your whole body) has disappeared.	0 1 2 3 4 5 6 7 8 9 10
173. Suddenly finding yourself somewhere (for example, at the beach, at work, in a nightclub, in your car, etc.) with no memory of how you got there.	0 1 2 3 4 5 6 7 8 9 10
174. Feeling that there is another person inside you who can come out and speak if it wants.	0 1 2 3 4 5 6 7 8 9 10
175. Being willing to do or say almost anything to get somebody to feel that you are 'special.'	0 1 2 3 4 5 6 7 8 9 10
176. Having nightmares about a trauma from your past.	0 1 2 3 4 5 6 7 8 9 10
177. People noticing your blank stare and the fact that you are 'gone.'	0 1 2 3 4 5 6 7 8 9 10
178. Being pleased by the concern and sympathy of others when they hear about the traumas that you have suffered.	0 1 2 3 4 5 6 7 8 9 10
179. 'Coming to' and finding that you have done something you don't remember doing (for example, smashed something, cut yourself, cleaned the whole house, etc.).	0 1 2 3 4 5 6 7 8 9 10
180. Having thoughts that don't really seem to belong to you.	0 1 2 3 4 5 6 7 8 9 10
181. Having pain while urinating (for no known medical reason).	0 1 2 3 4 5 6 7 8 9 10
182. Switching back and forth between feeling like a human and feeling like a member of some other species (for example, a cat, a dog, a squirrel, etc.).	0 1 2 3 4 5 6 7 8 9 10
183. Having 'tunnel vision' (where your visual field narrows down to just a tunnel) (for no known medical reason).	0 1 2 3 4 5 6 7 8 9 10
184. Having difficulty staying out of trance.	0 1 2 3 4 5 6 7 8 9 10
185. Your mood changing rapidly without any reason.	0 1 2 3 4 5 6 7 8 9 10
186. Discovering that you have attempted suicide, but having no memory of having done it.	0 1 2 3 4 5 6 7 8 9 10
187. Finding things that you must have written (or drawn), but with no memory of having done so.	0 1 2 3 4 5 6 7 8 9 10
188. Suddenly feeling very small, like a young child.	0 1 2 3 4 5 6 7 8 9 10
189. Suddenly not knowing how to do your job.	0 1 2 3 4 5 6 7 8 9 10
190. Feeling as if there is a struggle going on inside of you about who you really are.	0 1 2 3 4 5 6 7 8 9 10
191. Your body suddenly feeling as if it isn't really yours.	0 1 2 3 4 5 6 7 8 9 10
192. Being bothered by flashbacks for several days in a row.	0 1 2 3 4 5 6 7 8 9 10
193. Being confused or puzzled by your emotions.	0 1 2 3 4 5 6 7 8 9 10

194. Not remembering what happens when you drive a familiar route in your car.	0 1 2 3 4 5 6 7 8 9 10
195. Distinct changes in your handwriting.	0 1 2 3 4 5 6 7 8 9 10
196. Very strong feelings (for example, fear, or anger, or emotional pain and hurt) that suddenly go away.	0 1 2 3 4 5 6 7 8 9 10
197. Looking in the mirror and seeing someone other than yourself.	0 1 2 3 4 5 6 7 8 9 10
198. Some thoughts are suddenly 'taken away from you.'	0 1 2 3 4 5 6 7 8 9 10
199. Hearing a voice in your head that tells you to "shut up."	0 1 2 3 4 5 6 7 8 9 10
200. People telling you that you sometimes act so differently that you seem like another person.	0 1 2 3 4 5 6 7 8 9 10
201. Switching back and forth between feeling like a man and feeling like a woman.	0 1 2 3 4 5 6 7 8 9 10
202. Having another part inside that has different memories, behaviors, and feelings than you do.	0 1 2 3 4 5 6 7 8 9 10
203. Feeling that your feet or hands (or other parts of your body) have changed in size.	0 1 2 3 4 5 6 7 8 9 10
204. There were times when you 'came to' and found pills or a razor blade (or something else to hurt yourself with) in your hand.	0 1 2 3 4 5 6 7 8 9 10
205. Finding writings at your home in handwriting that you don't recognize.	0 1 2 3 4 5 6 7 8 9 10
206. Having flashbacks of poor episodes of your favorite TV show.	0 1 2 3 4 5 6 7 8 9 10
207. Hearing a voice in your head that calls you no good, worthless, or a failure.	0 1 2 3 4 5 6 7 8 9 10
208. Having a very angry part that 'comes out' and says and does things that you would never do or say.	0 1 2 3 4 5 6 7 8 9 10
209. Feeling like some of your thoughts are removed from your mind — by some force or by some other part of you.	0 1 2 3 4 5 6 7 8 9 10
210. Feeling a struggle inside you about what to think, how to feel, what you should do.	0 1 2 3 4 5 6 7 8 9 10
211. Not remembering where you were the day before.	0 1 2 3 4 5 6 7 8 9 10
212. Feeling that another part or entity inside you tries to stop you from doing or saying something.	0 1 2 3 4 5 6 7 8 9 10
213. Wishing that someone would finally realize how much you hurt.	0 1 2 3 4 5 6 7 8 9 10
214. More than one part of you has been reacting to these questions.	0 1 2 3 4 5 6 7 8 9 10
215. Feeling the presence of an angry part in your head that seems to hate you.	0 1 2 3 4 5 6 7 8 9 10
216. Hearing a voice in your head that is soothing, helpful, or protective.	0 1 2 3 4 5 6 7 8 9 10
217. Things in your home disappear or get moved around (and you don't know how this is happening).	0 1 2 3 4 5 6 7 8 9 10
218. Noticing the presence of a child inside you.	0 1 2 3 4 5 6 7 8 9 10

THE INTERNATIONAL SOCIETY FOR THE STUDY OF TRAUMA AND DISSOCIATION (ISSTD)

The International Society for the Study of Trauma and Dissociation (ISSTD) was founded in 1984. The Society has held an Annual Meeting every year since 1984. It publishes a newsletter, a membership directory, and an official journal, *The Journal of Trauma and Dissociation*. As well, the Society provides education and training for professionals through its web site, a series of psychotherapy training courses, videos and other forms of education. It has a mandate for education of the general public in addition to its focus on mental health professionals.

There are a number of Study Groups and Component Societies operating under the banner of the ISSTD. These provide opportunities for consultation, training and peer support in different regions of the United States and in other countries. The ISSTD is the best source of information on dissociation. We recommend that all professionals interested in trauma and dissociation join the ISSTD and takes advantage of its offerings. Dr. Ross is a Past President of the ISSTD and has received several awards from the Society.

The ISSTD has produced Treatment Guidelines for dissociative identity disorder in children and adults. We recommend that all professionals treating dissociative disorders obtain and read these guidelines. Contact information for the ISSTD is:

International Society for the Study of Trauma and Dissociation
60 Revere Drive, Suite 500
Northbrook, IL 60062
Phone: 847-480-0899
FAX: 847-480-9282
issd@isst-d.org
www.isst-d.org

The Journal of Trauma and Dissociation is published by Haworth Press. Information about it and a range of related journals is available at www.haworthpress.com. At the web page, click on Imprints, then click on Haworth Maltreatment and Trauma Press.

The ISSTD Treatment Guidelines for Adult DID were published as:

Chu, J. (2005). Guidelines for treating dissociative identity disorder in adults (2005). *Journal of Trauma and Dissociation*, 6, 69-149.

REFERENCES

The following books and papers are cited as references in *Trauma Model Therapy: Treatment Techniques For Trauma and Dissociation*:

Ellason, J.W., & Ross, C.A. (1996). Millon Clinical Multiaxial Inventory-II follow-up of patients with dissociative identity disorder. *Psychological Reports*, 78, 707-716.

Ellason, J.W., & Ross, C.A. (1997). Two-year follow-up of inpatients with dissociative identity disorder. *American Journal of Psychiatry*, 154, 832-839.

Ellason, J.W., & Ross, C.A. (200x). SCL-90-R norms for dissociative identity disorder. *Journal of Trauma and Dissociation*,

Pincus, H.A., Rush, A.J., First, M.B., & McQueen, L.E. (2000). *Handbook of psychiatric measures*. Washington, DC: American Psychiatric Association.

Ross, C.A. (1989). *Multiple personality disorder. Diagnosis, clinical features, and treatment*. New York: John Wiley & Sons.

Ross, C.A. (1994). *The Osiris complex: Case studies in multiple personality disorder*. Toronto: University of Toronto Press.

Ross, C.A. (1995). *Satanic ritual abuse: Principles of treatment*. Toronto: University of Toronto Press.

Ross, C.A. (1997). *Dissociative identity disorder. Diagnosis, clinical features, and treatment of multiple personality. (2nd ed.)*. New York: John Wiley & Sons.

Ross, C.A. (2004). *Schizophrenia: Innovations in diagnosis and treatment*. New York: Haworth Press.

Ross, C.A. (2007). *The trauma model: A solution to the problem of comorbidity in psychiatry*. Richardson, TX: Manitou Communications.

Ross, C.A., & Dua, V. (1993). Psychiatric health care costs of multiple personality disorder. *American Journal of Psychotherapy*, 47, 103-112.

Ross, C.A., & Ellason, J.W. (2001). Acute stabilization in an inpatient trauma program. *Journal of Trauma and Dissociation*, 2, 83-87.

Ross, C.A., & Haley, C. (2001). Acute stabilization in a trauma program. Paper presented at the Annual Meeting of the International Society for the Study of Dissociation.

Rotter, J.B. (1954). *Social learning and clinical psychology*. New York: Prentice-Hall.

Spanos, N.PP. (1996). *Multiple identities and false memories. A sociocognitive perspective*. Washington, DC: American Psychological Association.

Terr, L. (1992). *Too scared to cry: Psychic trauma in childhood*. New York: Basic Books.

West, C. (1999). *First Person Plural: My Life As a Multiple*. New York: Hyperion.

RECOMMENDED READING

The following is a list of recommended books in the trauma and dissociative disorders fields. Additional references are available in Ross (1997; 2004; 2007):

Allen, J. (2001). *Traumatic relationships and serious mental disorders.* Chichester, England: John Wiley & Sons.

Allen, J. G. & Fonagy, P. (2006). *Handbook of mentalizing-based treatment.* New York: John Wiley & Sons.

Allen, J.G., & Smith, W.H. (1995). *Diagnosis and treatment of dissociative disorders.* Northvale, NJ: Jason Aronson.

Alexander, P.C. (1993). The differential effects of abuse characteristics and attachment in the prediction of the long-term effects of sexual abuse, *Journal of Interpersonal Violence,* 8, 346-362.

Appelbaum, P. S., Uyehara, L. A., & Elin, M. R. (1997). *Trauma and memory: Clinical and legal controversies.* Oxford: Oxford University Press.

Barach, P.M.M. (1991). MPD as an attachment disorder. *Dissociation,* 4, 117-123.

Ben Ari, A., & Somer, E. (2004). The aftermath of therapist-client sex: Exploited women struggle with the consequences. *Clinical Psychology and Psychotherapy.* 11, 126-136.

Blizzard, R. (2003). Disorganized attachment: Development of dissociated self states and a relational approach to treatment. *Journal of Trauma and Dissociation,* 4(3), 27-50.

Boon, S. (1997). The treatment of traumatic memories in DID: Indications and contraindications. *Dissociation,* 10, 65-79.

Boon, S., & Draijer, N. (1993). *Multiple personality disorder in the Netherlands.* Amsterdam: Swets & Zeitlinger.

Braude, S. E. (1995). *First person plural: Multiple personality and the philosophy of mind.* Lanham, MD: Rowman & Littlefield Publishers.

Braun, B.G. (1986). *Treatment of multiple personality disorder.* Washington, DC: American Psychiatric Press.

Bremner, J.D. (2002). *Does stress damage the brain?* New York: W.W. Norton.

Bremner, J.D., & Marmar, C.R. (1998). *Trauma, memory, and dissociation.* Washington, DC: American Psychiatric Press.

Brewin, C. R. (2003). Post-*traumatic stress disorder: Malady or myth?* New Haven: Yale University Press.

Briere, J. (1989). *Therapy for adults molested as children: Beyond survival.* New York: Springer Publishing Co.

Briere, J. (1991). *Treating victims of child sexual abuse. New Directions for Mental Health Services series.* San Francisco: Jossey-Bass.

Briere, J. (1992). *Child abuse trauma: Theory and treatment of the lasting effects.* Newbury Park, CA: Sage Publications

Briere, J. (1994). *Assessing and treating victims of violence. New Directions for Mental Health Services series.* San Francisco: Jossey-Bass.

Briere, J. (1996). *Therapy for adults molested as children, Second edition.* New York: Springer Publishing Co.

Briere, J. (1997). *Psychological assessment of adult posttraumatic states.* Washington, D.C.: American Psychological Association.

Briere, J. (2004). *Psychological assessment of adult posttraumatic states: Phenomenology, diagnosis, and measurement, 2nd edition.* Washington, D.C.: American Psychological Association.

Briere, J., & Scott, C. (2006). *Principles of trauma therapy: A guide to symptoms, evaluation and treatment.* Newbury Park, CA: Sage Publications.

Briere, J. & Spinazzola, J. (2005). Phenomenological and psychological assessment of complex posttraumatic states. *Journal of Traumatic Stress*, 18 (5), 401-412.

Briere, J., Berliner, L., Bulkley, J., Jenny, C., & Reid, T. (1996). *The APSAC handbook on child maltreatment.* Newbury Park, CA: Sage Publications.

Brisch, K. H. (2002). Treating attachment disorders: From theory to therapy. New York: Guilford Press.

Bromberg, P. M. (2001). *Standing in the spaces: Essays on clinical process, trauma, and dissociation.* Mahwah, NJ: The Analytic Press.

Brown, D., Scheflin, A., & Hammond, C. (1998). *Memory, trauma treatment, and the law*. New York: W. W. Norton.

Brown, L.S. (2008). *Cultural competence in trauma therapy: Beyond the flashback.* Washington, DC: American Psychological Association.

Bursen, H. A. (1978). *Dismantling the memory machine: A philosophical investigation of machine theories of memory.* London: D. Reidel Publishing Company.
21st International Fall Conference, New Orleans, Louisiana, November 18-20.

Caldwelll, M. (2004). The 'Spectrum of Emotions.' International Society for the Study of Dissociation
21st International Fall Conference, New Orleans, Louisiana, November 18-20.

Calof, D.L. (1995). Chronic self-injury in adult survivors of childhood abuse: Sources, motivations, and functions of self-injury (Part 1). *Treating Abuse Today*, 5 (3), 11-17.

Calof, D.L. (1995). Chronic self-injury in adult survivors of childhood abuse: Sources, morivations, and functions of self-injury (Part II). *Treating Abuse Today*, 5 (4,5), 31-36.

Calof, D.L. (1996). Chronic self-injury in adult survivors of childhood abuse: Developmental processes of anger in relation to self-injury (Part I). *Treating Abuse Today*, 5 (6)/6 (1), 61-67.

Carey, L.J., & Rubin, J. (2006). *Expressive and creative arts methods for trauma survivors*. London: Jessica Kingsley Publishers.

Carlson, E. (1997). *Trauma assessments: A clinician's guide.* New York: Guilford Press.

Carlson, E.A. (1998). A prospective longitudinal study of disorganized/disoriented attachment. *Child Development*, 69, 1970-1979.

Cassidy, J., & Shaver, P.R. (2008). *Handbook of attachment: Theory, research, and clinical applications.* New York: Guilford Press..

Chefetz, R. A. (2005). Neuroscientific and therapeutic advances in dissociative disorders. *Psychiatric Annals*, 35, 8.

Chu, J. (1988). Ten traps for therapists in the treatment of trauma survivors. *Dissociation*, 1, 24-32.

Chu, J. (1998). *Rebuilding shattered lives: The responsible treatment of complex post-traumatic and dissociative disorders*. New York: John Wiley & Sons.

Cloitre, M., Cohen, L. R., & Koenen, K. C. (2006). *Treating survivors of childhood abuse: Psychotherapy for the interrupted life.* New York: Guilford Press.

Cohen, L., Berzoff, J., Elin, M. (1995). *Dissociative identity disorder: Theoretical and treatment controversies.* Northvale, NJ: Jason Aronson.

Courtois, C. A. (1988). *Healing the incest wound: Adult survivors in therapy.* New York: W. W. Norton.

Courtois, C. A. (1999). *Recollections of sexual abuse: Treatment principles and guidelines.* New York: W. W. Norton.

Courtois, C. A. (2002). Implications of the memory controversy for clinical practice: An overview of treatment recommendations and guidelines. *Journal of Child Sexual Abuse*, 9, 183-210.

Courtois, C. (2004). Complex trauma, complex reactions: Assessment and treatment.

Psychotherapy: Theory, Research, Practice, and Training, 41, 412-425.

Courtois, C.A., & Ford, J.D. (2009). *Treating complex traumatic stress disorders: An evidence-based guide.* New York: Routledge Mental Health.

Creamer, M., Burgess, P. M., McFarlane, A. C. (2001). Posttraumatic stress disorder: Findings for the Australian National Survey of Mental Health and Well-Being, *Psychological Medicine,* 31, 1237-1247.

Dalenberg, C. (2000). *Countertransference and the treatment of trauma.* Washington, DC: American Psychological Association.

Damasio, A. (1999). *The feeling of what happens.* New York: Harcourt Brace & Company.

Davies, J., & Frawley, M. G. (1994). *Treating the adult survivor of childhood sexual abuse: A psychoanalytic perspective.* New York: Basic Books.

Deiter, P.J., Nicholls, S.S., & Pearlman, L.A. (2000). Self-injury and self capacities: Assisting an individual in crisis. *Journal of Clinical Psychology,* 56, 1173-1191.

Dolan, Y. M. (1990). *Resolving sexual abuse: Solution-focused therapy and Ericksonian hypnosis for adult survivors.* New York: W.W. Norton.

Ellenberger, H. F. (1970). *The discovery of the unconscious.* New York: Basic Books.

Figley, C. R. (1985). *Trauma and its wake: The study and treatment of post-traumatic stress disorder.* New York: Brunner/Mazel.

Figley, C. R. (1995). *Compassion fatigue: Coping with secondary traumatic stress disorder in those who treat the traumatized.* New York: Brunner/Mazel.

Foa, E. B., Keane, T. M., & Friedman, M. J. (2000). *Effective treatments for PTSD.* New York: Guilford Press.

Follette, V. & J. I. Ruzek. (2007). *Cognitive behavioral therapies for trauma, Second edition.* New York: Guilford Press.

Fonagy, P., Gergely,G, Jurist, E., & Target, M. (2002). *Affect regulation, mentalization, and the development of the self other.* New York: Other Press.

Ford, J.D. & Kidd, P. (1998). Childhood trauma and disorders of extreme stress as predictors of treatment outcome with chronic posttraumatic stress disorder. *Journal of Traumatic Stress,* 11, 731-761.

Ford, J., Courtois, C., Steele, K., Van der Hart, O., & Nijenhuis, E. (2005). Treatment of complex posttraumatic self-dysregulation. *Journal of Traumatic Stress,* 18, 437-448.

Ford, J.D. & Courtois, C (Ed), (2009) *Treating Complex Trauma Disorders* Guilford Publications

Fosha, D. (2000). *The transforming power of affect: A model for accelerated change.* New York: Basic Books.

Freyd, J.J. (1996). *Betrayal trauma: The logic of forgetting childhood abuse.* Cambridge, MA: Harvard University Press.

Gabbard, G. & Wilkinson, S. (1994). *Management of countertransference with borderline patients.* Washington, DC: American Psychiatric Press.

Gelinas, D. J. (2003). Integrating EMDR into phase-oriented treatment for trauma. *Journal of Trauma & Dissociation,* 4(3), 91-135.

Gil, E. (1988). *Treatment of adult survivors of childhood abuse.* Walnut Creek: Launch Press.

Gold, S.N. (2000). *Not trauma alone, Therapy for child abuse survivors in family and social context.* Lillington, NC: Edwards Brothers.

Goodwin, J. M., & Attias, R. (1999). *Splintered reflections: Images of the body in trauma.* New York: Basic Books.

Herman, J. L. (1981). *Father-daughter incest.* Cambridge, MA: Harvard University Press.

Herman, J. L. (1992). Complex PTSD: A syndrome in survivors of prolonged and repeated trauma. *Journal of Traumatic Stress,* 3, 377-391.

Herman, J. L. (1992). *Trauma and recovery: The aftermath of violence-from domestic to political terror*. New York: Basic Books.

Herman, J. L., Perry, J. C., & van der Kolk, B. A. (1989). Childhood trauma in borderline personality disorder. *American Journal of Psychiatry*, 146, 490-495.

Holmes, J. (1996). *Attachment, intimacy, autonomy: Using attachment theory in adult psychotherapy.* Northvale, NJ: Jason Aronson.

Howell, E. F. (2005). *The dissociative mind*. Hillsdale, NJ: The Analytic Press.

International Society for the Study of Dissociation (2005). Guidelines for treating dissociative identity disorder in adults. *Journal of Trauma & Dissociation, 6*, 69-149.

Jehu, D. (1988). *Beyond sexual abuse: Therapy with women who were childhood victims.* New York: John Wiley & Sons.

Johnson, S. M. (2002). *Emotionally focused couple therapy with trauma survivors: Strengthening attachment bonds.* New York: Guilford Press.

Kepner, J. I. (1995). *Healing tasks: Psychotherapy with adult survivors of childhood abuse.* San Francisco: Jossey-Bass.

Kluft, R. P. (2006). Dealing with alters: A pragmatic clinical perspective. *Psychiatric Clinics of North America*, 29, 281-304.

Kluft, R. P. (1985). *Childhood antecedents of multiple personality*. Washington, DC: American Psychiatric Press.

Kluft, R. P. (1990). *Incest-related syndromes of adult psychopathology*. Washington, D.C.: American Psychiatric Press.

Kluft, R. P. (2000). The psychoanalytic psychotherapy of dissociative identity disorder in the context of trauma therapy. *Psychoanalytic Inquiry*, 20, 259-86.

Kluft, R. P. & Fine, C. G. (1993). *Clinical perspectives on multiple personality disorder*. Washington, D.C.: American Psychiatric Press.

Krippner, S., & Powers, S.M. (1997). *Broken images, broken selves: dissociative narratives in clinical practice.* Wahington, DC: Brunner/Mazel.

Kroll, J. (1993). *PSTD/Borderlines in therapy: Finding the balance.* New York: W. W. Norton.

Lewis, M. (1992). *Shame:The exposed self*. New York: Free Press.

Linehan, M. (1993). *Cognitive-behavioral treatment of borderline personality disorder*. New York: Guilford Press.

Lynn, S.J., & Rhue, J.W. (1994). *Dissociation: Clinical and theoretical perspectives.* New York: Guilford.

Martinez-Taboas, A. (1995). *Multiple personality: An Hispanic perspective.* San Juan, Puerto Rico: Puemte Publications.

McCann, I. L., & Pearlman, L.A. (1990). *Psychological trauma and the adult survivor: Theory, therapy, and transformation.* New York: Brunner/Mazel.

Michelson, L. K. &. Ray, W.J *Handbook of dissociation: Theoretical, empirical, and clinical perspectives.* New York: Plenum.

Middleton, W. (2004) Anna O and Hanna Q'. *Australasian psychiatry: bulletin of Royal Australian and New Zealand College of Psychiatrists* 2004; 12 (3):239-44

Middleton, W. (2004) Dissociative Disorders: A personal 'work in progress'. *Australasian psychiatry: bulletin of Royal Australian and New Zealand College of Psychiatrists* 2004; 12 (3):245-52

Middleton, W. (2005) Owning the past, claiming the present: perspectives on the treatment of dissociative disorders. *Australasian psychiatry: bulletin of Royal Australian and New Zealand College of Psychiatrists* 2005; 13 (1):40-9

Middleton, W., De Marni Cromer, L., Freyd, J.J. (2005) Remembering the Past, anticipating a future. *Australasian psychiatry: bulletin of Royal Australian and New Zealand College of Psychiatrists* 2005; 13 (3): 223-33

Mills, J. (2005). *Treating attachment pathology*. New York: Jason Aronson.

Myers, J.E.B., Berliner, L., Briere, J., Hendrix, C.T., Jenny, C.. & Reid, T. (2002). *The APSAC handbook on child maltreatment, 2nd edition.* Newbury Park, CA: Sage Publications.

Neumann, D. A., Houskamp, B. M., Pollock, V. E., & Briere, J. (1996). The long-term sequelae of childhood sexual abuse in women: A meta-analytic review. *Child Maltreatment,* 1, 6-17.

Nijenhuis, E. R.S. (2005). *Somatoform dissociation.* Oxford: Oxford University Press.

Nijenhuis, E. R. S., Spinhoven, P., & Vanderlinden, J. (1998). Animal defensive reactions as a model for dissociative reactions. *Journal of Traumatic Stress,* 11, 243-260.

Ogawa, J.R., Sroufe, L.A., Weinfeld, N.S., Carlson, E.A. & Egeland, B. (1997) Development and the fragmented self: Longitudinal study of dissociative symptomatology in a nonclinical sample. *Development and Psychopathology,* 9, 855-880.

Ogden, P., Minton, K., & Pain, C. (2006). *Trauma and the body: A sensorimotor approach to psychotherapy.* New York: W.W. Norton.

Panksepp, J. (1998). *Affective neuroscience: The foundations of human and animal emotions.* New York: Oxford University Press.

Pearlman, L.A. (2003). *Trauma and Attachment Belief Scale (TABS) manual.* Los Angeles, CA: Western Psychological Services.

Pearlman, L.A., & Courtois, C.A. (2005). Clinical applications of the attachment framework: Relational treatment of complex trauma. *Journal of Traumatic Stress,* 18, 449-460.

Pearlman, L. A., & Saakvitne, K. W. (1995). *Trauma and the therapist: Countertransference and vicarious traumatization in psychotherapy with incest survivors.* New York: W. W. Norton.

Pelcovitz, D., van der Kolk, B.A., Roth, S.,Mandel, F., Kaplan,S., & Resick, P. (1997). Development of a criteria set and a structured interview for disorders of extreme stress (SIDES). *Journal of Traumatic Stress,* 10, 3-16.

Perry, B. (1993). Neurodevelopment and the neurophysiology of trauma II: Clinical work along the alarm-fear-terror continuum. *The APSAC Advisor,* 6, 14-20.

Perry, B. (1993). Neurodevelopment and the neurophysiology of trauma: Conceptual considerations for clinical work with maltreated children. *The APSAC Advisor,* 6, 14-18.

Perry, B. (2007). *The boy who was raised as a dog.* New York: Basic Books.

Phillips, M., & Frederick, C. (1995). *Healing the divided self: Hypnotherapy for post-traumatic and dissociative conditions.* New York: W. W. Norton.

Polusny, M.M. & Follette, V. M. (1995). Long-term correlates of child sexual abuse: Theory and review of the empirical literature. *Applied and Preventive Psychology,* 4, 143-166.

Potter-Efron, R., & Potter-Efron, P. (1989). *Letting go of shame: Understanding how shame affects your life.* Center City, MN: Hazelden Press.

Putnam, F. W. (1989). *Diagnosis and treatment of multiple personality disorder.* New York: Guilford Press.

Putnam, F. W. (1997). *Dissociation in children and adolescents: A developmental perspective.* New York: Guilford Press.

Rivera, M. (1996). *More alike than different: treating severely dissociative trauma survivors.* Toronto: University of Toronto Press.

Ross, C. A. (1997). *Dissociative identity disorder: Diagnosis, clinical features and treatment of multiple personality, Second edition.* New York: John Wiley & Sons.

Ross, C. A. (2004). *Schizophrenia: Innovations in diagnosis and treatment.* New York: Haworth Press.

Ross, C. A. (2007). *The trauma model, A solution to the problem of comorbidity in psychiatry.* Richardson, TX:, Manitou Communications.

Roth, S., Newman, E., Pelcovitz, D., van der Kolk, B. & Mandel, F.S. (1997). Complex PTSD in victims exposed to sexual and physical abuse: Results from the DSM-IV field trial for posttraumatic stress disorder. *Journal of Traumatic Stress,* 10, 539-55.

Rothschild, B. (2000). T*he body remembers: The psychophysiology of trauma and trauma treatment.* New York: John Wiley& Sons.

Rothschild, B. (2003). *The body remembers: Casebook unifying methods and models in the treatment of trauma and PTSD.* New York: W. W. Norton.

Rothschild, B. (2006). *Help for the helper: The psychophysiology of compassion fatigue and vicarious trauma.* New York: W.W. Norton.

Saakvitne, K.W., Gamble, S.G., Pearlman, L.A., & Lev, B.T. (2000). *Risking connection: A training curriculum for working with survivors of childhood abuse.* Lutherville, MD: Sidran Press.

Sable, P. (2000). *Attachment and adult psychotherapy.* Northvale, NJ: Jason Aronson.

Schore, A. N. (2003). Affect regulation and the origin of the self. Mahwah, NJ: Earlbaum.

Schore, A. N. (2003). Affect dysregulation and disorders of the self. New York: W. W. Norton.

Schore, A. N. (2003). Affect regulation and the repair of the self. New York: W. W. Norton.

Schwartz , H. L. (2000). *Dialogues with forgotten voices: Relational perspectives on child abuse trauma and treatment of dissociative disorders.* New York: Basic Books.

Siegel, D. J. (1999). *The developing mind: Toward a neurobiology of interpersonal experience.* New York: Guilford Press.

Silberg, J. (1996). *The dissociative child.* Lutherville, MD: Sidran Press.

Smucker, M. R., & Dancu, C. V. (1999). *Cognitive-behavioral treatment for adult survivors of childhood trauma: Imagery rescripting and reprocessing.* Northvale, NJ: Jason Aronson.

Solomon, J. & George, C. (1999). *Attachment disorganization.* New York: Guilford Press.

Solomon, M. F., & Siegel, D. J. (2003). *Healing trauma: Attachment, mind, body, and brain.* New York: W. W. Norton.

Somer, E., Buchbinder, E. Peled-Avram, M. & Ben-Yizhack, Y. (2004). The stress and coping of Israeli emergency room social workers following terrorist attacks. *Qualitative Health Research,* 14, 1077-1093.

Spiegel, D. (1993). *Dissociative disorders: A clinical review.* Lutherville, MD: Sidran Press.

Spiegel, D. (1994). *Dissociation: Culture, mind, and body.* Washington, DC: American Psychiatric Press.

Spinazzola, J., Blaustein, M., & Van der Kolk, B. A. (2005). Posttraumatic stress disorder treatment outcome research: The study of unrepresentative samples? *Journal of Traumatic Stress,* 18, 425-436.

Spira, J.L. (1996). *Treating dissociative identity disorder.* San Francisco: Jossey-Bass.

Sroufe, A, Egeland, B., Carlson, E. A., & Collins, W. A. (2005). *The development of the person.: The Minnesota study of risk and adaptation from birth to adulthood.* New York: Guilford Press.

Stamm, B. H. (Ed.). (1995). *Secondary traumatic stress: Self-care issues for clinicians, researchers, & educators.* Lutherville, MD: Sidran Press.

Steele, K., Van der Hart, O., & Nijenhuis, E. R. S. (2001). Dependency in the treatment of complex posttraumatic stress disorder and dissociative disorders. *Journal of Trauma and Dissociation,* 2, 79-116.

Steele, K., Van der Hart, O., & Nijenhuis, E. R. S. (2005). Phase-oriented treatment of structural dissociation in complex traumatization: Overcoming trauma-related phobias. *Journal of Trauma & Dissociation,* 6, 11-53.

Steinberg, M. (1995). *Handbook for the assessment of dissociation. A clinical guide.* Washington, DC: American Psychiatric Press.

Stien, P.T., & Kendall, J. (2004). *Psychological trauma and the developing brain.* New York: Haworth Press.

Suryani, L.K., & Jensen, G.D. (1993). *Trance and possession in Bali: A window on western multiple personality, possession disorder, and suicide.* Oxford: Oxford University Press.

Twombly, J. H. (2005). EMDR for clients with dissociative identity disorder, DDNOS, and ego states. In R. Shapiro (Ed.), *EMDR solutions: Pathways to healing* (pp. 86-120). New York: W.W. Norton.

van der Hart, O., Brown, P., & Van der Kolk, B. A. (1989). Pierre Janet's treatment of post-traumatic stress. *Journal of Traumatic Stress*, 2, 379-396.

van der Hart, O., Nijenhuis, E. R. S., & Steele, K. (2006). *The haunted self: Structural dissociation and the treatment of chronic traumatization.* New York: W.W. Norton.

van der Kolk, B. (1994). The body keeps the score: Memory and the evolving psychobiology of post traumatic stress. *Harvard Review of Psychiatry*, 1, 253-265.

van der Kolk, B. (1987). *Psychological trauma*. Washington, DC: American Psychiatric Press.

van der Kolk, B. & McFarlane, A. (1996). *Traumatic stress: Human adaptation to overwhelming experience*. New York: Guilford Press.

Vanderlinden, J. (1993). *Dissociative experiences, trauma and hypnosis. Research findings & clinical implications in eating disorders.* Deltf, The Netherlands: Uitgeverij Eburon.

Waites, E.A., (1993). *Trauma and survival: Post-traumatic and dissociative disorders in women.* New York: W. W. Norton.

Wang, S., Wilson, J. P., & Mason, J. W. (1996). Stages of decompensation in combat-related posttraumatic stress disorder: A new conceptual model. *Integrative Physiological and Behavioral Science*, 11, 237-253.

Wilson, J. P., Friedman, M. J., & Lindy, J. D. (2002). *Treating psychological trauma and PTSD.* New York: Guilford Press.

Wilson, J. P., & Keane. T. M. (2004). *Assessing psychological trauma and PTSD. Second edition.* New York: Guilford Press

Wilson, J. P., & Lindy, J. (Eds.) (1994). *Countertransference in the treatment of PTSD.* New York: Guilford Press.

Zlotnick, C., Zakriski, A.L., Shea, M.T., Costello, E., Begin, A., Pearlstein, T. & Simpson, E. (1996). The long-term sequelae of sexual abuse: Support for a complex posttraumatic stress disorder. *Journal of Traumatic Stress*, 9, 195-205.

The following books deal with spirituality and counseling:

Bachelard M. (2008). *Behind the Exclusive Brethren.* Melbourne: Scribe Publications.

Batchelor, S. (1997). *Buddhism Without Beliefs: A Contemporary Guide to Awakening.* New York: Riverhead.

Burke M.T., Chauvin J.C., & Miranti J.G. (2005). *Religious & Spiritual Issues in Counselling: Applications Across Diverse Populations*. New York: Brunner-Routledge

Chödrön, P. (2000). *When Things Fall Apart: Heart Advice for Difficult Times.* Boston: Shambhala Classics.

Faiver C., Ingersol, R.E., O'Brien, E., & McNally, C. (2001). *Explorations in Counseling and Spirituality: Philosophical, Practical, & Personal Reflections.* Florence, KY: Brooks/Cole.

Germer, C.J., Siegel, R.D., & Fulton, P.R. (2005). *Mindfulness and Psychotherapy.* New York: Guilford Press.

Gunaratana, B.H. (2002). *Mindfulness in Plain English.* Boston: Wisdom.

Greenspan, M. (2003). *Healing Through The Dark Emotions: The Wisdom of Grief, Fear, and Despair.* Boston: Shambhala

Griffith, J.L, & Griffith, M. E. (2003). *Encountering The Sacred In Psychotherapy: How To Talk With People About Their Spiritual Lives.* New York: Guilford Press

Hahn, T.N. (1997). *The Miracle of Mindfulness.* Boston: Beacon.

Helmeke, K.B., & Ford, S.C. (2006). *The Therapist's Notebook for Integrating Spirituality in*

Counselling. New York: The Haworth Press

Kabat-Zinn, J. (2005). *Wherever You Go, There You Are: Mindfulness Meditation in Everyday Life* . New York: Hyperion.

Kornfield, J. (1993). *A Path with Heart: A Guide Through the Perils and Promises of Spiritual Life.* New York: Bantam.

Lines, D. (2006). *Spirituality in Counseling and Psychotherapy.* Thousand Oaks, CA: Sage.

May, G.G. (2005). *The Dark Night Of The Soul.* San Francisco: Harper.

Michie, D. (2004). *Buddhism for Busy People: Finding Happiness In An Uncertain World.* Sydney: Allen & Unwin.

Michie, D. (2008). *Hurry Up and Meditate: Your Starter Kit for Inner Peace and Better Health.* Sydney: Allen & Unwin

Miller, D. (2003). *Your Surviving Spirit: A Spiritual Workbook for Coping With Ttrauma.* Oakland CA: New Harbinger Publications.

Miller, G. (2003). *Incorporating Spirituality in Counseling & Psychotherapy: Theory & Technique.* New York: John Wiley & Sons.

Moore, T. (1992). *Care Of The Soul: A Guide For Cultivating Depth And Sacredness In Everyday Life.* New York: Harper Perennial

Moore, T. (2005). *Dark Nights of the Soul: A Guide to Finding Your Way Through Life's Ordeals.* New York: Gotham Books.

Olson, R.P. (2002). *Religious Theories of Personality And Psychotherapy: East Meets West.* New York: Haworth Press

Pargament, K.I. (2007). *Spiritually Integrated Psychotherapy: Understanding & Addressing The Sacred.* New York: Guilford Press.

Pargament, K.I. (1997). *The Psychology of Religion and Coping.* New York: Guilford Press.

Richards, S. P., & Bergin, A.E. (2005). *A Spiritual Strategy for Counseling and Psychotherapy - 2nd Edition.* Washington, DC: American Psychological Association.

Richo, D. (2005). *The 5 Things We Cannot Change: and the Happiness We Find by Embracing Them.* Boston: Shambhala

Schreurs, A. (2002). *Psychotherapy and Spirituality: Integrating the Spiritual Dimension into Therapeutic Practice. London:* Jessica Kingsley Publishers.

Tacey, D. (2003). *The Spirituality Revolution: The Emergence Of Contemporary Spirituality.* New York: Harper Collins

Tolle, E. (2004). *The Power of Now: A Guide to Spiritual Enlightenment.* Novato, CA: New World Library.

Tolle, E. (2005). *A New Earth: Awakening to Your Life's Purpose.* New York: Michael Joseph, Ltd.

Young-Eisendrath, P (1996) *The Gifts of Suffering: Finding Insight, Compassion, and Renewal* Addison Wesley

The following articles and book chapters deal with spirituality and counseling:

Daaleman, T.P., & Nease, D.E. (1994). Patient attitudes regarding physician inquiry into spiritual and religious issues. *Journal of Family Practice*, 39, 564-567.

Dein, S., & Stygal, J. (1997). Does being religious help or hinder coping with chronic illness? A critical literature review. *Palliative Medicine,* 11, 291-298.

De Mello, F.O. (1998). Religious experience and psychoanalysis: From man-as-god to man-with-god. *International Journal of Psychoanalysis* 79, 113-131.

Emmons, R.A., & Paloutzian, R. F. (2003). The psychology of religion. *Annual Review of Psychology* 54, 377-402.

Frazier, R.E., & Hansen, N.D. (2009). Religous /spiritual psychotherapy behaviors: Do we do what we believe to be important? *Professional Psychology: Research and Practice*, 40, 81-87.

Miller, W. R., & Thoresen, C. .E (2003). Spirituality, religion and health. An emerging field. *American Psychologist*, 58, 14-35.

Pargament, K., Ano, G.G., & Wachholtz, A.B. (2005). The religious dimension of coping: Advances in theory, research and practice. In, R.F. Paloutzian & C.L Park (Eds.), *Handbook of the Psychology of Religion and Spirituality* (pp. 479-495). New York: Guilford Press.

Park, C. L. (2005). Religion and meaning. In R.F. Paloutzian & C.L. Park C L. (Eds.), *Handbook of the Psychology of Religion and Spirituality* (pp. 295-314). New York: Guilford Press.

Passmore, N. L. (2003). Religious issues in counseling: Are Australian psychologists "dragging the chain"? *Australian Psychologist*, 38, 183-192.

Plante, T.G. (2008). "What do the spiritual and religious traditions offer the practicing psychologist?" *Pastoral Psychology*, 56, 429-444.

Rose, E. M., Westfeld, J.S., & Ansley, T. (2001). Spiritual issues in counseling: Client's beliefs and preferences. *Journal of Counseling Psychology*, 48, 1, 61-71.

Schieman, S. (2008). The religious role and the sense of personal control. *Sociology of Religion*, 69, 273-296.

Simmonds, J.G. (2004). Heart and spirit: Research with psychoanalysts and psychoanalytic psychotherapists about spirituality. *International Journal of Psychoanalysis*, 85, 951-971.

Smith, A.F. (2007). Do clients want their spiritual and religious beliefs to be discussed in therapy? *Psychotherapy In Australia*, 14 (1), 55-59.

Smith, A.F., & Simmonds, J.G. (2006). Help-seeking and paranormal beliefs in adherents of mainstream religion, alternative religion, and no religion. *Counseling Psychology Quarterly.* 19, 331-341.

Somer, E. (2004). Trance possession disorder in Judaism: Sixteenth-century dybbuks in the Near-East. *Journal of Trauma and Dissociation* 5 (2), 131-146.

Spilka, B. (2005). Religious practice, ritual and prayer. In R.F. Paloutzian & C.L. Park (Eds.), *Handbook of the psychology of religion and spirituality* (pp.365-377). New York: Guilford Press.

STATEMENTS OF PROFESSIONAL ASSOCIATIONS CONCERNING TRAUMA, DISSOCIATION, HYPNOSIS, AND MEMORY

American Medical Association Council on Scientific Affairs. (1995). Report on memories of child abuse. *International Journal of Clinical and Experimental Hypnosis*, 43, 114-117.

Hammond, D.C., Garver, R., Mutter, C.B., Crasilneck, H.B., Frischholz, E., Gravitz, M.A., Hibler, N.S., Olson, J., Scheflin, A., Spiegel, H., Wester, W. (1994). *Clinical hypnosis and memory: Guidelines for clinicians and for forensic hypnosis.* American Society of Clinical Hypnosis.

INDEX